THE MAVERICK METHOD

MATT SWYERS

THE MAVERICK METHOD

HOW TO WIN THE STARTUP GAME

Maverick Method Enterprises, LLC

CONTENTS

To what matters most in the world to me -
my family: Madison and Kennedy, my children,
Andrea and Jerry, my parents.
the wonderful people of The Trademark Company,
TTC Business Solutions, and the Swyers Law Firm, past and present

Nothing would have been possible or worthwhile
without your love, support, and dedication.

Thank you for the honor to be known as your dad, son, and co-worker.

First Printing, 2021 | Revised & Expanded, 2022

FORWARD

Fifty percent of all new businesses fail within the first five years. Fifty-percent! That means that if you start a business, and a friend or family member starts a business, on average, one of you is destined to fail. Why? Why do so many fail, while others succeed?

By the time I was 45 years old, I had founded two multi-million-dollar businesses that, in turn, have assisted thousands of other small businesses in getting their respective start. As such, over the past twenty years, I have been blessed with the perfect focus group to study what works and what doesn't when starting a business.

After years of toying with the idea, and with more than a little encouragement from friends in the industry, I sat down and put pen to paper. In the following pages, I have attempted to impart, to the best of my ability, that which I have learned from running my companies and helping launch over 100,000 startups.

My goal is that by sharing these concepts with you, your new business will be positioned not only to be in the 50% of businesses that survive past that initial 5-year mark, but will thrive throughout the life of the business.

We will explore these concepts in greater detail in the chapters to come. But to wet your whistle, here are the Maverick Method's Top Ten Rules to win in the startup game.

Top 10 Rules to Win the Startup Game

RULE 1: Create a Product People Want

Seems obvious, right? But as you will soon read, 50% of all business fail in the first five years because a shocking 43% have no market for their product. This means that over 20% of businesses fail in the first five years (50% overall, five-year failure rate x 43% = 21.5%) because they simply created a product no one wanted.

RULE 2: Make it Legal

Once you have a product people want, protect it, and yourself, legally. Secure any patents, copyrights, or trademarks (a.k.a intellectual property) that are unique about your offering to make sure what is yours stays yours. Most importantly, protect yourself by forming an LLC to run the business, which will protect your personal assets from the business's liabilities. Lastly, get insurance for the business and your products or services. This adds an extra layer of protection, should things ever hit the fan.

RULE 3: Build it to Scale

Write every system down, every formula, every manner for running your business. Create manuals as if you will franchise your business one day (even if you are not). Once pen has been put to paper, future employees can be trained to perform the requisite roles in the business, so it can be easily scaled.

RULE 4: Shamelessly Market Your Product

They can't buy it if they don't know about it. Even if you make the greatest widget in the history of widgets, no one will buy one if they do not know it exists. So, if you make it, make sure everyone knows about it!

RULE 5: Build a Great Team

You can't pull the cart by yourself. Invest in creating and sustaining amazing teams. Take care of your people, and they will take care of your customers.

RULE 6: Ignore the Naysayers and Work Your Ass Off

Along your journey as an entrepreneur, you will encounter people who will criticize you and your vision. Learn how to distinguish between those who know what they are talking about and those who do not. Only heed the advice of people who know what they are talking about, and who have your best interests in mind. And, more than anything else, roll up those sleeves and work your ass off!

RULE 7: Cash is King

The lifeblood of a business is money. Without positive cash flow, your business will cease to exist. A business's purpose is to profit. Thus, your revenues must exceed your costs. Period. When they do, put away a percentage of your profits for strategic reserves. If your revenues do not exceed your expenses, and you do not have a realistic plan to get them there, you must shut the business down.

RULE 8: Innovate and Refresh

Even if you come to market with a completely innovative or fresh product, create an innovation schedule to push out new products, innovations, or fresh updates several times per year. You are either growing, or you are dying.

RULE 9: Captain Your Ship

Determine your leadership style and captain your business. Plan for the best, but prepare for the eventual storms that may arise.

RULE 10: Plan to Succeed

Success does not occur by accident. Success is a product of design. Create and regularly update an Annual Business Map (ABM), charting out the steps you need to achieve your business goals. Maintain a daily checklist of tasks you must accomplish to keep focused on, and accomplish the higher-level goals in your ABM.

INTRODUCTION

WHAT'S IN A NAME?

Maverick? What an ass you're probably thinking. I mean, calling yourself Maverick? Who do you think you are? Tom Cruise and his iconic character from the 1986 blockbuster movie *Top Gun*? "I feel the need, the need for speed..." "Talk to me Goose.... talk to me." Are you serious?

Well, if you're reading the book or perhaps just flipping through the first few pages at one of our last remaining physical bookstores in the U.S., you've gotten through that initial objection and I've piqued your interest, if only a little. P.S., please don't spill any coffee on the book before you buy it. Gracias!

Admit it, you want to know why I settled upon this title, and how it all fits into me and my philosophy in helping thousands of businesses to get their start. More importantly, how can it benefit you? We both know you want to know these answers, so let's get on with it.

The reality is it has nothing to do with Mr. Cruise, *Top Gun*, or even being a traditional rebel. I've only had two nicknames in my life, Maverick and The Hammer. For the purposes of this book, we'll focus on the former, although, admittedly, the latter may be more entertaining. But that's for another book and another time and, well, Tipper Gore may want to put a rating on that one. So sorry folks, it's not Hammer time. It's all about Maverick now. But I digress.

The nickname Maverick was hung on me a few years ago by author Adam Smith while he was writing an article for *The World Trademark Review,* a specialized global industry publication for trademark geeks—I mean lawyers—around the world. If you search it, it's still out there somewhere in cyberspace. But at that time, my first company, a niche trademark law firm, had rocketed near the top, or, depending on who you ask, made it to the top of our industry and was redefining the marketplace for trademark services. "In what?", you might ask. Trademark legal services. You know, trademarks.

You see, trademarks are your brand, like Coca-Cola, Apple, or Google. To get a trademark, you generally need to come up with what you want your company or product to be called, search the name to make sure it's available—in other words, make sure that someone else is not already using that name—and then register it with the proper government agency.

Up until about the year 2000, you could do this by yourself, but it was highly technical, and if you wanted help, only a small, select group of high-priced law firms specialized in securing people's trademarks. So, if you need their services, be prepared to fork over plenty of cash to one of these law firms.

Well, we came along and changed everything. We brought reasonably-priced trademark services to the masses and created a niche industry where none had existed before. In so doing, we opened trademark services to the masses.

So, during our conversation, the reporter kept asking me for answers as to how we were disrupting our industry, how we had brought this dramatic change and were experiencing such amazing growth. Initially, I simply tried to answer his questions with my typical 50,000-foot overview speech given to so many clients and potential investors over the years.

"How?" I responded. "Name one industry that rewards customer loyalty by raising the customers' prices every year? Lawyers. We simply infused customer service into an industry in desperate need of the same."

If you've ever worked at a law firm and watched this happen, it is fascinating. Almost every year, lawyers go to their customers, clients in the legal field, and raise their rates! Let me say that again, in case you weren't paying attention or are otherwise not familiar with this practice: lawyers and law firms reward customer loyalty with an annual or periodic raising of their rates! Wow. I mean, thanks?

"Well, this year Partner XYZ's rate is increasing to ten trillion dollars per hour... so, thanks for your 15 years of being a dedicated client ... next year it will cost you an arm, a leg, and hey... is that a spare kidney?"

I mean really, thanks for your business. Here's an even bigger bill! You're welcome.

WHERE'S THE FUN IN BEING A LEMMING?

So, while most industries create incentives and programs to reward customers for their loyalty, law firms act as if the customer is the lucky one to be allowed the firm's legal assistance. What an awesome racket. And it works, so long as everyone in the industry goose steps to the beat of the same drum. Well, here's the problem. I've just never been that guy. I've always been blessed with my own, independent beat. I'm not what you call someone who is going to conform just because someone else next to me did.

Lemming: "Come on everybody, we're jumpin' off that bridge!"

Me: "Wait, why?"

Lemming: "Everyone else is doing it. Come on. It's gonna be the greatest thing ever!"

Me: "Again, wait, um, why?"

Lemming: "Because... well ... I dunno .. they're doing it."

Me: "OK then. Cool beans. I'm um ... just gonna hang here and watch you lemmings prove the doppler effect on your way down. Say hi to Jim Jones when you get to the bottom! Gracias and buh-bye!"

Dissatisfied with my original answer that we simply infused customer service into an industry in desperate need of the same, Adam pushed me for more. Finally, I relented. I asked him if he had ever seen a 1994 Western movie co-starring Mel Gibson and Jodi Foster. Being from the UK, he conceded he had not.

I LIKE TO WATCH

In the film, Mr. Gibson plays a card player in the American Old West, making his way to a huge poker tournament with a massive cash payout. To do so, he must journey across the West while securing enough cash to buy into the game along the way. The movie follows Mel throughout his travels, as he plays in lesser games, calls in loans from friends, and, of course, has the occasional run in with the mysterious bad guys trying to keep him from the tournament.

In one of the more memorable scenes, Mel asks to join a host of local card players in a game of poker, in a small-town saloon. The players are reluctant to let the slick-dressed Gibson into their poker game, concerned he'll easily take their money, leaving them with nothing but broken hopes and dreams and the smell of defeat.

Well, after flashing that famous smile, our hero Mel is allowed to play—with a catch. He promises to lose for the first hour he's at the table. Lose for the first hour? Who wouldn't take that deal in poker? I mean, if you have an ante (the money every player at the table must put in at the beginning of each hand) that is guaranteed money in the other players' pockets, right? Well Mr. Gibson, let me dust off this chair for you, right by me! Can I get you a drink? Maybe some peanuts? How about a steak sandwich? Or another steak sandwich? Sorry, I had to insert at least one reference to the movie *Fletch*. I am a kid of the 80s after all, what can I say?

Anyways, Mel's character does exactly what he says. He starts to lose. And he loses again, and again, and again. Now, during this time-lapsed sequence, we see Mel glance occasionally at his handy-dandy pocket watch. Obviously drunk on the excitement of winning, the other players lose track of time. And eventually, the big movie moment comes when another player goes to rake in what they think is their winnings...only to see Gibson flip down the winning hand. Of course, the other player is a little confused by our leading man, as the tension quickly rises. But as Gibson smugly reminds them, "I promised to lose for the first hour gentleman. The hour is up."

The players play on. As they do, the montage turns to one of Gibson just cleaning house. He rakes in pile after pile of money to his side of the table until, in a very dramatic moment, one of the other players accuses him of "cheatin'". Guns are drawn. Tension mounts. After all, this is the Old West. After some quick-witted dialogue, Gibson finally reveals his secret.

"Guys, what did you think I was doing for the first hour? I wasn't just losing. I was studying you all, learning your tells, learning how to beat you. Now do we want to fight, or do we want to play some poker?"

Well, if you don't know by now, the name of Mel's character was Bret Maverick. The movie: Richard Donner's classic 1994 western *Maverick*.

Bringing this back into focus. How did I do what I did? Well, sit back and listen, I continued with the reporter. It all started when I was at the U.S. Patent & Trademark Office (USPTO), working as a trademark-examining attorney. For years, I had been told I was not good enough to join one of those fancy, niche, prestigious law firms that practiced trademark law. I would apply, and they'd say, "No thanks." I'd apply again, I'd get the same response. I think I applied to work for most of them in the industry. And the answer was always the same. Thanks, but we're good.

Dejected, but resolved to get into the industry, I enrolled at George Washington University School of Law to secure my LLM. In short, my plan was to get a Master's Degree in trademark law. With that, I left my original job as a personal injury attorney and went to work as an examining attorney for the U.S. Patent and Trademark Office (USPTO). I figured, with that experience, and an LLM in trademark law from the prestigious George Washington University School of Law, I'd be a shoe-in at those snooty firms, right?

Survey says.... X.

But then a strange thing happened along the way to realizing that goal. In the course and scope of my work for the USPTO, I was blessed with the opportunity to be able to review those law firms' work that had so frequently scoffed at my candidacy. And guess what I found? Their work was replete with errors and mistakes. Shoddy work. These lawyers, whose ranks I had been killing myself to join, weren't that great after all. I mean, if you pitch to your clients your brilliance and expertise, why were they making these routine errors? And not just once or twice. All the time. I was stunned.

When thinking about it, I could only come to two possible conclusions as to why the level of their work was not what I thought it should be. First, they simply weren't that great. The proof is in the pudding, right? I mean, if you tell me you're awesome, shouldn't your work reflect it? Shouldn't you get things right the first time and not have to correct them at the request of the USPTO time and time again? If you charge someone a premium because your work allegedly deserves it, shouldn't your work reflect that alleged expertise and skill? Following me on this? At a minimum, please don't make common grammatical errors and mistakes. You're better than that, right? I mean, that's what you're charging the big bucks for, right?

The other possibility was far worse. Were they intentionally making errors to charge their clients more? Gouging their clients on purpose? Noooo. Not a lawyer. Say it isn't so. People love lawyers, and their bills are always so reasonable. I mean, when most people open their legal bills, their first reaction is, "Oh my, how affordable. How did they do so much for so little!" Right? If you've ever hired a lawyer, you get the sarcasm. If you've never hired a lawyer, but someday will, you'll get it then. If you never have to hire a lawyer, God bless you, and please call me to tell me your secret. But again, I digress.

Back to the "quality" of these law firms' work: these were simple errors. Stuff that should not be done by these premiere law firms. But guess what? When the USPTO sends a letter to counsel asking them for clarification of some issue, guess who gets to charge money for reading that letter? The big firm lawyer. And guess who gets to bill for writing the client telling them about the letter? The big firm lawyer. And guess who gets to bill for fixing the error they shouldn't have made in the first place? The big firm lawyer. Are you picking up on the theme here? Bill. Bill. Bill. Now, don't get me wrong. Bill, Bill, Bill is fine when you're at a Shakespeare look-a-like festival, but not when you're paying for legal services. Come on. And it's certainly not fine when those bills are to pay for the correction of errors which should not have occurred in the first place. Capiche?

What a racket, I thought. And this second alternative is even worse, right? I mean, that's a very dangerous road to go down. Intentionally creating errors in clients' applications to bill more? Hello, state bar associations? I think we have some relatively large issues we need to address.

So, while working at the USPTO, I decided the practice of law, or at least in my little corner of it, trademarks, had to change. We could build a better mousetrap. After a brief stop at another DC firm, I made the fateful decision to put my money where my mouth was, make the leap, and hang out my own proverbial shingle.

OH LORD, IT'S HARD TO BE HUMBLE...

In September of 2003, I founded The Trademark Company from the basement of my Northern Virginia home. It was a dark, musty basement that had not been updated since the house's construction in 1970. I mean, 8-foot-high popcorn ceilings, with my desk situated under an HVAC return that hung down to only 4 to 5 feet off the ground. Water-stained carpeting and wood panels that cautioned "Highly flammable. Avoid exposure to flames." The basement was also clearly lacking well-sealed doors and windows to the outside, as every morning I'd have to clean up the dead bugs on the floor before getting to work. On an aside, ever wonder why bugs crawl into your house to die in the middle of the floor? I mean, it's sort of strange, right? Here they made it in from the cold, only to perish on the relatively warm floor of your home. What's up with that? Are they committing bug suicide, or bugicide if you will, and just want you to know? I mean, really. Alright, back to our regularly scheduled programming.

You get the point. To say the conditions were spartan in my basement would be an understatement. No more Class A glass office buildings on K Street in Washington, D.C. No more power lunches downtown with other lawyers and business friends sniffing each other's business cards. No more being stalked by James Carville of the Clinton campaign near the Farragut West Metro stop. I swear, there was a two-month period in my life where, every time I turned around, he was right behind me. Startling, really. I can still feel his presence. But nope. I said goodbye to all of that, James included, and set up shop in a tiny, musty basement in my 1970s fixer-upper. Talk about keeping you humble.

At the time, I walked away from a law firm job that was paying me a salary of about $50,000 per year. By DC standards, this was modest. That said, it's far easier to start your own business when you only need to cover a $50,000 price tag as opposed to $100,000 or $130,000 like the salaries my friends at those big firms were making. In fact, if I had been making the big bucks at the time, I probably would never have ventured out, as I couldn't have taken the pay cut to do so. But at $50,000, well, that was not so bad. In short, with virtually no overhead like the premiere office space, I only needed to make about $1,000 per week to replace my salary. No problemo, I thought.

When I left I had two things going for me. First, the most prolific trademark attorney at the time was giving me all the litigation from his then-largest trademark filing practice. In short, he didn't want to get into litigation or go to court for his clients, so he gave all that work to me. And man, did this guy have the life. He lived on Miami Beach. He'd wake up, get a few hours of work done. Head to the beach. Have a nice lunch. Then walk back for some late afternoon work. Knocking off about 5, he'd then head to dinner and out to the clubs, dancing away his evenings with the lovely ladies of South Beach. And the next morning, he'd do it all over again. So why have the stress of litigation? He was only too happy to send it my way. And it was a lot. Again, if he ever reads this and did not hear it from me at the time, thank you! You helped me start my amazing journey.

Second, I had started to figure out how to generate my own business, contacting and retaining clients in the legal industry, when I was at my last law firm. New and innovative ways that no one had figured out. Again, you'll hear about those later in the book. But I've always fancied myself to be a bit of a tinkerer. Someone who just looks at something and says, how do we make it better? How do we accomplish this? I know no one else has done it. Doesn't mean we can't. So how? And then you do. That's how we innovate. Ask a question as to why something can't be improved and allow everything, no matter how far-fetched it may seem, to be placed on the table. And then you work towards implementing one of those solutions. It's simple once you get the hang of it.

In any event, a marketing company called Blue Dog Design out of Chicago was my first major client. Their founder, Michelle, wrote me a retainer check that was about the size of half a year's salary from my then-current position to file lawsuits against multiple defendants throughout the country. Things just don't get any easier when you open a business, to have half a year's salary in the bank.

With this big customer and huge referral source, I settled down in my musty basement and got to work. To match my salary at my billable rate of $200 per hour, I merely needed to make sure I had about 5 billable hours of work per week. Now, mind you, billable hours are the work attorneys do once they have a client, and are billing that client at their rate for services rendered. As any attorney who is a rainmaker will tell you, the devil is in the figuring out how to get more clients, the time it takes to retain them, and to keep those billable hours flowing.

Quick career tip for you fledgling attorneys out there. The fastest route to making partner at a law firm is to focus on bringing in your own clients and building a practice within your firm, not to focus on billing the most hours. Anyone can work on another person's client's work. Anyone can bill 2,500 hours a year. But build your own, portable, bank of business and you'll rocket to the front of the partnership line. Why? Because if you leave, your clients go with you! In short, when you turn into someone who is paying for yourself and others, who work for the clients that would leave with you if you left, you are far more valuable to the firm than just someone who works someone else's book of business. But again, I digress.

Needing to bill only about 5 hours per week to cover my former salary, I began spending vast amounts of time reading business books and studying how to make that better mousetrap. How to get better at attracting and retaining clients. How to build my practice from that dank, musty basement in Northern Virginia.

Coming full circle: during those initial years, I studied what the big firms were doing. I worked in silence. I created 350-page operations manual for how to run and easily execute a top caliber trademark law firm that, with the proper training, could be handled by anyone. I set a fair, flat rate for legal services and shamelessly marketed the same. I planned and worked in silence until the model was ready, then launched it on the world.

MAVERICK? DID YOUR PARENTS NOT LIKE YOU?

Where did it lead? How did it work? Well, remember all those big law firms that wouldn't hire me? Once the model was launched, it took off. Slowly at first, but over a few years, it gained steam. After two years, The Trademark Company would appear on many lists as one of the top trademark filers in the United States. The next year, as news of what we were doing spread, we climbed the list further.

By 2013, we reached the pinnacle of our industry and were named the Top Trademark Law Firm in the United States by *Intellectual Property Today* magazine. And the best part: we did all of this while helping thousands of businesses get their start, and realize their own American Dream.

So how did we do it? We studied in silence what the industry leaders were doing for years. We learned how to develop systems that improved upon everything they were doing. We created massive value for the customer that no one else had created. We expanded the market for trademark legal services to a new consumer base. I became our industry's Bret Maverick.

"So does that give you a little better background?" I asked the reporter, Adam Smith. He just stood there in silence. After a moment or two of flipping through his notes, he responded, "You're Maverick." A few weeks later, his article was published, pinning me with the nickname and, years later, the title of this book. So, without further ado, I present to you what I've learned from building my own business and helping over 100,000 other businesses to get their start.

I present to you: The Maverick Method: How to Win the Startup Game.

IF YOU BUILD IT, WILL THEY COME?

Create a Product People Want. Price it Right.

FAILURE IS NOT AN OPTION, BUT IT IS A POSSIBILITY

Twenty percent of small businesses fail within the first year. Twenty percent! The statistics get even worse at the five-year mark. After five years, fifty percent of all new small businesses fail. And if you're lucky enough to make it to your tenth anniversary, congratulations! Because a whopping sixty-five percent of all new small businesses fail by that time. Sixty-five percent!

That means, for anyone who picked up a copy of this book and is thinking about starting a business for the first time, twenty percent of your businesses will fail within the first five years. One out of five of you will leave the safety and security of a regular paycheck from someone else's business and, within a year or so, need to go crawling back to the companies you had abandoned. So, from the onset, don't burn those bridges!

Oh, and for another thirty percent of you, it gets worse. You'll have the illusion of success for a few years, until reality sets in and your business begins to fail before the five-year mark. And if you think it's painful trying to get back after a year, just wait until the five-year mark. I mean, unless you're Tom Hanks's character from *Cast Away*, it's not going to happen. And those who fail after five years are more likely to have burned through their savings, 401Ks, and other assets trying to prop up a failing business, because they once had the illusion of success and refuse to walk away from the dream of entrepreneurship which has slowly turned into a nightmare.

And congratulations! If you make it past five, the odds actually start to swing in your favor. But still, another fifteen percent of businesses will fail by the ten-year mark. So, if you make it to the five, great job. Your proof of concept worked! Only 7.5% of the remaining 50% fail by the 10-year mark. But looking back, sixty-five percent will fail. That means that two thirds of you that set out to get your piece of the American Dream won't make it before you are ready to retire to Ft. Lauderdale, start eating dinner at two, lunch at ten, breakfast the night before, and to spend your days looking for the ultimate soft yogurt and wondering why the kids never call. Credit to Billy Crystal from *City Slickers*.

But why do they fail? That's the big question, isn't it? And what can you do to make sure your business does not fail, ever. That's why I wrote *The Maverick Method*.

I used to work for someone else. And like you, I dreamed of a better tomorrow. A tomorrow where I was in charge and could make the decisions that affected my life, outside of someone else's control. Working for someone else, I was subject to their whims on who to keep employed and who to let go when there was an economic downturn. I had to deal with their often-arbitrary internal policies and get rated poorly on criteria that I didn't even know I was being judged on. I had to kiss up to people I loathed, because they were ahead of me in the company. Sound familiar?

I walked out nearly twenty years ago, and never looked back. And I have been blessed to have made it past the 1-year mark, then the five, and the ten. But it was not without extreme challenges. It was not without pain. And unlike so many, my business is in the business of starting and helping other businesses to get started. So, we can talk statistics all day long and into the night. But when you've literally helped thousands and thousands of businesses during the start-up phase and have witnessed the successes and failures behind those statistics, you acquire a unique perspective that others simply don't have, by merely looking at numbers and theorizing why businesses succeed, and why they fail.

And that's what this book is about. I'm here to share with you what I've learned from this experience, so that as you go down the road to owning your own business, or continue down that road, as the case may be, you don't become one of the nearly two-thirds of businesses that fail. That you get to that coveted position of being in the 1/3 that get past the ten-year mark. That you get to build your business successfully and not someone else's. In short, that you get your slice of the American Dream!

So why do they fail? A recent study found 20 primary reasons why startups fail. These include:

- No market need – 42%
- Ran out of cash – 29%
- Wrong team – 23%
- Outcompeted – 19%
- Pricing or cost issues – 18%
- Unfriendly user product – 17%
- Product without a business model – 17%
- Poor marketing – 14%
- Ignored customers – 14%
- Mistimed product- 13%
- Lost focus – 13%
- Disharmony among team and/or investors – 13%
- Pivot gone bad – 10%
- Lack of passion – 9%
- Failed geographical expansion – 9%
- No financing or investor interest – 8%
- Legal challenges – 8%
- Didn't use network – 8%
- Burned out – 8%
- Failure to pivot – 7%

Whew, that's a lot. And we're going to get to most if not all of these, because I want your business to succeed. And that's what we are here to do. But with over 18 years of helping new businesses get off the ground, I am still stunned to read (and, unfortunately, know all too well from experience) that the number one reason new businesses fail is that there is simply no market or need for their goods or services.

Look at the top of the list. According to the study, a stunning 42% of businesses fail because there was no market need for their product. 42%! This means that 42% of people starting a business, putting in all that blood, sweat, and tears, are doing so only to find out, when they launch, that no one will care, no one will buy their product.

IF YOU BUILD IT, WILL THEY COME?

This statistic always reminds me of a line from one of my favorite movies. The year is 1989, and the movie is *Field of Dreams,* starring the world's then-biggest movie star, Kevin Costner, pre-*Waterworld*, of course. Kevin plays the role of Ray Kinsella, a farmer who lives with his wife, Annie, and daughter, Karin, on their corn farm in rural Iowa. Ray has daddy issues, and is haunted by the relationship with his late father, a devoted baseball fan.

Walking through his cornfield one evening, Ray hears a voice whisper, "If you build it, he will come". Of course, like any sane individual, Ray believes he is slowly losing his mind. I mean, corn does not talk. And if it did, how terrifying would that be? Trying to eat corn on the cob while it screams "Noooooooooo!" But I digress.

As the movie progresses, the voice continues to haunt him. At some point, he sees a vision of a baseball diamond in his field of corn and an image of the great Shoeless Joe Jackson, a disgraced former major league player for the Chicago White Sox.

Who?

Alrighty then, time for a little actual U.S. history. The year is 1919 and World War I – the War to End All Wars - had just ended. America, like the rest of the world, was looking forward to a time of peace and prosperity heading into the Roaring Twenties. The 18th Amendment is passed, ushering in Prohibition. Later, the 19th Amendment is passed, giving women the right to vote. Of course, no wild parties could be held to celebrate the 19th, given that pesky 18th just one amendment prior. Should have planned that one better. I mean, really.

That year, the Chicago White Sox lost the World Series to the Cincinnati Reds, you know, one of those red teams from the current National League Central. But the Reds' victory, and, better stated, the Sox's loss, was awash in controversy. Joe Jackson, now known infamously as Shoeless Joe Jackson, and seven of his White Sox teammates, were accused of accepting $5,000 each to throw the World Series to the Cincinnati Reds. Criminal charges were brought against the eight, but all of them were acquitted. I mean, this is Chicago after all. That town is not famous for putting criminals behind bars, you know.

Despite their acquittals, however, the then-new commissioner of major league baseball, eager to flex a little muscle, issued a lifetime ban on the players for their involvement in the scandal. In short, their baseball careers were over. They were never allowed to set foot on a baseball diamond again, well, at least one controlled by Major League Baseball. Wonder what he would have done with the 2017 Houston Astros? Bet it wouldn't have just been fines.

Returning to *Field of Dreams*: as the movie progresses, Ray begins to piece together that if he builds a baseball field in his Iowa cornfield, Shoeless Joe, his father's idol, will once again be able to play baseball. That, in turn, will bring him somehow closer to his deceased father. Following this? I mean, it makes sense. And not far-fetched at all.

Now, why are the disgraced eight from the 1919 Chicago White Sox hanging out in a corn field in Iowa in 1989? I don't know. Watch the movie. It's great, I promise you!

Skipping forward just a bit: Ray builds the field. It was his vision. He was confident that, if he built it, they would come. And sure enough, when he builds it, they do. One at first, and you guessed it, yes, it's Shoeless Joe Jackson, played by a young Ray Liotta. Who, coincidentally, looked like a now- older Ray Liotta. That man has looked the same for thirty years. What gives? Figure that one out. Maybe someone should write a sci-fi plot based on that.

Anyways, as they finish their game of catch and Shoeless Joe heads back into the corn, he asks Ray if, tomorrow, he can bring the others? Of course. And before long, all eight of the disgraced White Sox are playing games on the new field, built by Ray on his corn farm in Iowa. Trust me, despite my quips, it's magical.

Not everyone believed in Ray's vision. And that, as you will learn, is OK. But Ray believed it. And in Ray's *Field of Dreams,* there is a very important lesson for all aspiring entrepreneurs. A fundamental question everyone must answer before walking through that cornfield on their own, searching for your vision: *If you build it, will they come?*

You see, many people are in love with the concept of being an entrepreneur, but not actually being an entrepreneur. Most people fall in love with the perception of freedom that comes with entrepreneurship. Being your own boss. Setting your own hours. Rising and falling on your own merit.

But few have the constitution to truly make it work, to understand what it takes to develop a product, market it, price it right, and sell it. We look at the icons of entrepreneurship: Steve Jobs, Elon Musk, Bill Gates, Phil Knight, and Sir Richard Branson, and think, "*I'll be the next self-made billionaire!*" But before they all started, they had to ask one fundamental question, if I build it, will they come?

As we are all aware, Steve had a hand in constructing some of the greatest hardware and software in the history of computing. From an early age, he believed he could deliver a personal computing experience to the masses, and transformed an industry. Later, he would transform the company he founded by revolutionizing the personal music device industry, then the cell phone industry.

Elon changed the way payments are accepted over the Internet. Later, he transformed the car industry by making the world's first sexy electric car. And, as I write this chapter, his Dragon capsule, launched through his SpaceX company, has just delivered the first two US astronauts from US soil to the International Space Station.

Bill looked at the way computers operate and said we can do better. He created a revolutionary user interface for computing that made him one of the wealthiest men in the history of the world.

Phil created a good shoe, then captured the market by some of the greatest marketing campaigns in history, securing the paid endorsements of almost every athletic superstar to peddle his line of shoes. “Just Do It”!

And, of course, there’s Sir Richard. Richard started with a record store, then a record label, then an airline, and has now expanded his brand into trains, cruise ships, banking and other industries, just to name a few. A true marketing genius, his Virgin Brand is known worldwide as a symbol of raucous sophistication, harkening back to the glory days of the 1960s in Great Britain.

But Steve, Elon, Bill, Phil, and Sir Richard had one thing in common: they understood the first step along the entrepreneurship path is to ask that fundamental question: *If I build it, will they come?*

All too often in my career I have witnessed countless individuals in love with the concept of being an entrepreneur yet failing to ask that fundamental question before starting down the path. The result? You build it, and no one comes.

A FRICKIN' BAD IDEA

Years ago, I had the pleasure of assisting a small start-up with protecting their brand for a new label of beer they had envisioned: Frickin' Beer. Yup, you heard me right, Frickin' Beer. So how did they come up with the name for the product? Well, sit back and have a listen.

One night, my customers, who were all in the marketing industry, were sitting around tossing back a few cold ones. As they tell the story, at some point the evening got, well, a little rambunctious. During their alcohol-fueled revelry, you know, where most great ideas are launched, someone yelled out, "Gimme another Frickin' Beer", and the rest is history. Well, not good history. Not to be outdone, one of the other boozers doubles down and exclaims "That's genius!" The others asked, "What?" And here it is, "We need to start a beer company and the name of the beer will be, "Frickin' Beer!"

Yeah!!!! All the guys shouted as, no doubt, they started dreaming of the riches they would soon have with their new label. Mind you, none of them had ever worked for a brewery, the beverage industry, or even a restaurant. In fact, no one had ever even brewed beer at home with their own kit. OK, let's face it, the entirety of their beer experience was drinking it and, on some nights, maybe a tad too much. Now most of us get up the next day, take a few aspirins, and say, "Damn, we are not doing that again, well, at least until next Friday. By the way, where the hell are we?"

These guys, despite no relevant experience whatsoever, woke up and, and—you can almost hear it now—shouted in unison,

"Give me a Frickin' Beer!!!" I mean, if I were involved earlier on in the process, I would have told them that stealing Mike Tyson's tiger would have been a better plan. Undaunted, we began efforts to secure the brand. That was my part. And admittedly, we had a fight on our hands to do it.

But the larger issue was this: they'd never brewed beer. They had no experience brewing beer. They did not even know what type of beer they wanted to bottle. In short, they did not know what their product was going to be. They had merely come up with a name for the product, without developing the product itself. That would be like Elon Musk saying he was going to found Tesla, but then had no idea what would make his cars special, or what type of cars he wanted to produce. Like Phil Knight founding Nike, having no idea if he wanted to make sneakers, loafers, or dress shoes.

All the guys knew at Frickin' was that they thought the brand was funny. And because of that, everyone would flock to buying the brand. So, they worked on the label. They worked on marketing. But somewhat amazingly, in last place on their "to do" list was the actual product itself, the beer. Did they think they were going to be the next Boston Beer Company, makers of Samuel Adams? If you have ever seen their commercials, what do they emphasize? The brew masters, and their love for making a great beer. The fresh barley and hops that go into the beer. In other words, the *beer*!

But the Frickin' guys, well, they thought it was just about the name. Perhaps if you're selling in little tourist towns such as Key West, Wilmington, NC, or Virginia Beach, you'll sell some products on humor alone. But to be more concerned about the name without a tested product? Not a good strategy. Again, though, recall from whence this strategy came—over one too many Frickin' beers.

Well, in the end, they were never able to decide upon a Frickin' product to go in their Frickin' bottles sufficient that they thought consumers would Frickin' buy it. So, the whole Frickin' company went to hell and eventually Frickin' closed.

The first step in your journey must always to be to, in a well-reasoned, preferably sober manner, come up with a product that people want. But the Frickin' guys are not alone. This can happen to anyone. Even the author of this book.

THE SOFTWARE THAT NO ONE WANTED

When The Trademark Company first launched for business in 2003, we specialized in one thing and one thing only: Registering Federal Trademarks. From the initial filings to responses to refusals—that's a thing—that is what I wanted to do. That was my vision. That was my dream. And we did it well. Arguably better than anyone else, ever.

But as the years went along, despite adding tangential services to our core offerings, we just seemed to keep hitting a ceiling with our growth. Originally, it was simply replacing my $50,000 per year salary. Add some employees, then we needed more. I can still remember the first year we eclipsed $1 million in revenue. Then $2 million, $3 million. But for some reason, we kept hitting that ceiling. And it was frustrating.

There are a couple of different ways to get past the proverbial ceiling. First, we could grab a larger market share. In short, we knew the pie, at the time, was about 200,000 trademark filings per year. And, at our height, we were only 1 or 2% of that market. So right there, we could increase our slice of the pie. That was option one.

Second, we could create and/or grow the market for trademarks by educating consumers on the need for a federally registered trademark and, assuming our market share percentage remained constant, growing the pie for all via education, thus increasing our overall business. In short, if we were to grow the overall market for federal trademarks from 200,000 to 300,000 per year, assuming we could maintain that 1-2% share, we would increase our business by 50%!

Third, we could enter vertical markets by expanding our product lines and offering tangential or complimentary services to those already offered, such as business training and other related business services. Well, one of the challenges of competing in a niche industry is the limited opportunity for growth. At the time The Trademark Company was founded, only 200,000 federal trademarks were filed per year. But at that same time, about 6 million small businesses were formed every year. So which industry do you think offered more growth?

We settled on option three. It had the lowest up-front cost and, we figured, we could make an easy entry into the market by simply building out the services, then offering them online.

To this end, we developed basic software to assist our customers to write their own business plans. The consumer was asked about 10 critical questions, everything from the name of the business, their marketplace and top competitors, and how they intended to enter and secure a market share. When we launched the software in 2016, I expected big things would result. I mean, how cool is this? Fill in a few blanks and a custom, 30-page business plan would be generated. Who wouldn't buy one?

Well, as it turns out, nobody. We never sold one business plan package. Not one! Zero. Nada. Get the picture? It was a complete disaster. And to think: all that time and effort developing the software, only to see it fail. It was like watching the movie *Field of Dreams,* only in the end, we yelled back to that voice from the corn, "Well, we built it, where the hell are they?"

Allow me to pause here, as many of you may be questioning why you are reading a book from someone who, like me, has failed when launching a product. After all, why would you take advice from a loser? But, as the adage goes, don't be afraid to fail. We learn more from our failures than our successes. And I have failed, a lot. But my victories in business and in life far outweigh my losses. As Thomas Edison once famously replied when asked about how many times he failed when making the light bulb, "I haven't failed – I've just found 10,000 ways that won't work." So never be afraid to fail. Be afraid to fail and not get up and try again. Then, when you stay down and don't get up, that is the only true failure.

Back to our Business Plan Software. So why did it fail? The product was solid. Check. The ease-of-use perfect. Check. But were we offering a product that was too, well, 1980s? Do businesses still need a business plan? Today's younger generation especially questions the concept. And perhaps, ironically, what we failed to recognize in rolling out this software was that the world has moved away from stodgy, traditional business plans and, instead, to the more dynamic concept of a business map. We'll chat about that a little later in the book.

While we built an amazing software package to help us enter the business filings market, we failed to determine, prior to all that effort, whether there was an actual market for our product. In short, perhaps based upon some form of failed assumption, we moved forward with the software and had a full operational platform only to find out, the hard way, there was no one interested in the same.

Accordingly, before you launch your product, before you walk into the man's office, fist held high, and quit your day job and storm out to the applause you believe will happen when you move on, make sure you ask yourself one critical question: If I build it, will they come?

A ROBOT THAT WAS BEHIND THE TIMES

Years ago, we had the good fortune to assist a young inventor who had solved a problem she had witnessed on a very personal level. Her grandmother had been a life-long smoker who, as a result of that pastime, had been rewarded with chronic COPD as well as emphysema, a couple of parting gifts brought to you by your friendly neighborhood cigarette manufacturer.

What is COPD you might ask? Well, to answer that question, let's take a walk down human anatomy lane. Have you ever wondered how you breathe? I mean, sure, we all take it for granted, right? In the time you just read the last two or three sentences you've probably inhaled and exhaled 2 or 3 times without ever thinking about it. But what happened in those moments, and why did your brain tell you to do it almost without thinking?

The answer lies in our basic human physiology. In short, we as humans largely need three things to live. Food, water, and oxygen. This is easy to remember if you have ever heard of the rule of 3s. Thirty days without food, you're gone. Three days without water, you're gone. Three minutes without oxygen, you're gone. It's that simple.

Well, we all know how we get food and water into our system. That's called your digestive track. We learn about this in school from a very early age. The food and water go in the pie hole. They are typically broken up first by your teeth and saliva. They drop down your esophagus and into your stomach. Or, as Fat Bastard, would quip from the Austin Powers series, *Get in my belly!*

The acid of your stomach starts the process of breaking it down further, then it drops into your intestines where the real magic happens. Like a FedEx sorting facility, your intestines figure out which nutrients go where and distribute them throughout your body as they are absorbed. Anything left over, well, you know what happens with that, especially if you're a fan of the Home Wrecker Burrito from Moe's. But I digress.

But back to your lungs: what's going on in there? In school, most of us were simply taught that you breathe in and presto, oxygen in your body. But, in reality, it is so much cooler than that. What are your lungs anyways? Most of us think of them as these two elastic bags that simply fill up and down every time you breathe and exhale. But the reality— what's going on in there at a cellular level—is so cool I've got to share it with you.

Your lungs are made up of 5 lobes and 5 independent chambers, each of which contain millions of these little, tiny air sacks called alveolar sacks. Why 5? I don't know. Most likely to have left room for your heart on one side, but also to provide redundancy in the system if you lose a lobe or two, prior to the days when we had surgery that could, to some degree, repair damage to the same. These little, tiny alveolar sacks, in turn, are what fills up with air, and oxygen, every time you breathe in.

Every time you breathe in—and now you are thinking about it—millions of little air bags are filling up with air and oxygen, and almost as quickly as you breathe it in, you breathe it out and repeat the process. In, and out. In, and out. Well for most of us, that's easy.

But imagine if that ease of breathing, the simple in-out you've been doing, was suddenly taken away. Welcome to the wonderful world of COPD, or Chronic Obstructive Pulmonary Disorder.

One of the awesome benefits of smoking, aside from lung cancer (higher rates of all cancers) smoker's mouth, etc., is that the tar from the cigarettes (yes even filtered cigarettes) eventually makes its way all the way to your alveolar sacks. This, in turn, clogs up those sacks one at a time, leading to diminished lung capacity. Maybe you don't notice it on day one. But eventually, that's why we see those old jokes about smokers climbing stairs and huffing and puffing. It's because they have damaged their lungs to the point the alveolar sacks are working overtime just to get in enough O2 to power muscles to go up a simple flight of stairs. Ha ha ha. Slow, asphyxiating death is so hysterical. Anyways.

Coming all the way back to our story: my customer's grandmother had been a life-long smoker and had developed COPD as a result. So that she could survive and get enough oxygen into her bloodstream, she was required to be on oxygen from a tank for the rest of her life. Well, for anyone who has seen this from the old days, people would have a tank in one room of the house, and then would simply have like a 100-foot cord so they could walk around anywhere in their homes. Of course, you can imagine the drawback of this.

If you've ever seen a dog on a long leash, there you go. The cords get wrapped around anything in the house. They knock stuff over. If you're not expecting it, and they get tangled on a piece of furniture, they can suddenly rip your mask right off your face. Not pleasant.

My customer had a great idea: I'm going to build granny a robot that follows her around with her oxygen tank. And, as her thought developed, I bet others will want this too! And she was right. Fixing a problem is one of the easiest ways to find a market for your goods and services. If you provide a fix to a known issue, people will come and buy it!

Now most of you are probably thinking about a robot like those in Will Smith's classic *iRobot* that would follow her around, talk with her, and give her O2 when needed. Yeah, no. Nothing that complicated. Rather, she did something brilliantly simple. For any of you familiar with the company *iRobot* and their product Roomba, she used an old Roomba as her prototype base for her O2 robot.

iRobot was originally a defense contractor, and manufactured robots for military use. Their robots were primarily used to sweep mines in battlefields throughout the world. At some point, the company added a commercial line of robots to clean your floors. Yup, the technology transferred from saving lives to saving people from dust bunnies. Their robots resemble little round discs that drive around your home in varying patterns vacuuming your floors. Candidly, I've had several over the years. They are amazing!

Watching her grandmother amble around her apartment, constantly fighting to keep her oxygen cord free from entanglements, my customer had her eureka moment: what if I took a Roomba and outfitted it with a holder for an oxygen tank, further adding some electronics so that wherever granny walked, it followed her like Mary and her little lamb? And she did.

Using an early model Roomba she fashioned a positional location system on it—I have no idea how—so that it would follow her grandma wherever she walked, carrying her oxygen tank always within a few feet of her. No more cord entanglements. No more frustrated granny.

The prototype worked great. We took care of all the branding. A patent lawyer helped her with some of the other aspects of what she had created. Once all the legal stuff was squared away, she began setting up meetings with potential angel investors. After all, this was an innovative product at the time. She was set to make a bundle. And then it happened. A small company came up with a shoulder-held, small oxygen generating device that was more innovative than what my customer had invented. And, in that moment, her product—innovative in and of itself—was leap-frogged by greater innovation. And before it could see the light of day, of being offered to the marketplace, the market left her innovation in the rear-view mirror. And no one ever saw the product again.

If you build it, will they come, is the first critical question you must ask. And, as we have seen above, if you create software without considering the market, you're wasting your time. If you're an innovator, you can be leap-frogged by another's innovation. You must understand why they are going to buy it from you, and get it to market when it is still relevant.

IT'S GOTTA BE DA SHOES, MONEY!

I can't tell you how many people have come to me over the years saying they want to be the next clothing or branding mogul like Damon John of Shark Tank fame, P Diddy, or anyone else who has just built a brand to the point people flock to their clothing. If I had to guess, I'd put the number between five and six thousand. And, with few exceptions, when I've asked them the question "OK, so why is someone going to buy your stuff?", 99% of them cannot answer that question. But there is that 1% out there. And the best one I recall was Blake Mycoskie.

In 2006, Blake was already a successful entrepreneur, having founded and sold a few companies. While visiting Argentina in 2006, Blake met an American woman who was part of a volunteer organization providing shoes for children in need. "Shoes?" He thought. "Hadn't realized lack of proper footwear was an issue." Blake then spent several days travelling from village to village with the group, as well as to some villages on his own. "I witnessed the intense pockets of poverty just outside the bustling capital," he wrote in a 2011 article for *The Business Insider*. "It dramatically heightened my awareness. Yes, I knew somewhere in the back of my mind that poor children around the world often went barefoot, but now, for the first time, I saw the real effects of being shoeless: the blisters, the sores, the infections."

Inspired, Blake returned to the United States and founded *Shoes for Better Tomorrows*. Although it was designed as a for-profit business, its mission was to continually give new shoes to disadvantaged children. Specifically, he created the "One for One" business model: the company would donate a new pair of shoes for every pair of shoes sold. The initial model of shoe, like the Argentinian Alpargata, was created to appeal to a worldwide audience, which would both sustain the company's mission and generate a profit.. The name of the company, *Shoes For A Better Tomorrow*, would later be shortened to its more famous name, *TOMS*, upon which I was honored to have worked.

So unlike so many who want to be the next FUBU, Polo, or even JUICY, but who don't have a clue as to how they will generate interest in their brand once launched, Blake knew from the start. One of the first great examples of how social entrepreneurship can lead to great success. And has TOMS been a success?

By 2019, TOMS, and its concept of One for One, had proven so successful that the company has now donated 93 million pairs of shoes since inception–not to mention also giving millions of dollars to causes, as well. The company donates between 40-50% of net profits, the highest percentage of any U.S. company!

BE THE SEXIEST PERSON AT THE BAR

What have we learned? Looking back, we saw blood, sweat, and tears go into software that no one wanted, a robot that was made irrelevant before it could get to market, and a Frickin' bad idea for beer. But what did we see go right? We saw an experienced entrepreneur, and one of the people who was really one of the initial greats of social entrepreneurship, take the market by storm. Zero product sold for the first three years. Over 93 million pairs of shoes have been given away by Blake's TOMS to date. Hopefully this will jump off the page for you by now. So how are you going to be the sexiest person at the bar?

Wait, what? Where is he going with this now? Sexiest person in the bar? I thought we were talking about product development. I thought we were talking about being an entrepreneur. Well, check and check. But as I always explain to every salesperson whom I've ever hired, when you're selling something, it's no different from trying to meet people at a bar, and it's a lot easier to do that when you're the sexiest person at the bar. Huh? you may say. Let me explain.

OK, I'll give you an example. Seems like we have an abundance of sexy actors named Chris right now. From our *Guardian of the Galaxy* Chris Pratt to Captain Kirk Chris Pine. And who can forget Captain America Chris Evans or the God of Thunder Thor, Chris

Hemsworth. For the purpose of our lesson, I'll just let you insert your own "Chris" into the story.

Two guys go to a bar one night hoping to meet a prospective date. On the one hand, we have Chris. Chris is 6 foot 1 inches tall. Physically fit. Full head of perfectly groomed hair. A smile that just lights up the room whenever he flashes it. And, moreover, he has a presence about him that's just, for lack of other terminology, cool. He's just wrapped shooting his latest flick and is jazzed about life and his career. Oh, and his payday for his work? A cool $20 million.

On the other hand, we have Phil. Phil is 5 foot, 3 inches tall. He's wearing a shirt that is comically too tight around the midsection and has let himself go in the last few years. Hairline is receding, but rather than shave it down and own it, he is starting to do the comb over thing. His smile still has a piece of chicken hanging out from between two teeth from the buffalo wings he had before coming to the bar. He sits in the corner, by himself, and almost fades into the darkness. He hates his low-paying career, and will complain to anyone who will listen about how he can't wait to find somewhere else to work.

At the end of the night, if you had to put your money on the line, your actual hard-earned money, who would you bet would have more dates? Pretty easy when you think about it, right? And no, the answer is not Phil! I know. I know.

Stunner, right? But I have got to tell you, any one of those Chris's is probably going to beat out Phil. Even Pratt's Andy character from *Parks and Rec*, who was one sandwich short of being fat. So why? Well, when you go through our thought process, aren't we all just looking for Chris in every decision that we make? I mean,

I want the Chris of beer, the one that tastes good to me and that I enjoy. I want the Chris of cars, one that looks great and is fun to drive. I want the Chris of everything. OK, this analogy is getting a little weird. But hopefully the point has been driven home. Does anyone ever want to truly settle for Phil? No! Why? Because Phil is not the sexiest person in the bar. That's why.

Coming full circle, you must think about making your product the proverbial sexiest person in the bar. Ask from the very start: why is anyone going to buy this from me? You've got to be able to answer that question. If you cannot, stop what you are doing and figure out the answer. It is the single most important question that, in my experience of helping thousands and thousands of individuals and businesses get their start, is overlooked way too often. And, according to the research set forth above, it is the reason that over 40% of new businesses fail. There is simply no market need for your product. You built it, and they did not come. You built Phil!

So, before you leave that lucrative job, or one that just pays the bills, you must ask yourself, are you selling Chris, or are you trying to sell Phil? Which would you rather broker if given the choice? So how do you know when you have a Chris? Well, there are some time-tested models that will help you guide you to this answer.

In general, when you come up with a new product or service, you must be able to identify yourself as one of three categories of offerings to be able to drum up interest, and sales, in your product. If you can't, you need to be able to figure out how to get into one of the categories to truly see a market for your product. Let's look at them now. The categories are:

1. A New or Better Concept.
2. An Innovation.
3. The Low-Cost Provider.

A BLISSFUL EXPERIENCE

A few years back, I was approached to help with the branding of a new ice cream company's flagship trademark *SHEER BLISS: Ultra Superior Premium Ice Cream*. The gentlemen had little experience in the ice cream market, but had discovered that current packaging for ice cream, primarily variants of paper and cardboard, led to the degradation of the ice cream's flavor. They came up with the concept of packaging their ice cream, the SHEER BLISS product, in metal tins which preserved the flavor to a greater degree than the inferior paper packaging standard in the industry. They began production of the product, we secured the names for them, and away they went.

What was their innovation? Why would people buy their product? I mean, have you ever been concerned about the packaging of your ice cream? Probably not. Just the flavor, right? Recognizing this challenge from the onset, they set out on a campaign of educating the consumer as to why their ice cream tasted better than all the rest. I can still remember their big breakthrough like it was yesterday.

Gary, Sheer Bliss's CEO, had made it on to the Today Show with Matt Lauer and Anne Curry. They were doing taste tests of various ice creams, and on the table was Gary's Sheer Bliss Pomegranate with Dark Chocolate Chips. When the hosts of the show got to his ice cream, he had a moment to explain about the metal packaging. And, one by one, as they tasted his ice cream, they all exclaimed how amazing it was. How wonderful it tasted. How it was the best ice cream they had ever had.

At that moment, Gary had done it. They had created a fantastic product and had distinguished themselves with an innovation, the metal can, and got the word out through the hosts of the most-watched morning show, exclaiming how amazing the ice cream was. In the days that followed, orders skyrocketed. Sheer Bliss had made it!

What did they do right? They produced a product, namely ice cream. Well, so does everyone else! Or at least a lot of companies do. So how did they distinguish themselves from the others? I mean, if they just produced ice cream, who would care? Who would buy it? But they added in the innovation of the metal can that made the ice cream taste better. But they did not stop there. They then made sure everyone knew about it, and did they ever. Going on the Today Show, educating the consumers, then having the hosts exclaim 'This is the best ice cream I've ever had!' Now that's a plan. And that's what you need when you launch. If you build it, will they come, and why?

On a larger scale, years before, we saw this happen in the United States from a kid from Brooklyn. The young man simply has a passion for the Italian Cafe experience. In the mid-1980s, he fell in love with the allure of little neighborhood coffee shops sprinkled throughout the cities of Italy. He loved how they were gathering places where people could enjoy a beverage of choice, hang out and just relax. He felt if he could only bring that concept to the U.S. and reach the American consumer, perhaps they, too, would fall in love with the romance of coffee like the that shared by our neighbors in Italy.

And so began his quest to educate the U.S. consumer and build a brand. At the time, we had specialty coffee shops, but nothing that really captured his vision. He founded a line of stores named Il Giornale to capitalize on what he felt was a great idea. Although they did well, they truly did not capture the experience that he was looking for. His search led him to a small coffee-roasting company in the Pacific Northwest, specifically Seattle. They were operating a few stores then, but were more into roasting the beans than delivering the finished Italian Cafe product he wanted.

In time, Il Giornale merged with this coffee-roasting company from Seattle, adopting their name, as he felt it was the look and feel he was aiming for. The name, of course, Starbucks. Heard of them? The kid from Brooklyn? self-made billionaire and Starbucks visionary Howard Schultz.

But like Gary of Sheer Bliss, Howard knew he had to educate the consumers on the love of coffee, the romance of his vision. So, he did. He took an ordinary, everyday commodity that was just a staple, and made it sexy. He made it cool to get a cup of coffee, or a latte, or whatever else Starbucks made. It's not just coffee, it's now an idea, a status symbol.

So, did *Sheer Bliss* just sell ice cream? Does Starbucks just sell coffee? No! They sell ultra-premium ice cream, and the romance of coffee and Italian coffee shops. Obviously, Gary, and to a dramatically larger scale, Howard, got it.

If you build it, will they come? Well, if you are an innovator and market the hell out of that innovation, the answer is yes!

INNOVATE AN ENTIRELY NEW PRODUCT

Another great way to make sure someone will buy your offering is to provide that solution through innovation or technology, something that no one has ever seen before.

A few years back, we at The Trademark Company recognized a need for our customers, and the market, for an alternative to the more expensive, traditional legal representation in trademark registration. You see, up until that point, filing for new businesses and trademarks was relatively simple. There's a fill-in-the blank form, where the customer provides the information. It's uploaded to the proper government entity. BAM! They get their business formed, or their trademark registered. Well, sort of. In the trademark world, nothing is ever guaranteed.

In short, once the application is filed, it must be examined by a human, then they decide if it is worthy of registration. Most of the time trademarks get at least a minor rejection, asking the applicant to clarify some minor issue before it can be approved. But other times, trademarks get outright rejected because they either look too much like another trademark, or just aren't something the office thinks should be registered.

When one of these big refusals is issued, you need to have a custom response filed that addresses the reasons for the refusal, and makes an argument that the trademark should be registered. Well, custom argument? Legal analysis? These are things traditionally left to attorneys, right? Attorneys that charge lots of money to make these custom arguments, whether they work or not.

But what if someone could design software that assembles custom responses to those office actions? What if someone could make a TurboTax-like, user-friendly interface that, when a customer untrained in the law, just answers easy questions, it assembles a custom response to the refusal that works to get their trademark registered a significant amount of the time? What if?

After looking around for the right platform upon which to build this software, we finally found it. A few hiccups had to be ironed out, but now, using this innovative software, 95% of our customers can assemble responses to even the most complex of legal refusals, all at a fraction of the price for what a law firm would charge. Has it been a hit? Oh yes, it has. We've been able to help so many of our customers get past refusals from the U.S. Patent and Trademark Office using this innovation, so they too can get their trademark and continue with their American Dream.

Innovation pays. It truly does.

BATTER UP...

One of my favorite stories about innovation is about our customer Rob Vito and his company Unequal Technologies. Rob is one of the greatest guys I've ever met, and just an absolute joy to be around. By training, Rob is a scientist from Penn State University, who embodies the adage of "You never know where life will take you." If memory serves me correctly, many years ago Rob was approached by Penn State's legendary football coach Joe Paterno, prior to the scandal that would cost him his job and legacy. Penn State had a big game that week, and their starting quarterback had busted up his ribs in the preceding game.

Joe asked Rob if he could fashion something that would allow him to play without fear of further injury. Rob thought about it and agreed. It took him a little while to come up with the prototype, but he created an anti-compression Kevlar vest for the Penn

State QB that protected him from those pesky Big Ten defenders. The result? The quarterback was able to play the game, played well, and notched another victory for Joe Pa's then-storied legacy.

Here is where it starts to get interesting, and I hope that I remember this correctly. After this initial success, Rob was toying around with whether such a product would have commercial success. In other words, was there a market for this type of protective gear in sports? One day, he gets a call from some guy named Jerry Jones. As the story goes, after some initial introductions Jerry asked, "Hey, our QB ... Tony ... you know Tony Romo ... he's got some dinged-up ribs. Can you fandangle us one of those things you did at PSU?"

"Sure," Rob replied. And this is where it gets *really* interesting.

Rob fashions the new flak jacket for Tony. Of course, he makes a couple of spares. He flies out to the game to fit Tony and watch his creation. Just prior to the game, the press gets wind of this and asks Rob to demonstrate the product. Rob straps on the vest, then hands the report a baseball bat. The reporter looks at him, on live TV, in disbelief. Rob says, “Hit me.” Swing away! So, he does. Rob barely felt a thing. A legend was born! Unequal Technologies was born! Don't believe me? Just search Rob Vito and baseball bat on YouTube. It's there.

Rob had innovated an entirely new line of products. Within just a few months, they went from being just a little start-up to getting their first round of Venture Capital, then second, and so on. This chance company has changed Rob's life in ways you can hardly imagine. His Unequal Technologies company is now valued in the hundreds of millions. In addition to their traditional protective equipment, they are at the forefront of the war against concussions in athletics. And with Rob's mind, I'm confident he'll have them solved soon.

As an aside, one of the coolest things that happened to him along the way was when he took yet another call. Gotta tell you, he has received a lot of cool calls. As the story goes on this occasion, he picked up his cellphone and a voice on the other end of the phone said, "Is this Rob Vito?"

"Yes, it is," he replied.

"Hey Rob, this is Tom Cruise, do you know who I am?"

For a minute Rob thought, no way, someone is messing with me. But as he has been taught so many times before, go with it and see where it leads you. Turns out it *was* Tom; he was working on a project and wanted Rob to build the suits for him and for the other actors in the movie. Rob agreed and got to spend two weeks on the set with Tom, fitting him, refitting him, and making sure everything worked smoothly on the suits he constructed. The movie: *Edge of Tomorrow*.

THE APPLE OF JOBS' EYE

Behind every successful product lies a problem in search of a solution. The now iconic iPod was born out of the pitiful state of the young MP3 player market in the late 1990s. By that time, portable MP3s had been in the market for several years, but Apple found that all the then-existing products on the market offered a truly lackluster user experience. In his classic fashion, Steve Jobs had a simple term that perfectly summed up his view for gadgets like that: "Crap". All at Apple agreed.

Flash memory-based players of the era held only about a CD's worth of songs. Hard drive players held far more but were relatively big, heavy, and they sported user interfaces that were difficult and that didn't scale well when scrolling through tons of songs. Moreover, most portable media players used a pokey USB 1.1 standard to transfer music from a host computer to the player, making the user wait up to five minutes to transfer a CD's worth of songs. Want to move thousands of songs? Settle in, as the transfer time would shoot up to several hours.

Considering the poor state of the market, Jobs decided that Apple should create its own MP3 player, one that played well with iTunes and would attract more customers to the Mac platform. He assigned Jon Rubinstein, then Apple's senior VP of hardware, to the new project.

Rubinstein began his research on the MP3 project. Almost from the beginning, he identified two ingredients that the current market players were lacking: a speedy FireWire interface to solve the transfer problem, and tiny 5GB hard drive that would make Apple's music device smaller than any other hard drive-based player on the market. With most of Apple's teams tied up in Mac-related projects, Rubinstein sought help from outside the company. Rubenstein turned to Tony Fadell to help design and engineer the new MP3 player.

Fadell's initial design had the iPod's face dominated by a simple rectangular display and the now-iconic scroll wheel, which, unlike later models, physically moved when you spun it. After six months of hard work, the iPod began to come together. The concentrated and well-organized efforts of Apple's various iPod teams proved that they could finish the product in time.

Other MP3 players used plus and minus buttons that would move, one item at a time, through a list of songs, which would grow tedious if the unit held a thousand songs—basically, you'd have to push the button a thousand times. With a wheel, a quick flick of the finger would navigate through the list at any rate the user wanted—especially since Apple would make the scroll speed accelerate the longer you spun the wheel.

The iPod team met its deadline, shipping the first iPod in November 2001. To date, Apple has now sold more than 304 million iPods.

In sum, innovation sells. So long as it is still innovative by the time you get it to market, and you get the word out, it's going to sell. But what if you're not an innovator? What other models are out there that you can use to push your product?

THE LOWEST COST PROVIDER: A RECIPE FOR FAILURE?

Let's say you want to sell widgets. The only issue? There are 27 other on-line widget companies, all with the same idea, who already have their own market share. There's nothing special about your widgets. Yet you are still attracted to the market. One way to enter an existing market is to immediately adopt a lowest cost provider (LCP) model. What's that? Well, it's simple. It means that you enter the market with the lowest-price widget among all your competitors. And, if you get the word out, this is typically a pretty good model, for a while. However, it has a significant downside, known as the race to the bottom.

In short, it's easy to be the lowest cost provider on the block. Just look at the prices of your competitors, and lower yours until they are lower than the other guys, right? Pretty easy, huh? Well, not so fast, my young padawan. Let's say your competitor doesn't like you swiping all his business by lowering his prices. What does he do in return? One guess. If you said, "Lower his prices to a point below that of yours", congratulations! You win the prize!

Suddenly, you're losing those customers that you'd sort of stolen, by being the LCP! Well, you're not the type of person to take that lying down

You drop your prices again, and grab back that market share. But this time, you start running the numbers and realize that you've dropped your prices so low, you may be losing money. And guess what? Your competitor drops his prices again. It's the classic LCP in which no one wins and, eventually, someone loses big.

Don't think it happens? Take a listen.

TRADEMARK WARS

For years, the market for consumer trademarks was dominated by three major players. There were the nice folks whose original spokesman helped free OJ. Another company owned by *He who shall not be Named*, and yours truly at The Trademark Company. Now, in fairness, *Free OJ* was the market leader by a long shot. Their share was probably 5 times Lord Voldemort's, and 10 times ours. Damn it, I said his name. Well, not his real name. And for years, we had a peaceful co-existence, enjoying our respective market shares with 2 out of 3 of us focusing on customer service. You know *Voldemort*, he's never been much a people person. Damn it, said it again. Anyways.

Well, over the years, this peaceful co-existence went on. From time to time, we would have another player enter the market and try to wedge themselves in by becoming the LCP. And they'd come. They'd grab a little market share. But then, inevitably, they couldn't sustain their razor-thin margins and would need to drop out of the market before bankruptcy set in. Our three-headed OJ-freeing, Voldemort-resembling, Trademark Company domination continued until a smooth-talking caballero from Texas road into our trademark town in 2017.

El Caballero, as we will call him, hailed from a land frozen in time called Houston. Unlike so many who had come before him, he was a veteran of online legal services, having successfully run one of the largest business formation companies in the U.S. In 2017, he quietly entered the market with a sleek new web site and a price offering of half of that of The Trademark Company, *Free OJ*, and, of course, *Lord Voldemort*. Damn it, said it again.

The market tilted dramatically towards El Caballero as he and his LCP model quickly gobbled up a greater and greater share. Of the three original market leaders, our market share declined. I'm unsure as to whether *Free OJ*'s did, but it stands to reason it must have. And, based upon his reactions, Voldemort was incensed because he, in all intensive accounts, lost the most. Maybe he should have tried to work on his people skills? Anyways.

Well, two out of three of us had to react. And what did we do? Yup, The Trademark Company and *Lord Voldemort* dropped prices to match *El Caballero*. Once this happened, business stabilized, but margins were low. Too low. In fact, they were so low, we wondered how long we could hold at this price level.

But wait, there's more! You see, there is lots of stuff that happens when you drop prices that, to the uninitiated, you don't consider. First, your margins are dramatically reduced, leading to less money in the bank. With less money in the bank, you often must reduce or lower starting salaries, which leads to a lower quality of work force. A lower quality of work force leads to a lower quality of work, unless you hire and insert more management over those workers to make sure they are doing it right.

But with what, a smile? We already established you have less money, so you must hire less skilled workers. You simply don't have the resources to hire that management structure. And that's just on your business's side. What about the type of consumers? Ever think about that?

When you are the LCP, you must also understand you are going to attract a different class of consumer. In the industry, there is a nice term for it: sophistication. Typically, the higher the price point, consumers are assumed to be more sophisticated, more educated. The lower the price point, the less educated. That's not to say you can't have educated consumers that are lacking resources. It's just to say that, on average, the cheaper a product is it opens the market to the masses, and the masses are often not the brightest.

The next compounding factor is the time you end up spending with those consumers. Sophisticated consumers tend to ask less questions, then retain what they are told with a general understanding of the value proposition you bring to the table. Unsophisticated consumers tend to ask more questions and take up more time, because they neither understand what you do, nor do they retain what you have told them or what they can read on your web site. Loving this LCP model yet? But wait, there's more!

With a clientele of unsophisticated consumers, you'll notice that your customer service and online complaints will start to tick up. Because they may not understand the service you provide, or be able to comprehend the expectations of the service they begin to complain. And they complain way more than a sophisticated customer. The challenge of many of their complaints is that you did everything you were supposed to have done under your Terms of Service, but they are still dissatisfied, so they complain. And, of course, the time to deal with their complaints will weigh on any company, especially one whose margins are already so low by being the LCP. But hey, why stop there? The dominoes continue to fall. Trust me.

When they don't get a resolution to a problem you cannot solve because it was in your Terms of Service, they take to social media. They bash you anywhere and everywhere they can: Google, Yelp, the Better Business Bureau. Negative after negative reviews. Some are so committed they'll use multiple accounts to leave you multiple 1-star ratings from the same person. The review sites don't care, but prospective customers do. Think they want to go to a company that has a 1.7 rating on Google or Yelp? Well, not the ones that are sophisticated enough to look at your reviews first. And for those who are not, well, they just keep coming, continuing this nasty downward spiral.

No way, you say. Way, I reply. I watched it happen at The Trademark Company as we fought against *El Caballero*. When I founded The Trademark Company in 2003, the original price for a trademark was about $225. This was the price for the standard package. Sure, you had other options at higher price points. But this was the baseline. Over the years the price for that standard package remained largely consistent. At one point, it moved down to $149, where it stayed for years. From time-to-time, it would even would swing all the way to $99 in slow seasons for sales, etc. But 2017 saw something we had never seen before: $69! That's right, *El Caballero* came in with an almost unheard-of $69!

Initially, we resisted. But as the weeks turned into months and we began to watch our online orders plummet, we felt we had to react. We had to do something to get back our customers. We had to drop to the dreaded $69! But as we dropped, so too did Lord

Voldemort. And suddenly, Trademark Wars had something it had never had before: not one, not two, but three amigos at a $69 price point. It worked for a while.

Online orders went up. Money started to flow once again. Life was good. Well, so we thought. After a few months of this lower price point, we began to see the cracks in the wall of LCP philosophy. First, although the company was working at full capacity, the bank accounts just never seemed to be that full. Every week it was a struggle to get enough money in the door to pay the bills as a function of our razor-thin margins. Yet we were working like dogs to answer all the questions flowing from our new consumer base, and get all the work done they were paying us for. It was truly exhausting.

Soon, the questions began morphing into complaints as that new, unsophisticated consumer base seemingly lacked the capacity to understand our role in the trademark process, blaming us for everything from not doing things for them we were never contracted to do to if their trademarks were rejected by the USPTO —which happens with some frequency. Adding to the already-inundated phone lines from new customers who took up more and more time with questions to our account managers, tons of existing customers called back with mounting consumer complaints. It began to overwhelm the system.

And when we could not get to all the calls coming in, what do you think happened? Did they go quietly into the night? Nope. They took to social media and review sites to bash us, and bash us good. "Fraud," or "A scam!", they would post. "They took my money and got my trademark rejected!" On one level, you understand their frustration. After all, they paid for a service to register their trademark, and it got rejected. On the other hand, both our

Terms of Service and our Account Representatives were always very clear: the $69 price tag does not guarantee registration, just that it will be filed. Then the USPTO must decide whether to register the trademark. But the $69 clientele simply lacked the capacity to understand this reality.

Our Account Managers were exhausted from being beaten up all day with the barrage of angry calls. Their morale was at an all-time low. To make matters worse, because we were following the LCP, the bank accounts had barely enough in them to manage our current payroll, let alone hire the additional customer service help we so desperately needed.

We were trapped in the LCP downward spiral. Too many customers paying too few dollars, all angry and lowering our company's reputation in the process. This, in turn, led to a loss of higher value customers who saw our reviews and demanded their money back, often before even giving us a chance to get their work done. The company was literally drowning in unsophisticated customers paying too little for services that they did not understand.

And then it happened! We reached a breaking point: enough was enough. We could no longer deal with the $69 customer. They were killing the business. We thought, what if we raised prices? Not to what they were. But higher than they had ever been. Could we attract a higher level of consumer? So long as we sold one of the higher priced packages instead of three $69ers, we'd make the same money, yet have fewer customers to service curing so many issues. Let *El Caballero* and *Lord Voldemort* have the $69ers. God Bless if they can deal with that mess.

On a fateful in March 2020, as the global pandemic was just gathering steam here in the U.S., we did what no one would have expected: we raised prices across the board. But as we did, the perception of the value of our services also rose. To our pleasant surprise, the volume of our orders stayed about the same, but we were immediately receiving orders from more sophisticated customers, customers who, upon explanation, understood the role we play and the services that we provide. All the while, we increased our margins, allowing us to get growing once again as the world's economies began to struggle.

We know what the LCP model does. It encourages a race-to-the-bottom nosedive that, if undertaken by a novice, can lead to the demise of the company. Rather than to ever adopt an LCP model, focus on value to the consumer and not cost. You'll be glad you did.

Which brings us to the next topic for discussion: how to price your product or service.

THE PRICE IS RIGHT

This is one of the most challenging decisions that must be made by each entrepreneur: how much should my widget cost? As we've mentioned above, the first absolute in pricing is that it must, at a minimum, be priced so that sales price, based upon actual sales, is sufficient to cover the costs of your company. If not, it's priced too low, and selling more will only mean compounding the losses of the business. On the other hand, if you price it too high, no one will buy it.

In economics, we use a relatively simple chart to demonstrate this concept known as a Supply and Demand Curve.

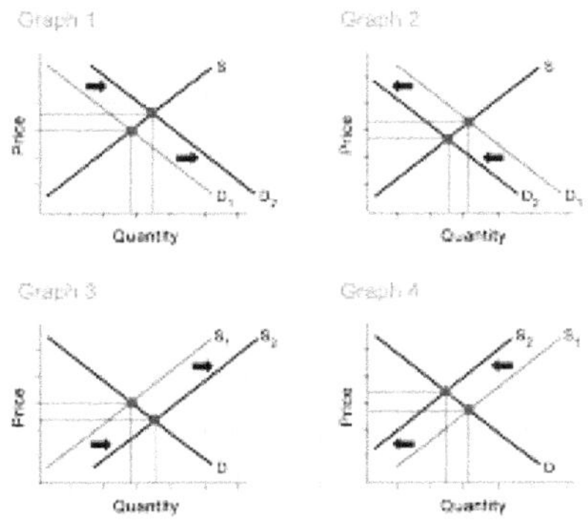

Figure A

In our curve, the vertical axis tracks price. The horizontal axis quantity. We then add in two lines to our graph representing Supply, how much of the product you and/or your competitors will be providing in the market, and Demand: how much the consumers want your product.

As we can see from all the graphs, your price point should, ideally, equal the point at which Supply transects Demand in the marketplace. Boring you enough yet? Didn't think we'd have a lesson in philosophical economics stuffed into the pages of this book, did you? Well, soak it up, because it's going to teach you very quickly about what you can charge for your products in just a few minutes.

So, as you can see, the price the market will tolerate for a product exists at the intersection of the Supply and Demand curves. If Supply remains constant, but Demand increases, the price that you can charge will increase (Graph 1). If Demand decreases while price remains constant, you must lower your price (Graph 2). Correspondingly, if Supply increases while Demand remains constant

(Graph 3) the price must go down. But if Supply decreases while the Demand remains constant the price will go up.

Now that your eyes are sufficiently crossed, what does this mean in real life?

KABBAGE PATCH ON DEMAND

Alrighty then, Graph 1 effectively shows the Kabbage Patch Doll scenario. Huh? you might say. Yup, the Kabbage Patch kids.

Way back in the 1980s, just before one Christmas, a series of dolls called the Kabbage Patch Kids caught fire in the marketplace. It was a national phenomenon. Everyone had to get a Kabbage Patch kid for their child. It was crazy. People would stand in line for hours waiting for stores to open that were rumored to have had a shipment of them overnight. They'd sprint to get one or two. They'd trip each other and, in some documented cases, even get into physical altercations over the last remaining dolls in a store's inventory. It was amazing. The phenomena inspired a segment on Saturday Night Live with Eddie Murphy getting in trouble for his famous character Mr. Robinson selling dolls with an actual cabbage for a head. It even inspired a movie with Arnold Schwarzenegger called *Jingle All the Way.* And I had a front-row ticket to the mayhem. How? Because a few years earlier, my mom and dad, as a side-gig, opened a toy store in Oakbrook Plaza in North Palm Beach, Florida.

Everyday we'd have crazed parents coming into our small, upscale toy store with their crazy eyes, their mouth frothing and yelling, "Do you have them? Do you have any Kabbage Patch Kids?" Now, as a small, specialty toy store, we generally did not sell mainstream stuff. And we had not ordered any of these dolls for the Christmas season. So, for much of the Christmas season, the answer was, "No, we do not." I can still recall the smell of failure as parents would turn and walk out of the store knowing that little Susy would not have her doll under the tree that year.

But then it happened. A Christmas miracle! One of the toy reps we used called my dad and said, "I can get 50 dolls. You want them?"

"Um, yeah" my dad said. And just like that, the stage was set for us to join the madness, to be one of those places they show on the news with people sprinting to the store where the dolls are displayed, bumping and tackling each other, and, on occasions, throwing punches. For a doll!

On an aside, I always wondered if some store owners purposefully set up their Kabbage Patch displays in the back of the store, just to watch the crazy Olympics trying to get back to them. I mean, they knew they would have a line of people sprinting to wherever they were. Why put them in the back left of the store, save for the amusement of the staff? Right?

Turning back to our Christmas Miracle: in Graph 1, we see what happens when supply remains constant but demand increases. The price of the goods can go up! Well, in the case of the Kabbage Patch kids, the demand curve couldn't exist on our graph it had shifted so far to the right. If I recall correctly, the suggested manufacturer's retail price for one of these dolls was $60 or $70 dollars. For a doll; $60 to $70 for some died fabric assembled in some foreign sweat shop. Wow. And remember, this was in the 80s!

To make matters more interesting, remember I mentioned we had a small, specialty toy store. Well, my dad had designed it in his own vision. He did not want a normal-looking toy store with your typical shelves. Nope, we had these cool, sleek-looking shelves built of a metal framework supporting . . . glass shelves.

Glass shelves! In a store for kids and toys! If we had one of those Kabbage Patch riots, man, there was going to be shattered glass and severed limbs everywhere. The horror!

Well, the day came when the Kabbage Patch Kids were set to arrive. Mind you, I think this was only days before Christmas and the country had lost its mind about these things. Demand was off the charts, and my dad probably could have charged $300 to $400 per doll. But he didn't. We opened that morning with no fanfare. We had not advertised we were getting about 50 of the dolls. Quietly, we started unpacking the boxes and putting them on those glass shelves. Mind you, this was in the days before social media, where word spread via word of mouth, literally.

I can still recall the face of the first person who walked into the store that morning when they saw the dolls sitting displayed on a shelf. It was like a person who had been wandering in the desert seeing an oasis and hoping it was not a mirage. They walked up, cocked their heads as they looked at the dolls, looked at me almost incredulously, then back at the dolls. And then the funniest thing they did, they actually poked one of the dolls with their index finger to see if it was real. I swear! They looked at me and said, "Are these really them?"

"They are" I replied. "Limit 2 per customer per our policy."

Before I could finish the sentence, he had already grabbed 2, and was reaching for his wallet. He rushed out of the store, and all was quiet for a few minutes... a few. It would not stay that way for long.

Word quickly spread. And did it spread. No riots, no fights, but those dolls sold out within an hour. To this day, I have rarely seen a better example of the demand curve being shifted so far to the right that you could charge whatever you wanted for a product.

Coming full circle to our lesson from a doll from the 1980s: where is the demand curve for your products or services? To truly price your product right, you must have some notion of where this is. But that's only half of the equation. Let's look at the other half.

TRADEMARK SUPPLY

I previously mentioned the story of The Trademark Company and our long-term competitors, the OJs and Lord Voldemort. That, in essence, is a perfect example of how supply can affect the market and price for a commodity.

During our years of competition, the demand for trademark services remained relatively constant. So too did the supply of those services. The OJs were always the biggest player in the industry, followed by us and LV. Sure, from time to time someone would ride in and pitch their tent in our space. But it was not until El Caballero rode into town that anyone Stuck. So, if you're scoring at home, we went from three primary providers to four.

Remember how I lamented that, when El Caballero rode in on his Jackass, he announced a new LCP price of $49 for a trademark application?! Well, maybe El Caballero was not as stupid as he seemed. In fact, if we look closely, it appears he may have had a course in Economics 101.

You see, El Caballero's entrance into the marketplace shifted the supply curve for trademark services to the right (Graph 3). And what does that do? Well assuming demand remains constant, as it must have, it lowers the price people are willing to pay for a good or service, due to the increased supply.

Think about it. It's no different than the oil industry, and what they used to do to the US every summer, in reverse (Graph 4). If you remember the George W. Bush administration, they had us all under the belief that oil prices, and specifically the cost of gas, had skyrocketed to around $3 to $5 per gallon, and that this was due to reduced supply in the marketplace. Hmmmm. And this was due to less oil in the ground? Um, no. Did the world's fleet of supertankers all sink in the same catastrophe? Nope. Well, what was it?

As it turns out, right before each summer driving season, oil companies would seemingly always need to perform maintenance on some of their U.S. refineries. Wow, what are the odds of this happening almost every year? Right before Memorial Day? Weird, right? And so, what happens when they shut down major refineries that turn crude oil into gasoline? It decreases the supply of gasoline in the US. Follow me? So, what does that do to the price of gas? Well, look back at Graph 4—prices shoot up. And they did. Every summer. Like clockwork. Until we got the oilman out of the oval office. Then price manipulation ended, and the price of gas has been far more stable since 2009.

Returning to the Trademark Wars. El Caballero's entrance into the market shifted the supply curve to the right. He likely foresaw this when he priced his service at $49. In short, since he knew he would be increasing the supply in the marketplace, why wait to follow the new price? Rather, understanding how supply and demand works, he set the price where he felt the supply and demand curves would meet, given the new supply curve his presence had altered in the industry. Wow. Not such a dumb cowboy, after all!

WHAT DOES ALL OF THIS MEAN FOR YOU?

Do you think El Caballero had a complex grasp of demand and supply curves? Maybe. Maybe not. More likely he just understood that there were three major players in the industry he was entering, and wanted to make a splash. What did he do? A little Internet research, most likely. All that he had to do was look at what the competitors were charging and, having decided on an LCP model, and knowing he would increase supply, he set his price at a level he knew would instantly attract a big chunk of the market. And it did.

So how do you make sure the price is right?

Now that you have a baseline understanding of simple economics and supply and demand curves, and know to look at what others are charging in the industry combined with what your entrance will do to supply, you can start to figure out how to price your goods or services.

Unfortunately, I can't tell you the ideal price for your product. Books lack that interactive feature. But knowing what you intend to offer here is what you should consider in setting your price:

Cost: What is the total cost that goes into each unit or service, based upon the amount of those units or services you expect to sell? Your price must always exceed this for you to be profitable, the goal of all businesses.

Volume: Together with cost, your cost per unit, and the price per unit you can charge, will depend on the volume you expect to sell in the marketplace, at that price. The lower the price, likely the higher the volume. The higher the price, you will tend to sell less, but with a higher margin. Where will you decide to be?

Competitors' Pricing: Always a great start is to look at your competitors, and see what they are charging for comparable services. If you are offering something less, price it lower. But if you are offering something better, consider pricing it higher, but explaining to the consumer why.

Supply & Demand Curves: Finally, you must understand the impact of your market entry on the supply curve. If you are entering a massive market, like the clothing industry, this is largely irrelevant, as the supply of 10,000 extra t-shirts will not move that supply needle. But if you are entering a far smaller market like the trademark industry, consider the effect on the supply curve, and your price.

Chapter Summary: Build it So They Will Come

- **Provide a Product or Services People Need**: Before investing your blood, sweat, and tears, develop a product or service people want, and are willing to pay for. Ask yourself why people need or want to buy what I will be selling.
- **Make it Competitive:** Know how your product or service will compete in the marketplace. Is it innovative? What problem does it solve?
- **Price it Right:** Set the price at a point where you are profitable after all expenses, but where the product will move in the marketplace.

Additional Suggested Reading:

The Pumpkin Plan, A Simple Strategy to Grow a Remarkable Business in Any Field, Mike Michalowicz, 2012

CHAPTER 2

LEGALESE

Bulletproof Your Business from the Start.

WHAT'S IN A NAME?

Now that you have a product and a good idea how to price it, you need to name it. Make sure that name is available, figure out what corporate structure is right for you, set up your company, and ensure the heck out of everything. These initial steps are crucial in setting you up for long-term success, but also in making sure that you are personally protected should things ever go south with the business. Why? Well let me explain.

Trademarks are my original bread and butter. With The Trademark Company, I have helped thousands and thousands of people to protect their trademarks, securing rights in the same. As such, I like to think I know a little bit about them, and can help you to understand the value of selecting and securing rights in your brand for your new product. But first off, let's make sure you know what a trademark is.

What's a trademark? In the plainest words possible, a trademark is your brand. It's how you identify your goods or services from those provided by someone else. It's names like Apple, Google, and Nike that, when you see them, you know instantly who the provider of the goods or services is just by seeing the name. Plain and simple.

SELECTING THE PERFECT TRADEMARK

So, as a former trademark-examining attorney for the U.S. Patent and Trademark Office, and founder of The Trademark Company, I am often asked for suggestions on how to select a great trademark by our start-up business customers. The response is always the same, “It depends. What do you want out of your trademark?”

There are two schools of thought in selecting a great trademark that every new business must consider. On one hand, do you want to use a completely new, self-coined name? Something that no one has ever heard of, such as Google or eBay?

On the other hand, do you want a trademark that creates instant interest in the product or service because it tells your prospective customers what you provide and what they'll get, such as Frosted Mini Wheats for cereal, or Vision Center for an eyewear store?

Both schools of thought have their benefits. Both also have their detriments. Which should you choose? Like I said above, it depends on what you are looking to get out of your trademark.

Coined trademarks, those that are completely made up, are the strongest form of trademarks and, in theory, the easiest to protect. Trademarks like Google, eBay, and Hulu. But beware, although easier to protect, such trademarks do not tell the consumer what you do, or what goods or services you provide. As such, if you intend to coin your own trademark, be ready to spend more to promote your brand, as there will be no instant recognition by consumers of what you do or provide.

Descriptive trademarks, on the other hand, provide the owner with instant recognition for what their brand does. "Trademarks" like New York Pizzeria for a pizza place in New York or Mexican Restaurant for, you guessed it, a restaurant serving Mexican food, are classic examples of descriptive trademarks. But picking a descriptive trademark comes at a cost.

Descriptive trademarks are difficult to enforce and, as a result, may not provide the owner with the ability to enforce their trademarks. In other words, the owner of NEW YORK PIZZERIA, more likely than not, cannot stop someone else from using NEW YORK CITY PIZZERIA, even though the trademarks are very similar. As such, if you are looking to adopt a trademark that instantly drums up interest in your goods or services, and will cost less to brand, adopting a descriptive trademark may be best for you. You simply need to know that the rights you will acquire in any such trademark may never entitle you to exclude others from the use of similar trademarks.

In the end, how do you select a great trademark? It depends. What are you looking for? And that decision is up to you.

McFRINGEMENT

There are a couple of key things you must know about trademarks as you get started. First, you can't use a trademark that is already being used by someone else on a product or service. This extends to similar trademarks as well, not just those that are identical to one that's already in use. Seems obvious, right? But a lot of people don't get it, so let's go into a bit.

One of the most famous trademarks of all time is McDonald's. Yup, the old golden arches. And they use it to let you know that just inside those doors are those delicious fries, shakes, and burgers. And yes, I'm 50 as I write this. And no, I am under no delusion that, if I eat McDonald's every day, I may put on a pound or two, six or even twenty. But it's not their fault for making such delicious food. That's their genius. A great product delivered with consistent, amazing speed.

Now, to protect the identity of some of the players involved, and for other legal reasons, I will, from time to time, slightly alter a story here or there. But know that everything I relay to you in these pages happened at one time or another, and the lessons remain the same.

I once had a customer who was trying to register the trademark McCatTreats for use in connection with—you guessed it—cat treats. Well, if you know anything about McDonalds, they are very protective of their "Mc" family of trademarks, believing that anything associated with the prefix "Mc" in conjunction with almost any other word is theirs for the taking. Candidly, given the fame of their brand, I sort of agree.

But one of my customers wanted to register McCatTreats and, despite my concern that she would likely get a letter from those nice folks in Illinois asking her to cease all use of the brand name, she filed anyways. To add insult to injury, after we had filed the application with the United States Patent & Trademark Office, she called me up and said "Matt, now I want to have you call

McDonald's to see if they will license the name from me so that they can then start selling 'McCatTreats' in their restaurants."

Sigh.

Well, if you know anything about McDonald's, they tend to only roll out products that have originated in their test kitchens from their main campus in Illinois. Sure, famously, one of their franchisees came up with the Big Mac, and another the Egg McMuffin, but for the most part, they like to develop their own products in their test kitchen and then, if successful, roll it out to select markets themselves for market testing.

Despite this knowledge, and the fact she was now largely admitting to having filed for a trademark that was clearly similar to the 'Mc' brands for the purpose of licensing it to— get this—the people who already owned that brand, she instructed me to call the nice people at McDonald's to see if we could negotiate a license for them to use her knock-off of their own trademark.

Sigh.

Now don't get me wrong, she did not have a malicious bone in her body. She was simply a sweet, cat-loving, McDonald's-eating fan who thought the idea of McCatTreats was something they should venture into, akin to a Puppiccino over at Starbucks.

Fortunately for her, I knew McDonald's' lawyers at the time. Candidly, they're just great lawyers. I know, I know. I just complimented a lawyer. Honestly, I cannot recall who they used as outside counsel. But whoever it was, they were just a pleasure to deal with. I think it stemmed from them being both a great lawyer and law firm, in conjunction with having a wonderful client in McDonald's.

Of course, not everyone is so fortunate to have great counsel, but in my experience with dealing with lawyers and in-house counsel for LA Gear, the NBA, CBS / Showtime, and, of course, McDonald's, it is so wonderful to deal with confident professionals that can truly get the job done for their clients in a pleasant and professional manner.

Anyways, despite my recommendation, I picked up the phone and called my buddy over at McDonald's.

"John", I said, " Got a minute?"

I then outlined my customer's plan for the McCatTreats brand, and asked if they would be interested in licensing it away from my client. I finished my pitch and braced for impact. There was a long pause on the other end of the phone. One of those pauses you could audibly hear him inhaling, as if to say, "I don't know where to start."

Fortunately for us, he did. "Matt", he started, "I want to make sure I get this straight. Your customer wants to register a knockoff of our trademark to license it back to us?" Sigh. Nothing gets by that guy. Nail. Head. Bing!

Over the next few minutes, we had a lovely conversation about McDonald's' brand history and their efforts to ensure that all things "Mc" in the food industry remained theirs, things I already knew. In the end, he very politely asked that our customer cease and desist all efforts to bring to market "McCatTreats," and refrain from any efforts in the future. I thanked him for his time and returned to my client with the news. As expected, she was dejected, but took the news well.

But you see, by learning that you cannot adopt, in whole or in part, someone else's brand, my customer learned a valuable lesson about trademarks, one that you should now understand: You can't use a trademark that is similar to an existing trademark. Pick a trademark and make sure it is unique! Otherwise, you will spend your blood, sweat, and tears developing your brand, only to find out you need to give it up and re-brand because it violates someone else's rights.

How do you make sure you haven't picked a trademark used by someone else? Have a trademark search performed, of course. It's that easy.

SEARCH AND YOU WILL FIND

In 2000, I was hired as a trademark examining attorney with the U.S. Patent & Trademark Office. In those days, you had to attend weeks of in-classroom training to learn not only about trademark law, but how to search and examine trademark applications to make sure that the desired trademarks were available and qualified for registration. Today, I'm pretty sure training is relegated to how to turn your computer on and off, and how not to trip down the stairs while walking. Let's just say the quality of their work has diminished over the years, as my contemporaries have grown into leadership roles at the office.

But back in the day, my class, which consisted of about 12 pie-eyed young attorneys, endured weeks of rigorous training, learning everything there was to know about the trademark world and system of examination. I'm not talking *Rocky III*-type training where, at the end, we raced our instructors down a Southern California beach with a symbolic victory and frolicked in the surf. To this day, I can still see Carl Weathers reading the script thinking, "Say what? Sly is going to beat me in a foot race? Sylvester Stallone beat me, Carl Weathers. Well, this is fiction." Anyways. Nope, I'm talking about real, hard book-learning, followed by practice, practice, practice.

Of all the things we practiced, perhaps the most significant was the ability to properly search to see if a trademark is available. It's not as simple as it seems. An applied-for trademark, let's say APPLE, could be blocked by a common misspelling like APLE, a plural trademark such as APPLES, or even a picture of an Apple. As such, an examining attorney's search must be broad enough to locate all such blocking trademarks. Why, you may ask, would the word ORANGE not block APPLE? Come on, people, because that's Apples and Oranges. Yeah, I went there. Anyways.

My instructor was a then-young attorney named Kevin Peska. A proud Gator from the University of Florida, Kevin was, and remains, a great credit to the USPTO and the legal profession overall. He spent hours meticulously teaching us how to properly search trademark records for blocking trademarks. He dealt with hundreds of questions, always with a smile, always with the patience of a wonderful parent teaching a child how to ride a bike.

I distinctly recall at one point having a trademark hit my desk which was merely two intersecting lines, like a plus sign, except the point of intersection had been erased. OK, in fairness, technically, that's really four lines, all sort of converging at a common point. But then I couldn't use the word intersection, and that is so much cooler than four pointy lines. Anyways, how could anyone else ever have come up with such a trademark design in the past? I thought.

I raised my hand and, with the patience of a Jedi Master, Kevin walked across the room to me. I said, "Instructor Peska, when you have a design that is this unique, do I really have to search for it?" Peska straightened a little, looked off to the distance, and said, "So sure are you in the ways of the trademark are you, hmm? Search it you must."

OK, in fairness, he did not say it like Yoda. But the point is: you've got to search, and make sure your trademark is available, even if you created it and think it is hyper unique.

Well, guess what? Damn, if someone else had not applied for the exact same trademark 3 weeks prior, meaning that it was blocked. No Registration for You! And that's why you've got to search to make sure the trademark you have selected is available, even if you think it is unique. With the amount of people applying for trademarks, especially these days, no matter how unique you think your idea is, someone else may have already had the same and applied for it. And if they apply for it first, often that will be enough, and you'll be out of luck. Just like Bonnie Dunn, one of my first clients, who had a scandalous time getting her trademark registered.

A SCANDALOUS TRADEMARK

Bonnie came to me years ago to help register her trademark for *Les Scandal*, the name of her off-Broadway burlesque show featuring a variety of unique acts from around the world. Bonnie herself was a throwback fan dancer from a day long since passed.

What is fan dancing, you may ask? Well, it's a sexy, stylish way to give the audience glimpses of the female form, almost in a teasing manner, made famous by Peggy Davis in closing scene of Tom Wolfe's *The Right Stuff*. In short, the dancer, usually dressed in a skin suit, OK not a skin suit like in *Silence of the Lambs*, "put the lotion in the basket" fame, but a skin-colored suit. Well, the skin-colored suit offers glimpses of the dancer's form behind large fans made of delicate feathers used to obstruct the view of her body, save for those occasional glimpses allowed by the performer. It's quite intoxicating.

Translated, *Les Scandal* simply means "The Scandal". When Bonnie came to us, she first asked that a trademark research report be performed. So, we did it. And guess what? Green light! All clear! File for the trademark! Save for one issue: for some reason Bonnie didn't want to move forward to register it just yet. Wait, huh? The trademark is available, register it now! Well, she waited. And waited. And months after the search was performed, she finally came to me and said, let's do this!

We filed for it. And guess what? One guess now, and only one... yup ... you guessed it... someone else had applied for the trademark in the time between the search report clearing it and the months later that she applied to register it!!! Sigh. OMG!

What could have been a very simple registration process, if acted upon promptly, turned into a 3-year slug fest for her rights with the other trademark filer, costing her multiple times what it should have spent if she would only have filed for it when the report came back clear. So please, when you find out your trademark is available, do not hesitate, do not think twice: get it on file ASAP to secure your brand before someone else does.

And this concludes the first section of this chapter regarding naming your business or product and securing the trademark rights to the same. Remember, when it comes to trademarks, time is not your friend. Here's a checklist as to how to adopt and protect your business's most valuable asset:

1. **Select a Trademark:** Pick a name to name your business or product. The best names are distinctive, meaning they don't simply describe the product as you cannot protect a trademark that is simply descriptive (e.g., RED SHOES for shoes that are red).

2. **Trademark Search:** Have a professional trademark search done. This will let you know if your trademark is available.
3. **Register It!**

But that's just the naming stuff. What about forming a new company? What about insuring it all? Aren't those equally as important? Yes! Yes, they are. Sit back, pour some more coffee, because away we go!

INCORPORATE!

Next up, once you decide upon your name and your trademark, you should incorporate or form your business as a separate company, apart from you as an individual. The most popular business form for start-up businesses is a limited liability company, better known as an LLC.

Why start a separate company? I mean, why can't you just go out, lease a storefront, hang out a sign and start selling whatever it is you want to sell under your own name. Well, technically you can. There is nothing stopping you from signing on the dotted line of a three-year lease, with your own personal name, and using your own credit cards as your business credit cards. Just taking whatever money you earn from the business and putting it right in your own pocket. There's also nothing stopping you from going out to the garage, grabbing that power drill, and performing brain surgery on yourself. Rest assured, both could lead to your ultimate demise.

The reasons to form a separate company truly boil down to this. First, in today's day and age, it's easy. I mean really freaking easy. In most states, the Secretary of State's web site is so easy to use, you can form your LLC in a matter of minutes. If you're intimated by the concept, there are websites and businesses out there, like The Trademark Company—yes, a shameless plug—that can do it for you quickly and easily all for a very low cost. So don't fail to do it because you're afraid to learn the ins and outs of how to. Just Do It!

Second, when you do it, and run your business through the LLC, or Corporation, if you want to get fancy, it creates a shield against personal liability for the debts or liabilities of the business. In short, that lease you sign will be in the name of the company. You'll be able to get credit cards in the business's name. And you'll pay yourself through the company's bank accounts. In the end, it is not drastically different than just having everything in your own name and running it as a sole proprietorship. But because you have that piece of paper from the Secretary of State that says JOHN DOE, LLC, the business's debts will remain the business's debts, apart from your personal assets.

This is the single most important reason why you form an LLC. Once you have that separate entity, or company, if you ever get sued, if your business goes under, your house, your car, your personal assets are all protected against liability and being taken by the people who are suing you. Even if you don't get sued, but simply default on that lease or can't make the payments on your business's equipment, they can't go after you personally. And that’s the value of running the business through an LLC!

Let's look at a few examples to emphasize this in practice.

RAIN DROPS AND THE CEILING KEEP FALLIN' ON MY HEAD

Years ago, I worked for a regional insurance defense law firm in the Washington, D.C. area. What is an insurance defense firm, you might ask? Well, when you get in a car accident and get sued, you contact your insurance company. Since they are the ones who insure you, meaning they pay the bill if you lose a lot of money, they hire a lawyer to defend you and, by extension, them. Typically, insurance carriers don't pay too well, and law firms that seek that type of work are a specialized breed. That's why law firms that are on retainer for them are colloquially called insurance defense firms. Now you know. So back to our story.

When I was working for the insurance defense firm, one of the partners, an amazingly skilled trial attorney, came to me and asked me to be her second chair in a case going to trial in just a few weeks. She was probably in her late 50s at the time, and had tried hundreds of civil cases. To say she was experienced was an understatement. So, in all likelihood, she did not need a second chair. But often it is nice to have a second chair just to see if you missed anything during a cross examination, to carry your proverbial bag, or, as was probably the case (remember my love of the practice of law) to maximize billable hours to the client. It's a recurring theme, isn't it?

Anyways, she invited me along to be her second chair. Of course, as a senior associate, I needed the billable hours. And getting in on a trial that would guarantee you 40 to 70 hours per week was a gold mine, especially when you were only the second chair. All the billables. Far less responsibility.

Our clients were the individual proprietor of the rental housing where the injury occurred. For the purposes of our book, we will call him Dirk Johnson, who formed the LLC in the District of Columbia to run his rental property business. I know you can probably see where this is going already. But stay with me, it will hammer home the point.

Well, Dirk's business owned and occupied certain highly affordable rental properties in the District of Columbia. In common vernacular, Dirk was a slum lord. You know, someone who owns properties they barely maintain because the rent they charge can barely cover the cost of the mortgage. Yeah, a slum. Well, at one of his properties, the ceiling had collapsed during a freak, highly intense rainstorm which inundated the gutters in the building, pouring rain into the ceiling above the renter's bedroom. The water flowing into the property caused the drywall to become saturated and collapse, injuring the tenant in the process.

The case alleged that Dirk and his company were negligent in their maintenance of the property and, as a result of not cleaning the gutters, the water was allowed to flow into the ceiling above the tenant's bedroom, causing it to collapse on her. Yup, that's why I went to law school. To argue about the standard of cleaning out gutters. Glamorous.

To say the trial was contentious would be an understatement. And from the get-go, it was apparent that the Plaintiff's lawyer was intent not about making this case about gutter maintenance, or even the evils of a slum lord, but the evils of a white slum lord victimizing the African American community. To say we had our hands full was an understatement.

Fortunately, however, the plaintiff's attorney was a highly skilled criminal defense lawyer, but not a plaintiff's personal injury lawyer. In short, he was amazing at thinking on his feet, directing a witness to pull tears from the jury, and cross-examining witnesses. But he lacked the focus to see the forest for the trees and how to satisfy certain required elements of his case against Dirk, the individual defendant.

You see, in order to win every case, be it criminal or civil, a lawyer must prove certain required elements. In its simplest form, in a negligence case, a lawyer must prove that a duty existed (e.g., you have a duty to drive carefully), there was a breach of that duty (e.g., you ran a stop sign), and the plaintiff's injury resulted from your breach of that duty (e.g., you injured someone in a car crash caused by your running the stop sign).

Well, in the case of when you sue a company for negligence, like Dirk's company, in order to "pierce the corporate veil" and sue Dirk directly for his acts running the company, like maintenance, that are within the company's role, you must establish that the individual defendant was using the LLC as a sham and that they, not the LLC, are the true bad guy. So, like the negligence standard above, there is a very specific way you do this. And, of course, our esteemed plaintiff's attorney had no clue.

One of the trial techniques I picked up over the years that has served me well is that it is not the volume of the person talking but what is said and what goes into the record which is important. I learned this from the late, great Joseph Koonz who was a trial legend in the District of Columbia for years. So, as part of my strategy, I would often lull opposing counsel into false confidence and, when they least expect it, hit them with a quick verbal motion or something else that truly crushes their case. This case was no different.

Following the conclusion of the evidence counsel, we were invited to judge's chambers to discuss which jury instructions should be given to the jury before closing arguments. Jury instructions? In every case prior to the lawyers making their closing arguments, the jury is read the law and the standards that apply to the allegations in the case. The lawyers then present closing arguments as to why the facts in evidence either support, or do not support, those respective elements.

Being the sneaky little weasel I am, I waited until my esteemed lead counsel and the plaintiff's counsel were battling over whether to use one instruction on a critical point or another. At that moment, having summed this chump up for about 5 days in trial, I knew it was time to make my move. When the judge looked up at me almost as if he were questioning his life's choices, I quickly blurted out: "Your honor, I have a quick oral motion." And for those of you with minds in the gutter, oral is what we lawyers use instead of "verbal".

"Your honor, I have a quick oral motion," I continued. "It doesn't appear that there has been any evidence to pierce the corporate veil in this case to keep Dirk as a defendant. Can we all agree just to dismiss him out so we can streamline this whole thing?"

The Judge looked at me, probably more in tune with the gravity of what I was asking. He turned to the Plaintiff's lawyer and said, "Sounds about right, what do you think?" Then he looked over at the plaintiff's lawyer, engrossed in his other thoughts while getting pounded by our lead counsel. And in an instant, the plaintiff's lawyer simply waived his hand and said something to the effect of, "Yeah, I don't need him, sounds good, judge." And just like that, Dirk was free! No personal liability at stake. The LLC had served its purpose!

What happened in that instant, you might ask? Well, the case went from possibly taking Dirk's car, his house, his very way of living ... to one of a case for insurance money only. You see, the LLC that was the only remaining defendant had no assets. It did not own the building. It did not own anything. It was just a shell. At that moment, Dirk was free. No fear of personal liability. And with only an insurance policy on the line, no possibility of settlement, as it was no longer his money at risk line.

I excused myself to handle some ministerial matters. I walked back into the courtroom and told him what we had been able to do. He dropped to his knees and started to cry. He was free of the nightmare of losing everything. He was free to know that, no matter what happened with the jury, he would survive. He was free, because he had formed an LLC and, while late, it would shield him from the personal exposure a person can have if they do not run their business through an LLC.

THE NCAA's DOMAIN

Years later, I would see the exact opposite happen when I opened my own place. To tell the story properly, first I must bore you with a little bit of background on the Internet, domain names, and the Anti-cybersquatting Consumer Protection Act or ACPA. Oh, go on, you say? Well away we gooooooooo. Weeeeeeeeee!

Back in the early days when Al Gore invented the Internet (sorry, could not resist) it was all about getting the best domain name. There was a veritable gold rush to register as many domain names as possible, in case this whole Internet thing ever caught on. Wait, what is a domain name, you might ask?

A domain name is effectively an address on the world wide web where a web host can, with the proper IP access, post your web site. How it works is: ICANN creates or licenses out "domain names" which can be virtually any characters followed by a top-level designator such as .com, .net, or any of the hundreds that are now officially licensed out. ICANN then approves certain vendors, such as GoDaddy.com, to register domain names in a paying customer's name for their exclusive use.

For those with foresight who knew the Internet would be big someday, when domains first hit the scene, savvy entrepreneurs would register hundreds and sometimes thousands of domains, ultimately for resale to people who were already using them as trademarks, or may wish to do so in the future. The problem? Was this trademark infringement? In this new Internet era could you register a domain name of a famous brand, like CocaCola.com, and then sell it to Coca-Cola for money?

In the early days, this question was largely unsettled, as the domain name pirates filled their chests with domain name gold. But then a few court rulings came down, stating that this type of warehousing and ransom of domain names was akin to trademark infringement. A movement was commenced by major brands to grab the registered domains of their famous trademarks, some Congress people got greased ... and, yadda yadda yadda, out popped the ACPA.

The ACPA made it illegal to register and "squat" on a domain name that was identical or confusingly similar to a registered or in-use trademark at the time the domain name was acquired. In short, even if it were available, I could not go out and register Microsoft.com and then turn to Microsoft and say, give me a gazillion dollars for the domain, as their lawyers would be able to do horrible things to me under the ACPA.

OK, now I have finally set the stage. And yes, this will come full circle about why you need an LLC, I promise!

Here's the story and, again, for our purposes, the name of my customer has been changed to protect the innocent.

Before the ACPA was a thing, my customer was one of those early domain name cowboys seeking his fortune online, as he forecast that this Internet thing would be big. At some point during the first couple of years, he registered hundreds of domain names, many of them admittedly being like famous brands that were already in existence. But, at the time, this was not illegal. What would become very relevant, however, is the fact that he did so in his own name, personally! He did not register them in the name of ABC Company or whatever, he did so in his name, John Q. Public. Yikes!

Let's just say he had a certain domain name registered. Hypothetically, let's say it was probably something associated with NCAA. Prior to my involvement, but slightly after the passing of the ACPA, he received a cease-and-desist letter from NCAA's lawyers demanding that he turn over the rights to the domain name immediately. Now, I want to be fair here and make sure you can follow me with this story, as there will be three law firms that represent the NCAA. To make it easy on you, we will call them Jack Ass Law Firm 1, Jack Ass Law Firm 2, and Jack Ass Law Firm 3. Hell let's abbreviate it to JALF 1, JALF 2, and JALF 3. Back to our story.

JALF 1 sends him a letter demanding that he turn over the domain name immediately. So, what does he do? Does he ignore JALF 1? Does he hire a lawyer? Does he tell them to go to hell? Nope, very respectfully, he responds to their email with a polite, "Let me know to whom you want it transferred, and I will make it happen today!" That's right, unfettered cooperation at his own expense. And, of course, does he hear back from JALF 1 or the NCAA? Nope. Nadda. Nothing. JALF!!!

A year or so later, and still having done nothing with the domain name at issue, he gets another letter from the NCAA's new law firm, JALF 2. This time they are a little more direct, and demand that he transfer the domain name immediately, or bad things will happen to him under the ACPA. Again, my customer says to them, "Like I told JALF 1 a year ago, and I'm telling you nice folks at JALF 2 now: just let me know who to transfer it to, and I will make it happen ASAP."

Crickets, again! No response. No nothing. Complete unfettered cooperation. And this is where it gets completely maddening. I'm looking at you NCAA and JALF 3!

About a year later, there is a knock at his door. He opens the door and, to his surprise, is served a federal lawsuit under the ACPA. Huh? What the F? he and I both think. Yup, that's right. The NCAA sued him to get the domain name that he had offered to JALF 1 and JALF 2, and had registered even before the ACPA was in effect. Seriously, WTF? Hire some attorneys that read their damn emails, NCAA.

In any event, because he held the domain names personally, guess what? He was sued, personally. Now the light bulb is going off for most of you. Although he had twice offered to transfer the domain name immediately, that was of no matter. JALF 3 came in, guns blazing, and sued his ass despite being a great guy who was 100% cooperating with the NCAA. They simply had crappy counsel in JALF 1 and JALF 2. And here's the kicker: he gave them the same offer as he had given to JALF 1 and JALF 2. And they declined. They replied, since the NCAA had had to spend money on the lawsuit, that they would only settle for a transfer of the domain name *And* $50,000, the cost of their legal representation thus far. Wait, what? JALF!!!!!!!!!!!!!!!!!! Are you kidding me? A man, who was not in violation when he registered the domain name, had twice offered to give this to you, and you are holding his feet to the fire because, at worst, your attorney's incompetence and, at best, because you all are just a bunch of jack assess. Man, until this point, I had never met someone from Indiana I did not like. Changed my whole opinion of the NCAA.

He asked, "Matt, what can I do? I can't afford $50,000 cash now. And it costs more to defend the case." A case that was caused because JALF 1 and JALF 2 did not do their jobs. Pathetic. And the NCAA knew it. But because the domain name wasn't held in his name, not an LLC, everything he had worked on for his entire life, his car, savings, etc., were on the line. Stunning.

Skipping forward, the case eventually resolved, and he had to pay some of those demanded attorney's fees. But, again, if he had only had an LLC in place, he may have simply been able to say FU JALF 1, 2, 3 and the NCAA. Oh, and while we are on the subject of the NCAA, pay your lawyers less and let colleges pay their players more, just sayin', JA (figure out that acronym).

HE WHO SHALL NOT BE NAMED . . . PART DEUX

But my experience in this arena is not simply limited to others. It has benefited me in the past as well, personally.

A few years back, Lord Voldemort sued my company and me, alleging various theories of stuff he thought we were doing that was anticompetitive. Now, it's one thing to sue the company, but he also went so far as to sue me personally in the lawsuit. To this day I can still remember the feeling. We were on a family trip back to Washington, D.C. where our kids were born. We were touring the Smithsonian's Air & Space Museum and had just come out of an exhibit for the Apollo Space program. As it so often does, my phone flashed with a preview of an inbound email.

Now, understand, I get about 300 emails a day. Sometimes they are so frequent my phone looks like a damn strobe light. But I digress.

Something about the preview on this one caught me. The subject line was something like *Lord Voldemort vs. The Trademark Company and Me, personally.* Do you know that feeling when you first see something that terrifies you and your heart falls into the pit of your stomach? Yup, that was me, at that moment. At that point, it gets a little fuzzy due to the adrenaline rush, but I believe I uttered something to the group like, "I'm going to step out and read something really quick," all the while being positive that I probably looked like I'd seen a ghost.

I found a place to collect myself and opened the email, revealing what I had feared: *Lord Voldemort* had indeed sued the company, but also me personally! Wait, what? Well, the kids and my wife at the time came out of the exhibit. I had to transition back to whatever shell of myself I could to try and enjoy the rest of the day with the family. Later, during the cab ride to dinner, I was able to download and read the entire lawsuit. Yup, clear, he had sued both me and the LLC. And, as a lawyer, I instantly knew the risk he'd put me and my family in.

You see, in theory, if he only sued the company, you could default on the lawsuit, never answer it, and the worst-case scenario is he gets to exercise a default judgment against the company. If the LLC holds no assets, or is in massive debt, good luck to you fella, and we'll just declare bankruptcy! Now I'm not suggesting this is a great plan, but if you get sued, at least the knowledge they cannot get to your personal assets can provide you with some comfort.

But when you personally are named, it is a whole different ballgame. Lose or default on that puppy, and one day you may see the Sheriff come to your home, evict you, and nail a sign in the front yard stating, "Public Auction in Two Weeks!" Yeah, it's real. Kudos to *Lord Voldemort*, he got my attention. From the get-go, goal number one was to protect my family and get me out of the case personally, as soon as possible.

There will be more about this below, but because of the nature of the lawsuit I immediately contacted my insurance carrier, requesting that they defend the case. After some hemming and hollering, they agreed to do so and, in their defense of my defense, hired an absolute top-tier, top-caliber law firm to defend the company and me.

Again, if you have read this far into this book, you know I am generally not a fan of lawyers or the legal profession anymore, due to stories like the NCAA above, etc. But when credit to the profession is due, credit is due. And the initial law firm that represented me in the case filed by *Lord Voldemort* was amazing. As an old legal joke goes, a good lawyer knows the law, a great lawyer knows the judge. But I always like to twist it just a little. A good lawyer knows the law. A great lawyer knows the law and, no matter the circumstances, should alleviate the stress of the client by constant assurances that they have everything under control and not to worry. And the big law firm my carrier hired for me did just that.

A few weeks later, I was sitting in the Corinthian Hotel in downtown London. I know, sounds like I travel a lot. But my former wife worked out of London then, and had invited the kids and I to join her for Spring Break there, as opposed to our traditional trip to a more tropical climate. If you ever have the chance to go, I strongly recommend it. Great town.

Anyways. Always sticking to my rule of trying to work when the rest are asleep, or playing video games, I can always recall the head partner of the California-based law firm and I having that initial consultation in the 11:00 pm hour, London time, as he was 8 hours behind me, near San Francisco. Without waiving privilege, he assured me that they had everything under control and that we would likely be able to dismiss most of the case during the initial motions phase. I've never had the opportunity to truly thank him, but what a credit to the profession. A calming influence, combined with substantive know-how, set my mind largely at ease.

Well, he and his fantastic associate got to work. And by the time I was on a flight home from London, they had filed a series of motions to start carving up Lord Voldemort's case like Harry Potter, stealing and destroying the horcruxes. In the end, on a fateful day some months later, the associate called me with the news: I was out! They had secured my personal dismissal from the case. They'd done it! I no longer had to worry about losing my house, my personal savings, everything I had worked for due to this lawsuit. The LLCs shield had worked, even if tested, and had done what it was designed to do.

In conclusion, run your business through a corporation or an LLC! Doing so protects you from personal liability. And, if tested, it may just save you as it did for me. But only if you heed my words. But, of course, there is one last component that you may have picked up on. That's right, insure it. And insure it to the max with every policy possible.

INSURE IT

Finally, you've got to get insurance. And I don't mean a little. I mean, insure against everything, for as much as you can afford. Trust me, someday you will need it. And when you do, you will be thrilled you listened to me.

When I was a fledgling attorney working for Koonz McKenney, my esteemed boss and I were once having lunch. And today, for the life of me, I cannot recall how we got on the subject. But as personal injury lawyers, I'm sure we were talking about some case somewhere, and what the policy limits were for the policy covering the defendant. Anyways, Pete asks me, "Do you know what your policy limits are?" I thought for a while. And as the proud son of a former service member, I knew I had USAA. I replied, "I think I have $1 million in coverage," thinking that was a lot.

Pete just shook his head. "What?" I asked, like the pie-eyed trainee I was.

Pete continued, "Always get the maximum policy they will write for you. I suggest at least $5 million." Perplexed, I asked the follow-up to keep the lesson going. "Why?" And so began the lesson.

"You see, if you get into an automobile accident, you can do a lot of damage, injure people badly. A good personal injury attorney can make a small case seem average, an average big, and a big case life changing. If you only have $1 million in coverage, they may be able to claim millions in damages. If that's the case, they'll never settle, they'll go to trial, and if they hit a $2 million dollar judgment and you only have $1 million in coverage, one guess who is responsible for the part not covered by your insurance."

"Wow," I recall exclaiming.

"Exactly", he continued. "But when you have the biggest policy —you can typically get about $5 million— there's almost no lawyer who will go to trial if the policy is surrendered."

"Surrendered?" I asked. "Yes, surrendered, meaning that the insurance carrier tenders, or offers, the entire policy if they agree to settle the case."

"So always keep the maximum amount of insurance you can have. That way, if you ever need it, it virtually guarantees you will not lose your house, car, and everything that you have worked for if something bad happens."

To this day, I have always heeded that advice. And I encourage you all to do the same. Insure yourself to the hilt.

A NOT SO BAD BABY

Many years ago, I had a friend who was an obstetrician practicing medicine in South Florida. For those of you who do not know, an obstetrician is a baby doctor. More specifically, they are the people who deliver babies and, on many occasions, need to be ready when everything does not go as planned to save the newborns' lives.

About my friend: one of the greatest, most intelligent guys you have ever met in your life. A dedicated family man, he came from middle class surroundings with loving parents who worked their asses off to send him to school. A little know-how, some hard work, and a stint in the Air Force to help pay for school got him accepted to a great medical school before he even graduated college. In fact, to this day, we still tease him that he technically never graduated college, because his medical school was so impressed with his resume, they took him after only three years. Yeah, that's the kind of guy we are talking about.

For years, my buddy practiced delivering thousands of babies and saving hundreds of lives. One of the things most of us take for granted is the process of delivering a child. So many things can go wrong in a moment that, for every reasons, should be one of the happiest in new parents' lives. I know this from personal experience: this friend largely saved my former wife and daughter's lives when things went south in their health forcing a dramatically premature delivery of our first child. Had it not been for my buddies' expertise, neither my daughter nor her mom would have made it. And we take these skills for granted every day. But once again, I digress.

My friend was set to deliver a woman's first child. Her husband was an old high school teammate of my brother's. In fact, he was sort of known as a hell-raiser in high school. Although no one in my family ever partook in anything of this nature, this guy—the father of the child—had never met a line of cocaine he didn't snort. It's rumored he snorted so much nose candy that he almost single-handedly kept the Medellin Cartel in business. I mean, they even crafted a first-of-its-kind frequent snorter's club card for this ass-wipe. I mean, every time you see him, you'd think, did he just eat a powdered sugar donut through his nose?

Getting the feeling I did not think highly of this ass-face? Read on.

His wife, who, for all intents and purposes, was a nice person and perhaps did not know the level of ass-wipe he was, was set to give birth to their first child. The big day came, and they checked into the hospital. My buddy met them there shortly thereafter, like all good OBs do, and explained what to expect from the inducement process, labor, and all the other fun-filled stuff in preparation for the next few hours of labor.

After being induced, a few hours later my pal was called back, as the wife was getting closer to that magical moment. My buddy arrived, said hello to the couple, then and went and scrubbed up. She and the ass-wipe were taken into the birthing room for the delivery of their child. My pal returned and, after about an hour of pushing, their little bundle of joy arrived. Everything was normal, or so they thought. As is the case, the newborn, after briefly being held by mom and dad, was taken by one of the nurses for a routine checkup in the next room. Everything was fine up until then. And that's when it started to go south.

A few minutes later, the nurse called out that the newborn was not behaving normally. There was some form of distress, and they needed an emergency consultation with a pediatrician ASAP. Picking up the phone, they immediately called for the on-call pediatrician. He arrived moments later, stabilized the baby, then that happy day for the couple turned into one that too many of us have experienced—will your new baby survive the day? The night? And, if so, will he or she be alright, or permanently disabled?

The baby survived the first day, and then the second, and soon it was clear he was out of the woods. However, for some reason it was very apparent early on that the child was having severe cognitive issues. How can they tell this at that age, I have no idea. But it was clear.

Well, before you could say, *But OJ Got it in the End with a Civil Suit*, ass-wipe and his wife had lawyered up and were preparing to file a medical malpractice case against my buddy, his practice, the nurse who took the baby, the hospital, and anyone else even remotely involved in the delivery of the child. Dominos was lucky they weren't delivering pizzas to the hospital that night. They probably would have been named as a defendant as well.

You see, this was South Florida, land of the lawsuit. Land of personal injury lawyers making a business of others' pain. All you have to do is drive down I-95 from Palm Beach to Miami. About every other Billboard is another PI Lawyer asking, "Have you Been Injured?" Land of the limitless verdicts that could bankrupt you in a split second, even if you'd done nothing wrong. In short, it was the Wild Wild West of personal injury jurisdictions. Glad the bar associations are so keen on keeping the profession upstanding and respected.

Within months they were all sued. As referenced above, if you've ever been served a lawsuit, it is breathtaking. When you first read the *ad damnum* (that's fancy lawyer speak for how much money they are demanding), your initial response is almost always to see that huge number and think, "My God, they are trying to take everything!" It's human nature. It's terrifying.

As the case progressed, it became apparent what was going on. Without going into too much detail (candidly, I can't recall the medical terminology), the child had a rapid onset condition after being born that would, in the eyes of the plaintiff's attorney and his experts, cost tens of millions of dollars in care over the life of the child. From an outsider's perspective, however, it was pure crap. I mean, the plaintiff's counsel had two separate and opposing theories:

First, that, during the prenatal treatment of the mother, my buddy had messed up in some capacity, resulting in the baby's infirmity. Second, that the baby was born completely fine, but had been dropped by the nurse when she took it away, injuring the child severely.

Well, although the plaintiff's attorney would never concede this, there actually is a third cause of the ailment, one that I felt would be a strong defense. The child's medical condition could have been caused by drug abuse by the father. Yup. That ass-wipe. In fact, most of the medical research supported this claim.

That being said, my buddy practiced in South Florida, the land of $100 million verdicts, where plaintiff's attorneys could routinely paint a guy who came from nothing, worked his ass off through school, served our country, dedicated his life to delivering and saving mothers and their children, as the bad guy! Oh, and paint as the victim the coked-up, loser ass-wipe who most likely caused the illness of his own child by snorting his way across South Florida. Think I still have strong feelings on this one?

And if you're still with me, trust me, I'm coming back to the tie-in on insurance. At some point, the case got all the way to the courtroom steps. In lawyer-speak, this means they were about a week out of trial, the witnesses were all lined up, and everything was ready to go. This is typically when cases settle, as there is risk on both sides, although often greater risk on the side of the defendant, especially if they think there is a chance the bell could be rung with a massive verdict.

But in this case, the Plaintiff still wasn't sure if it was my buddy that allegedly caused the damage, or the nurse. And, of course, it never crossed their mind it could have been Mr. McSnuffles-Snort-a-Lot. Nevertheless, they were barreling to trial, and would let the jury sort that out. But then it happened, the call came in. The Plaintiff's counsel made one last demand of my friend and, by extension, his medical malpractice insurance carrier. "Tender the $10 million policy and we're done with you," he said simply.

With a claim of $100 million in damages, but only having a $10 million dollar policy, guess who pays everything over $10 million, or files for bankruptcy, should a jury award that $100 million? Yup, my buddy.

I can still remember to this day the feeling of relief when that demand came in for my buddy. Of course, he did not take it that way. But me and another close friend of his, who is also a lawyer, sat him down and said, without reservation, "Take the deal!" As his eyes welled up with tears, something I had only seen once before when his father had passed, he said, "But I did not do anything wrong!" Putting my hand on his shoulder, I said, "I know. But it's not about right or wrong anymore. It's about surviving this financially. Make the deal."

Later that day, my buddy made the call to his attorney, and they inked the deal. Ass-wipe got a $10 million check. A few days later, they settled with the nurse and the hospital for a similar amount. I'm sure that ass-wipe had a party to end all parties that night.

Oh, and in case you're interested in the happy ending: turns out the baby was just fine. A few years after the settlement, word got back that she had been misdiagnosed. That she was completely OK. Today she is a proud graduate, with honors, from the University of Florida. Guess who paid for that? What an ass-wipe.

In the end, the story illustrates the value of insurance. It does not matter if the claim is valid or not. You insure yourself to the hilt so when, and if, this scenario, or a similar scenario unfolds, it does not end you. My buddy did not want to take the deal. He did not want to do anything that even looked like he had done something that could be construed as wrong. That's not what it is about.

Insurance is there to take care of these things when, and if, they occur. Whether or not you believe you are responsible does not matter. Just don't let them take away everything you have built. That's what it is for. Insure it!

THE WIGGLES

But even the best insurance company will try and wiggle out of their obligation to pay for your defense or the damages, if they can. They don't turn a profit by easily paying every claim and defending every lawsuit. That's the insurance game.

If you think you are insured if this occurs, be ready with a good coverage lawyer to put them in their place, and make sure they accept responsibility for defending the lawsuit you'd paid them to, with all those insurance policy premiums over the years.

Remember the story about when He Who Shall Not Be Named filed that wonderful lawsuit against me and my company? Well, I hope you can, as I just mentioned it a few paragraphs ago. In any event, part of his claims was that our company was advertising in a manner that violated the law by making false claims about the quality of our goods and services. Once I dug through the lawsuit, it was relatively clear that his claim fell under something called false advertising, or advertising injury.

Great! I thought, thinking that the claim was clearly covered, and that the insurance carrier would swoop right into the rescue and defend the heck out of this case. Well, remember, you must insure it for the reasons set forth above. But did you know that the average cost to defend a federal district lawsuit is about $300,000? Stunning, right? $300,000! And that's not paying the other side. That's the cost of your lawyers!

Win, lose, or draw, if you get sued, 9 out of 10 times the first thing that your carrier is going to do is to conduct a quick coverage audit, so they can try and wiggle out of the cost of defending the lawsuit. A what? A coverage audit. What's that, you might ask? You mean, just because I seemingly have insurance for this claim does not mean that they are going to cover it? As The Fonz would say, *Exacta Mundo!* Here's how it works.

You're relaxing on a family vacation, having a blast and enjoying all that you have worked so hard to achieve. Then you get notice that someone has filed a lawsuit against you. You go blank, and start thinking of all the doomsday scenarios that your life, as you know it, may be over. Then you recall, 'Wait one second, I have insurance for this!" You tender, or forward, the lawsuit to your insurance company. They look at it and, given their experience level, instantly know how much this is going to cost them to defend, even if the defense is successful. You see, they are an insurance company concerned with the bottom line. They are not a right or wrong company, and largely don't care if you're at fault. The rub is this, how much is it going to cost them? That's all they care about. And they use big words like "mitigation of loss" which, for our purposes, means if they can wiggle out of having to defend you in the case, they will!

While you are thinking, "Whew, glad I'm covered for this!" if the risk is too high—too much money—know that your carrier, those folks you've been paying all that money to in premiums over the years, will hire coverage counsel to try and find a way that the claim is not covered by their policy, thus wiggling out of their obligation to defend you. Don't let them get away with it!

One of my most terrifying days was when I learned this reality. Once I tendered the lawsuit to the carrier, they informed me they were sending it to their counsel in San Diego for further analysis. Further analysis, I thought. That's odd. The lawsuit was not even in San Diego. I mean, why would they send it to a law firm there?

At some point, it hit me. And the terror set in. They had sent it to the coverage counsel to try and wiggle out of their obligation to defend me in the case. If they did, a simple denial of coverage letter would be forthcoming. And, at the time, the letter probably would have sent me into bankruptcy, as I sincerely doubt I could have afforded a $300,000 tab.

To this day, I can still recall the letter coming into my email inbox. It came with a simple email, "Dear Mr. Swyers, Attached please find our firm's letter concerning coverage in the above-referenced matter". I quickly opened the attachment to a 15-page letter. My heart sunk, knowing that attorneys rarely spend 15 pages to tell you something good. Knowing how to read a coverage or other type letters, there was no use in reading the analysis. I quickly scrolled to the bottom of the letter, to the section labeled "Summary". And there it was. Some of the most wonderful words I have ever read, "... and for the reasons and based upon the analysis set forth above, the carrier will defend the referenced lawsuit."

I literally dropped to my knees at that moment, raised my hands in the air, and thanked God for my blessings and for the opinion of counsel. Wiping the tears of joy away from my face, I knew that by having insured the business properly, and having received a favorable coverage opinion, everything that I had worked so hard for in my life would likely be safe, that we would go on, that although I would be burdened with the time and emotions of a lawsuit, I would not be going through it alone. Amen!

The story goes on from here, and has many fascinating twists and turns, but for our purposes I will say just a few more words about the same. Should you ever get sued—and it is clearly within something your policy covers—make sure to immediately send the lawsuit to your insurance carrier to begin the defense of the matter. If, however, it is something that you are unsure whether it is covered, like an advertising injury claim, or if your insurance company sends it to coverage counsel, or issues a flat-out denial of coverage, know that it may be worth it to hire your own coverage lawyer to negotiate with them as to whether they will accept coverage.

For a few thousand dollars, a good coverage lawyer can often convince an insurance company, by threats or otherwise bad faith, that they must accept coverage of the case. So, although you may have to spend a few thousand to get it covered, it is well worth it, as who wouldn't want to spend $5,000 to get a $300,000 defense? I rest my case.

Chapter Summary: Make it Legal!

- **Trademark It**: Your trademark is your business's most valuable asset. Make sure it is available and register it!
- **Form an LLC**: Form a separate business entity. For most, the easiest structure is a Limited Liability Company (LLC). This will shelter your personal assets (e.g., car house) from your business liabilities (e.g., bills, debts, etc.). And, if possible, avoid personal guarantees secured with your personal assets. That's the point of the business structure, after all.
- **Insure It**: Find a local Insurance Broker and buy every foreseeable policy from them. And then, if you ever need them, remember, nothing personal: it's just business!

BUILD IT TO SCALE

Ready to Super-Size Your Business from the Start.

SUPERSIZE ME

In 1954, a multimixer salesman was surprised to receive a large order from a small restaurant in San Bernardino, California. Up until that point, he was fortunate if he could get a restaurant to buy a single multimixer, a mixer that could make 6 milkshakes at once. But the small restaurant ordered several. Intrigued by the thought that one restaurant could make such a large order and, moreover, require that amount of production for their milkshake business, he decided to take a visit to this new mysterious customer to see what was going on.

When he arrived, he was greeted by a long but quickly moving line where customers were placing their food orders through, of all places, a window. When it was his turn, he ordered his burger, fries, and shake. As he finished paying, he was astonished his meal was already being handed to him. The restaurant, run by two brothers, was a model of modern efficiency. Their key to success? A limited menu, concentrating on just a few items – burgers, fries and beverages – which allowed them to focus on systems that guaranteed maintaining high quality and unprecedented quick service.

They had systemized everything, from the toasting of the buns to the frying of the burgers and even how the condiments were added to each product. It was like watching the original assembly line created by Henry Ford, only in a restaurant! To make things even more efficient, they anticipated the volume of food orders based upon the time of day and the number of people in the line, so that food was hot and ready, deliverable within moments of an order being placed.

Until the brother's concept and applied innovations, eating at a restaurant, even a drive-in, which were so popular in the 1950s, was a more customized experience with a larger, more diverse menu. Place your order with the waitress, then she, in turn, relayed the order to a cook, the cook would read the order and then prepare your custom meal. Then the waitress would bring it back. Oh, the inefficiency!

Not here. Not in this San Bernardino establishment. As the multimixer salesman watched in amazement, there were no waitresses. The food was delivered right at the ordering counter. There were no tables. Get your food and go. Burgers were assembled in an assembly-line fashion and dropped down a chute, ready for bagging even before orders were taken. Fries were kept hot all throughout the day. And a shake could be delivered, thanks to its multimixers, faster than any other restaurant of the day.

Systems. Systems. Systems.

Well, by now you have probably deduced that the brothers were Dick and Mac McDonald, and that multimixer salesman, well, that was none other than the legend Ray Kroc. And that is how Ray Kroc met the McDonalds brothers. It was their innovative genius that led to the early systems that would propel the McDonalds fame. However, it was Kroc's genius as to how to replicate those systems and franchise them, well, everywhere.

Of course, if you really want to learn how it all came together, watch *The Founder* starring Michael Keaton as the man, the myth, the legend, Ray Kroc. It's a fascinating portrayal of how a conscious obsession with replicable systems led to the birth of the greatest franchise in the history of the world.

Most of us know the story of McDonalds and Mr. Kroc. But a relentless obsession with systems can be found in almost any successful business, even the business of government.

IN THE CLOSET

For instance, in my two stops working for the federal government, they had workable early systems that allowed us to easily construct form correspondence and legal pleadings, allowing for a quick and consistent result in every letter, and every legal decision depending upon what issue was being addressed. Yes, that's right, I said it: the federal government was more efficient than the private sector. They had created the Ford Model-T assembly line for correspondence and legal pleadings. Heck, you didn't even need to be a lawyer, they made it so easy.

You don't hear that often, do you? Now I've mentioned the USPTO previously, but when I first moved to the Washington D.C. area in 1993, I briefly worked on Capitol Hill as a Congressional

Intern for the 16th District out of Florida. This was my first experience working for the Federal Government.

Now, before I go on, I do have to share one story with you from that Summer. At the time, Congressman Fred Grandy represented Iowa's 6th District. Man, you may be saying to yourself, why do I know that name? Seems so familiar. Well, if you are of a certain age, you may remember Former Congressman Grandy from another acting role he performed for years, that of Gopher on the iconic series *The Love Boat*. Yup, that Gopher. What most people don't know is that Grandy is a graduate of Harvard University, yeah that Harvard, and had, prior to making it big on *The Love Boat*, been active in politics as a speech writer.

Well, as the story goes, one of my fellow interns—clearly not understanding his place in the pecking order—happened to get on an elevator with Congressman Grandy and several other staff members. Rumor has it that Representative Grandy nicely asked "What floor?" to the intern. The intern smugly replied, "Lido Deck!" Rumor also has it that was the intern's last day in Congress. Dude, know your place and don't be an ass. And by the way, I'm speaking about the intern.

Back to our regularly scheduled story. Now, as an intern, your life is not glamorous. In fact, have you ever heard someone complain that their office is the size of a closet? Well, I'm here to tell you that my "office" was literally a closet. And not a nice walk-in with shelving and a desk or something you would see in the *Real Housewives of Beverly Hills.* Nope, on my first day, we had two interns that started for the summer of 1993 program. I can remember like it was yesterday when they walked us into the main office.

To set the stage properly, you need to understand that at the time, a U.S. House of Representative's office in the Rayburn House

Office Building was about 3000 square feet largely divided into 3 1000-foot spaces. The first was the congressperson's private office, one of the finest offices I have ever seen. The middle third was the high-end reception area and higher staff like Chief of Staff, attractive receptionists, and personal secretaries. The final third was what can only be described as the pit, where 8 - 10 legislative assistants were crammed into an open working space with a multitude of desks, coping machines, water coolers, and truly unique smells that could only come from the sweat-stained shirts worn by over-caffeinated, underpaid, legislative drones.

When I showed up for my internship, I quickly deduced that the other intern was higher in the pecking order. I guess he was the fruit of the loins of a major donor or business owner in the Congressman's district. We walked to his lovely wooden desk in the uncrowded high-end section of the office near the Congressman's Chief of Staff and personal assistant. After some brief introductions, we left him in his space and opened the door to the pit. Now, it was not dirty or anything like that. But going from a pristine, top-caliber office space to walking through that door was like when Luke, Han, Lea, and Chewy slid down the trash shoot into the garbage soup pit in *Star Wars*. OK, maybe it wasn't that bad. After all, there was no one-eyed garbage snake stalking us. But it truly was like walking into the movies' version of every police station in any big city, where you see the criminals handcuffed to metal desks while they are being interrogated by some grungy detective who had not shaved in days and was in desperate need of a shower. And here, the parts of the grungy detectives were being played by those dedicated legislative assistants.

As we walked by desk after desk, none of them were vacant. They were all occupied with legislative assistants busy drafting legislation and correspondence for congressman. Most were too busy to even look up or acknowledge me. Getting to the end of the row of desks, the Congressman's personal assistant gave me a little smile and said, "Here's where you will be working this Summer."

I looked around. No desk. No chair. Just louvered sliding doors to what appeared to be a small reach-in closet. She placed her hands on the two small knobs and pulled apart the accordion doors. To my surprise, they had actually fit a 2' by 6' piece of unfinished wood on cyder blocks in the closet.

"Here's your desk!" she said. She then reached in, pulled out the metal folding chair for me and pointed towards a computer that was so old it looked like something used by NASA during the Apollo lunar landings. As my son and I now often joke, "That computer's so old it has a pull string to start it."

"And this will be your computer," she said as she turned and excused herself from the pit, probably to go get showered and remove the smell of despair and broken dreams.

Well, if you know anything about me at all, inside I may be like "What the hell?", but on the outside I'll always keep a stiff upper lip and carry on. I unfolded the folding chair and flipped on the large orange toggle to start the computer. I could swear a little black exhaust puffed out as it whirled to life and the green and black DOS screen began to glow.

As the computer continued to warm up, another staffer then came over and showed me the ropes. "In short", he said, "your job will be pretty easy this Summer". Pointing to a stack of opened letters on the far corner of the desk about three feet high: "Your job is to send responses to constituent correspondence the Congressman receives regarding various issues of the day."

Exciting I thought. "Great, so I just write them letters back? What do I do, take them in to the Congressman and ask him how I should respond?"

The staffer just looked at me with a slightly dumbfounded look. "Um, yeah, we don't bother the Congressman .... ever ... and you, well, may never even see him, ever." A wry little smile crossed his face.

"How it works," he continued, "is that we as staffers know there are generally only so many topics the Congressman will receive letters on at a specific time. For instance, Right now, the hot topic is gun control..."

OK people, amazing how years later that's still a hot topic, but again, I digress.

He continued, "So we have two form letters to respond to any correspondence we receive from constituents. One when they are for gun control and one for when they are against gun control. What you merely need to do is to access each letter, sort into pro or con gun control, then insert their name and addresses into the system and the computer will print out the proper response."

And this is what I did during the Summer of 1993. Fresh out of college. Waiting to attend law school. Sorting constituent correspondence into issues, then again by whether the author was pro or against that issue. Once sorted, I generated a "custom" form response, yeah, a custom form response. Go figure. All for the Congressman's signature. Oh, and guess what, I signed his name to all the letters! Yup. That was the most training I received. How to sign his name. And I could do it. Perfectly. Still can. Wanna see?

My first stint at the government taught me the first cog in what would become my *eMyth* systemized business: correspondence. We lawyers write hundreds if not thousands of letters each year. And after being in the private sector for some time, they generally were 85 - 90% the same. Why had no one I had worked for created a document management system for form letters? Oh right, because that would mean fewer billable hours. Ooops, was that another backhanded swipe at the legal profession? Truth hurts, lawyers!

Well, I knew my new shop was going to be a flat-fee law firm. As such, efficiency would be the name of the game. So, the first cog in the machine of The Trademark Company was decided upon. I would create a form manual with every potential letter and email that I would need to build the business and put them into a manual named *The Trademark Company Operations Manual 101*. And I did. And it was amazing.

BACK WHEN THE USPTO WAS GOOD

The second part of this efficiency model would come from the USPTO itself. As I've mentioned before, the whole concept for The Trademark Company arose out of witnessing the less-than-stellar work submitted by many of the big firms during my tenure there. But the other valuable skill that I picked up from the USPTO was how to systemize legal pleadings.

Today, our company's Artificial Intelligence (AI) technology is a tad more advanced than this original concept, and can literally create complex legal arguments and documents based upon limited user input. But in 2000, AI technology was future tech. But what the USPTO had done back in those days to ensure a consistent result in the examination of trademarks was sharp.

First, they created a form paragraph book, filled with every conceivable paragraph an examining attorney would need for their job. Everything from the initial salutations in correspondence to far more complex legal arguments citing specific case law and decisions. The paragraphs were then numbered and categorized by subject. Using these paragraphs, provided they did their job right, examining attorneys, over 300 of them at the time, would all produce a consistent product on every file they worked on, using the tools given.

Second, the USPTO trained us, and trained us well, in how to use the form book. Specifically, we went to school inside the USPTO for weeks to first learn the underlying law, then to learn how to learn how to use the form book once we were placed into service. It was more like a cooking class than anything legal. In short: when you see this issue, insert this paragraph. This issue gets this one, followed by this one, and then this one. It was not practicing law; it was more akin to a recipe for how to bake a cake. And it worked brilliantly. Everything from letters to complex legal pleadings could be constructed using this system. Whoever came up with this was well ahead of their time.

Unbelievably, the government, yes, I said it, the government, is where I picked up the concept of efficiency through building systems into your business. Wait, huh? How? Because law firms are, by their very nature, encouraged to make mistakes, or to be less efficient, because they get paid by the hour. Well, because of my dislike of business-as-usual at these mega firms, that was the other major selling point I intended to bring to the market: flat fees for everything!

When you bill by the hour, you don't want efficiency. Remember our discussion above, the one about asking that lawyer down the hall, then the client gets billed not only for your time but for his, and all of this because you don't know what you're doing? And again, why is a client paying you to learn your job? Isn't that why they are paying you big bucks per hour? Aren't you supposed to know it already? Absurd.

Well, in my model, a client would never again pay for a lawyer learning on the job. Everything, every service I provided, would've been done for a flat fee. In short, 95% of the issues I was presented with I had seen hundreds of times. As such, why bill by the hour? Once systemized like a McDonald's operations manual, I could charge a flat fee for any legal services. Just look at their issue, as I did when working for the Congressman, determine which pigeonhole it fit into, and assemble correspondence, or a pleading, within minutes based on my form manual. Fast. Efficient. Effective.

No more billing surprises. No more people having to decide between legal fees and food for their children that month. And yes, I have heard that before. And yes, I have witnessed attorneys demand their bills be paid while families go hungry, then drive home in their new Mercedes. Nope. No more of that. This was going to be revolutionary. This was going to open high-caliber legal services to the masses. This was going to lead me to the top of my industry. And it eventually did.

THE GREAT FLOOD OF 2008

By now you've heard the iconic saying that most overnight success stories were 20 years in the making. It's easy to look at the giants of our industries and think, wow, they just hit it big! But the reality is typically far different. If you look behind the scenes, there were years of developing the business model, generating leads through advertising, and creating the systems to scale the business once there was proof of concept and profitable results.

Microsoft started in a garage. Google was originally just a school project. And Amazon, well, they just wanted to sell books online.

But over the years they grew into the titans of their industries that we know today. But that was no accident. You can't just get to billions and billions sold without having the infrastructure to service those orders. At some point, the businesses needed to scale.

What do you mean "scale"? They had to grow in a manner that kept their profit margins intact while adding more and more employees to the business, thus increasing their overall revenue. Scaling. And unless your intent is to run your business with just you and a few employees, and to keep it tiny for the life of the business, you need to know this fact now: Build Your Business from the Start to Scale.

In 2008, The Trademark Company was a scant 5 years old. I had a web site which generated leads for the business and arguably the second-highest web presence in our industry behind the OJs. What we did *not* have was size.

In fact, 5 years into the business, I had moved from Northern Virginia and the company's original office—in my basement—to the Raleigh-Durham area of North Carolina. At some point I had realized I needed to hire employees, but really did not have a hold on how to do that for the first time. I realized I did not want them working out of my house, that would seem too small. So, I rented what can only be described as the worst small office space in all of Raleigh! Worst? How so?

Well, it was clean. And, for the record, did not have pests or crime issues. But I can only assume it was a small area that must have been a mechanical room at some point in this large, class-A building in a suburb of Raleigh called Cary. It was a two-room space, shaped like a figure eight in which, as the boss, I took the back office away from the entrance door in the front office. Well, evidently, on the other side of that wall was the building's mechanical room, complete with water risers and a commercial fire alarm system. Mind you, this was in the days when remote computing and storing things in the cloud weren't quite the norm. Most of my work had to take place at a big desktop I had positioned in this office.

Well, I'm not one that enjoys a lot of background noise when I work. Bad choice of offices. First, on a good day, the water rushing through those risers could only be described as annoying. I mean, typically, the sound of water is soothing, right? No. It was like water rushing through pipes while thousands of pieces of broken glass slowly shredded small woodland creatures. The noise was horrendous. And that was a good day!

At least two days a week, the system's main fire alarm would report a fault. Now, for the other tenants of the building, they had no idea. The fire alarms did not go off. But the control panel, evidently on the other side of the thinnest sheet of drywall in the history of construction, would start making an alarm that sounded like a cross between one of those European police sirens with an ice pick being shoved into your ear. It sucked.

Moreover, every time this thing went off, the building's maintenance company (great guys) would have to stop what they were doing, jump in their trucks, and drive 45 minutes to shut it off. I tried to justify it by telling myself, This is what you get for $1,000 a month, and you must grow your way out of this. But eventually, the last straw fell on the camel's back, and I broke the lease. What was that, you might ask?

Well, one fine morning I get a call from the Cary Fire Department at about 7 a.m. "Hello, is Mr. Swyers available?" the voice asked. "Yes, this is Matt Swyers," I replied. The voice on the other end of the phone explained how they had responded to a report of water coming out of the main doors of the Class A building that we were in, and were investigating if the source of the water was our office. More specifically, one of the high-pressure risers had ruptured with sufficient force, had blown through the drywall and was shooting a geyser of water into my little space. At the time they arrived, there was 3 inches of standing water in the office, and it was rising fast. But they had acted quickly to shut down the water to the building.

I threw on some clothes and rushed out the door, knowing my entire fledgling company was on a few hard drives sitting in that office. Sure, I had backups at home, but that would have meant days of downtime while specialty software companies shipped me new operating systems, then uploading the data. Yeesh. But when I arrived, they let me come into the office, despite the standing water. Wearing my trusty Timberlands, I went to the back office where the rupture had occurred, expecting the worst. To my delight, the Cary Fire Department had acted so quickly, and, knowing we were a small business, had grabbed my computers and put them on furniture off the floor and away from the water. In short, they had helped save the business, or at least a significant hassle for the business. To the men and women of the Cary Fire Department and Fire Departments everywhere, again, thank you for all that you do!!! It is greatly appreciated.

But at that moment, it hit me: I had been running a business for 5 years that could have been taken out, possibly, by just a burst pipe. What was I doing? My livelihood, and that of my family's, was, in part, dependent on the strength of an aging waterline and the good men and women of the local fire department? No way. That's teetering on the edge. It was time to figure out how to scale the business and to grow it so that no small incident like that could ever threaten it again. I set off on my journey to learn how to scale a business.

THE RISE OF ATLANTIS

So often in life, metaphors intersect with reality. A few weeks after the flood, my former wife and I were scheduled to take our first trip away from both children, since our son had arrived in 2005. The destination: Atlantis on Paradise Island, in the Bahamas.

If you've never been to Atlantis, it should be on your list of destinations. It is a mega resort built right on some of the finest beaches in the Bahamas. It has casinos, shows, night life, every type of restaurant you can imagine, and literally the best water park I have ever seen, built right into the resort. Water Park in the morning, swim with the dolphins in the early afternoon. Later, grab an inner tube and float around the resort in one of the world's longest lazy rivers, or just grab some rays at the beach. Then a world-class dinner, a show, and a little gaming at the casino to conclude the day. It is an amazing experience.

During this trip, we were without kids for the first time in a few years. We stayed at The Cove, the most exclusive and hip of the resort's hotels, which contained an adults-only pool, akin to something that you would see on South Beach in Miami. It's not that there were a bunch of naked people running around, although the swimsuits were admittedly a tad smaller at this pool. It's just that, while you're enjoying an adult beverage on high-end lounge chairs —often on islands in the middle of the pool—or enjoying those same beverages while watching scantily-clad perfect 10s dance with each other in the shallows, you weren't concerned with suddenly getting hit in the face with a water gun, or being interrupted by the afternoon meltdowns kids invariably have like clockwork.

It was during this fateful trip, while at this uber-cool pool, that I picked up Robert Kiyosaki's 1997 masterpiece *Rich Dad Poor Dad.* If you have not read it, consider putting this book down immediately, go to Amazon.com, and order a copy. After you have ordered your copy, come back to this point and slog through the rest of my musings.

Anyways, if you are an entrepreneur, or even thinking about being an entrepreneur, it is the single most important book you will ever read. It's not so much a traditional "how to" book for business, or a certain aspect of business. Rather, it's great at explaining the proper mindset you need to be a successful entrepreneur and, more generally, financially sound in your business and personal life. From the millions of us whose lives you have transformed, thank you, Robert.

I was mesmerized by Kiyosaki's manner of thinking in *Rich Dad Poor Dad.* And, if you were not aware of this fact already, if you are an entrepreneur, or a business leader, you need to read as much as you can to keep the idea-flow going. Commit yourself to a lifetime of learning.

In any event, I breezed through *Rich Dad Poor Dad* at the pool and enjoyed it so much that I immediately started on his second book, *Cashflow Quadrant.* In this book, Kiyosaki explains in more detail his philosophy of how to establish a successful business structure for your life, ensuring a consistent cash flow. But for me, and perhaps of greatest significance in my life, *Cashflow Quadrant* specifically referenced and recommended the book that would change everything for me: *eMyth* by Michael E. Gerber.

In my opinion, if you are opening a business and only have time to read one book, ever, this is the one. This is the single most important book to build a scalable business ever written. Period. As

I read the book, it opened my eyes as to how to structure my new mousetrap, and how to build a better law firm. The book goes way beyond my forthcoming summary but, effectively, it teaches you how to systemize everything, as if you intended to franchise the business from day one to something like McDonald's or Starbucks. Everything is written down. Everything is put into a manual. Everything is a system. It is the systems that form the business. It is the systems that are the most important things in business. These concepts may be basic for some, but to a fledgling entrepreneur that did not go to business school, they were revolutionary.

So, armed with Kiyosaki's viewpoint and Gerber's "systemize everything," I set out to build a better mousetrap. I studied in silence everything everyone else was doing in my little industry, looking at what worked and what didn't. Once I had this general knowledge, I combined it into one easy-to-use operations manual as to how I, and later my entire small company, would operate on a day-to-day basis.

The first thing I set out to systemize was legal correspondence. Lawyers send out the same form letters every day. However, back in the early 2000s, at least at the two law firms where I had originally worked, there was no central repository for "form" correspondence. Now, by today's standards, every law firm has some form of document management system. Back then, well, that just did not happen.

If you had a particular subject, and asked around, the answer may be, "Well, see Andy down the hall. I think he had a similar issue a year ago, he may be able to help you." But coming full circle, what just happened at that moment? No repository of documents means that, every time the law firm must create a new letter or document, it is done from scratch. From scratch equates to more time. More time equals, well, you guessed it, more billable hours! The client is billed more. Oh, and in our example, you don't think Andy's time is free, do you? The 10 minutes he spends searching for the letter will appear on the client's next bill, as well. What a racket.

But after a few months of work, there it was, in all its glory. The Trademark Company Operations Manual 1.0. It had everything in it, from core concepts about our culture to every form imaginable. From emails to call scripts. From letters to form legal pleadings. In short, if it needed to be done in the company, it was somewhere in that manual.

Over the years, we have developed more manuals. A sales manual. A customer service manual. There was even a manual for accounting and litigation. Our entire business was written down in "how to" books. So, when we hired, it wasn't that difficult to bring someone on. We gave them some in-class training, and handed them the manual. And from there, if managed well, you will produce a consistent, quality product or service, so that all your customers know what to expect.

But all of this is for naught if it is not managed well, with those running the systems being held accountable.

THE KING IS DREAD

For almost two decades, every trainee at The Trademark Company has had to endure stories about my love for McDonald's. Sorry. But at the time I am authoring this book, even at the ripe old age of 50, I am (still) lovin' it. From the first time I had a hamburger, to their iconic Happy Meal, chicken nuggets, I loved it all. And let's face it, those fries ... they are to die for.

And who could forget those extra value meals? In 1993, when I moved to Washington D.C. I didn't have two nickels to rub together. I was broke. I didn't have enough for breakfast. So, I would walk to work across the D.C. mall to the Rayburn House Office Building, sipping free coffee from the lobby in the dirty little long-term hotel I was boarding in for the summer. I cannot recall what I would do for lunch. I think they had a cheap sandwich place in one of the buildings, and I could grab a sandwich.

But then, every night, for that entire summer, I would look forward to that walk home. I didn't know anyone, so I didn't worry about being asked out by friends. Heck, even if I did, I could not have afforded to go out. So, it was easy, and expected. About 3 blocks from my hotel, I would start smelling those fries, those glorious fries. Rounding the corner, my tummy would grumble in excited anticipation as those iconic golden arches would come into view.

As I swung the doors open, the smell of food—glorious McDonald's food—was too much to bear. I would walk up to the counter, order my meal, and hand the cashier a crinkled up $5 I had allotted for dinner. And within minutes there it was, right on the tray with the iconic paper insert, a Big Mac, large fries, and large Diet Coke, all for about $3!!! All steaming hot, fresh, and ready to satisfy my grumbling belly.

And you know what always stood out to me about that summer? Every meal at McDonald's was awesome. I mean, there are those who love McDonald's, and those who do not. You know where I stand. But without exception, for an entire summer, that meal was perfect. And I mean perfect. The fries were always hot. The hamburgers looked just like the commercials, and the Diet Coke a perfect match to wash it all down. It was a little bit of comfort at the end of an exhausting day working in that closet in the pit of the Congressman's office.

Want to know something else awesome? That McDonald's was just like every other McDonald's I have ever been to, no matter where, delivering a near perfect product consistently with a smile. It didn't matter if it were the first time I got a Happy Meal in South Florida, my first Happy Meal with Chicken Nuggets outside of Denver, Colorado, or just a wonderful burger after a series of less-than-inspiring British cuisine in London.

It is stunning how often they get it right and consistent at McDonald's. Why, might you ask? Because after they build the systems and put them into place, with manuals and other manners of adding consistency to the process, they manage the processes at an expert level to make sure those systems are followed with exacting precision, whether it's in South Florida, Denver, or London. It is a secret you must undertake when scaling a business. But don't take my word for it. Let's just look at McDonald's one-time biggest competitor: the tired old King.

A few years back, we were in the process of moving from Washington, D.C. to Raleigh, N.C. For those of you not too familiar with that hike, it's a straight shot south on I-95 for between 4 and 12 hours, depending on D.C. traffic. Yes, we once had close to an 8-hour delay. Thank you, wonderful world of Woodbridge! Technically it's not the town's fault. I mean, going from 8 lanes to 2 with DC-mindset drivers. Great planning, folks. Great planning!

At the midway point, there is one of those gas-and-feed places, you know, combined gas station and restaurant. I cannot recall the brand of the gas station, but the restaurant was Burger King. Well, the kids were hungry, and we needed gas, so we figured we'd kill two birds in one stone. Well, after trying to eat at that restaurant on that day, killing birds with a stone would have been a better option for food. I mean, really.

There was not a line in the restaurant which, I thought, was a little odd for fast food, but hey, faster for us, right? Um, yeah no.

"My son will have a 6-piece chicken tenders."

"Sorry sir, we don't have chicken tenders right now," came the reply.

I turned to my 2-year-old son, expecting a meltdown. "No worries, we'll have a cheeseburger meal."

"About that," the clerk replied, "we don't have any cheese."

I had never been faced with a fast-food restaurant that was out of stuff. I looked at him curiously. "Anything else you're out of?"

He looked at me and said, "Yeah, I'm sorry, we only have the larger burger sizes for the Whoppers. No fries, no chicken. Our delivery truck didn't get here ... yesterday."

I was floored. I mean these things happen. But we were not in a pandemic. It was not a holiday. Nothing. Just, they didn't have stuff on the menu. Wow. To me, an instant red flag on the management of the business went up. How could they be open without food to serve? Undaunted, we ordered cheeseless Whoppers, grabbed some water—did I mention their fountain drinks were down too?—and went on our way.

Fast forward a few months: we are swinging down to check on the progress of our home. Lightning can't strike twice, can it? We pull into our favorite gas-and-feed. As we started to fuel the truck up, I walked over to grab the family a few sacks of BK goodness.

"Goooooood afternoon," I said with a big smile. "Can I have a Whooper, Jr. meal with Onion Rings?"

The cashier stopped me, "Are fries OK? We are out of onion rings."

"Of course," I replied. "Anything else I should stay away from?" I then went on to recount my prior experience, and we had a good laugh about how, at that location, they were always getting shorted by the supply truck and had just gotten used to having to tell customers they were out of some major item on the menu. But on that day, the only thing they did not have were the onion rings.

And in that moment, and in this little story, hopefully you can glean the distinction between what I consider to be a well-managed organization in McDonald's and one that is less professionally managed in Burger King. They both have similar franchise models. They both have similar training manuals. They both have similar menus. But, in the end, you must add in that third critical element to those systems: a management structure that ensures that the systems are followed, and followed with exacting precision.

Think about it. I have never walked into a McDonalds anywhere in the world and been told they are out of something. The bathrooms are always clean, the restaurants tidy, and the food served hot and on schedule. Compare this to Burger King, where on multiple occasions I have walked in and they are out of products, the cleanliness of the restaurants varies widely—in my opinion, of course—and the overall experience is simply not as good as that of the Golden Arches. Now that is not because of those wonderful kids working at the register or prepping your meal. It's due to a lack of proper management structure to ensure that the original model, as updated, is provided consistently to every customer around the globe

So, when building your business from the start, create that scalable model and put everything down in a manual, as if you were going to franchise the same. Then, as you grow, you must continue to delegate and manage the work performed within your model to ensure that your product, whatever it may be, is delivered with the same quality and attention to detail as you set down in the original plan.

Chapter Summary: Build it to Scale

- **Create Your Scalable Model:** Create your business model, and everything you will do to make it successful. From your product or service, how it is made or delivered, to your ideal customers. Then create your dream position organization chart, which addresses every aspect of the four main divisions of a business: (1) marketing; (2) sales; (3) operations; and (4) accounting. Understand that, depending upon the initial scale of your business, you yourself may need to fill some, if not all, those positions. But as you grow, you know which positions you need to fill to scale the business to your dream size. Define each role, and what they will do with detailed job descriptions.
- **Reduce it to a Franchise Manual:** Everything must be put down into a detailed "how to" manual, from how you market, sales emails and scripts, how the goods or services are delivered, to the accounting aspects of the business. This will not only make sure that you develop a consistent product, but that you can hire people and scale the business consistently with the way the business is required to run.
- **Delegate, Manage & Hold Accountable:** Finally, build it and, provided it is profitable (as we continue to discuss below), add the cogs to your organizational chart. Make sure

that you have a series of checks and balances in place to continuously ensure everyone in the organization is accomplishing the work they were hired to do. Hold them accountable to do so, and if they are not accountable, find someone else for the position who is.

Additional Suggested Reading:

The eMyth Revisited, Michael Gerber, 1995

Secret Service, John R. Dijulius III, 2003

What's the Secret? To Providing a World-Class Customer Experience, John R. Dijulius III, 2008

Additional Suggested Resource:

Trainual.com

SHAMELESSLY MARKET YOURSELF

They Can't Buy It if They Don't Know It Exists.

THE KING OF MARKETING

I grew up in South Florida. More specifically, I lived in a little town called North Palm Beach, about 90 minutes north of Miami. It was a great little city and, in the mid-to-late 1970s, just bustling with young families. As I remember it, it was like something out of a movie. Gangs of kids riding their bikes to Twin City Mall to play at the local video arcade or catch a movie. A little further up was the 7-Eleven where we'd grab a mid-afternoon Slurpee and perhaps a treat before heading home to have dinner with the family.

It was a simpler time then. There were no cell phones. You knew to come home when the sun went down. If all else failed, you would listen for dad's whistle. Some dads would call out. Guess they hadn't mastered the two-fingered whistle. I myself never could. But my dad had, and it was the loudest thing ever. It was the most deafening whistle which, I swear, you could hear from the next county. When my brother and I heard that, you knew you had better be on your way home, and fast. Dinner was coming off the stove and being carried to the table. And you were not late for dinner, ever.

It was my hometown. The type of place that had a central ballpark with baseball fields in the summer that doubled as football and soccer fields in the fall. Where every Saturday the parks would begin bustling with activity in the early morning with back-to-back-to-back-to-back games that would go to the early evenings. Where, if your parents had multiple kids, you'd be parked for the day either warming up or playing your games, or hanging out or watching your siblings play. Between games, you'd hang with your buddies and maybe grab some candy. And lunch was always a slice of the world's worst pizza and a snow cone from the dedicated parents working the plywood, 8' by 12' concession stand, painted in that same drab green like every other park in the U.S. It was, in a word, America.

At that time television, you know, TV, wasn't massive yet. You couldn't just whip out your phone and in seconds be watching anything that has ever been recorded, ever! I mean sure, Saturday mornings you'd get up and watch cartoons. You see, back then, Saturday mornings were really the only time to see them. Of course, this had to be done before heading to the ballpark for the day. The classics in the old-style of animation. Bugs Bunny was always my favorite. Especially when they added the Coyote and Road Runner, Sylvester and Tweetee. And I don't know about you, but, perhaps as an early tell on the entrepreneurial spirit, I always rooted for the Coyote to figure out how to catch that anncying Road Runner. I mean, at his heart, Wiley was simply trying to solve a problem. He wanted to catch that arrogant, annoying Road Runner. *Beep Beep*! Man, if I got taunted with a Beep Beep and someone sticking their tongue out at me, I surely would have obsessed about how to solve the problem of getting them. Isn't that the spirit of most entrepreneurs?

OMG. I'm aware that I sound like my grandparents, who, amazingly, would tell stories about how they had to walk uphill in the snow for two miles to get to school, then back home uphill two miles in the snow. Hmmmmm. How'd that work again? I was always told never to call them out on that one But hopefully the OMG reference removes this from a complete curmudgeonly trip down memory lane in the late 1970s.

At night, when you'd get home from the ballpark, we'd watch a little *Hee Haw,* as mom and dad would retire to their bedroom to get dressed for their evening. And then, perhaps the best part of the week: a TV dinner! As kids, that meant mom and dad were heading out, and we got TV dinners! And by extension, TV! They were always great. From Salisbury steak, with those funky hard mashed potatoes and some form of Cobler or chocolate cake baked right in the tray, to fried chicken. It was always awesome. Man, our parents didn't know what they were missing!

Invariably, our babysitter would arrive, as we could barely make out mom and dad calling out, "Be good. We'll be home at blah blah blah blah," as their voices faded out the door. By that time, we were already tuned out. I mean the TV was on! And soon that magical tune would announce the beginning of the most popular show on TV.

"*Love, Life's Sweetest Reward* ..." Sing it along right now if you know it. It's OK. And you knew it was on! The *Love Boat,* and, if we could convince the babysitter—if one of her guy friends was not sneaking in, that is—we'd be able to stay up and watch *Fantasy Island*! A show about a mysterious tall man and his petite mini-man co-host. Perhaps the most mysterious part of that show was why they never really addressed Mr. Roark's and Tatoo's relationship. Just saying. Man, the simplicity of life then was wonderful.

And for those of you too young to remember this, those were the days you couldn't skip commercials. There was no Apple TV, no TIVO, no DVRs. Heck, we hadn't even heard of a VHS yet! Nope, if you wanted to watch TV, you watched what they put on and when they put it on. Imagine that, kids. And we liked it. And it was good! So back then, commercials were a part of life. They were inescapable. If you were hanging on to see who shot JR on *Dallas,* or whether the O'Malley's would be able to patch up their marriage on the *Love Boat* between Acapulco and Los Angeles, you had to watch them. And in my life, there was one line of commercials that reigned supreme! The King, if you will.

Sure, you had your iconic commercials of the 1970s that we all remember. *I'd like to buy the world a Coke.* I mean who could forget that? Genius. The Rainbow Apple Computer that I can remember when visiting this new concept of a "computer store," which would later morph into their famous “1984”-themed ad campaign. And, of course, the advertisements for Atari, which were never enough for us to have one in our house. Nope, we had the Apple 2e. And we could get games on it. But they just weren't the same.

But for my money, one ad campaign ruled them all. It was a regal ad. The monarch of the air waves. It was The Tire King! I know, I know what you're probably thinking. Rafiki walking slowly up

Pride Rock, raising his outstretched monkey hands, and proudly presenting a tire to the whoops and hollers of the animals gathered below. Oh wait, wrong king. I may owe Disney a nickel now. No, the commercials weren't that dramatic. But man, were they effective. The Tire King!

This guy dressed up as a king—you know, crown, scepter, robes —proclaiming that he had the best prices on tires around. The best service around. Because he was the best. He was... The Tire King. His business? Why, Tire Kingdom, of course.

A little background on the business: Tire Kingdom was founded by Chuck Curcio in 1972, starting with a single location in a farmer's market in West Palm Beach, Florida. In large part because of Chuck's (a.k.a The Tire King's) outlandish marketing efforts, business grew rapidly, and the organization started opening stores throughout Florida. He parodied popular shows of the time such as Miami Vice, all the while keeping to his theme of being the King of Tires. Did it work? From that single location, Chuck opened another store, then another, and another. By the late 1980s, Tire Kingdom had expanded through most major markets in Florida, with 34 locations by 1984 and 67 locations by late 1988. In subsequent years, the company expanded to Georgia, Louisiana, Vermont, Ohio, New Hampshire, the Carolinas, and the United States Virgin Islands.

Some thought Chuck was a fool, doing these outlandish and often embarrassing commercials. I can remember people making fun of him openly. Yet, you know what? Everyone remembered Tire Kingdom, and that crazy Chuck Curcio. And guess what? Part deux: most people went there for their tires. So outlandish, sure. Embarrassing? Maybe. Smart? All the way to the bank, baby.

Through his over-the-top marketing techniques, coupled with the expansion those efforts afforded, Curcio sold Tire Kingdom to the Michelin group, and an investment group headed by Goldman Sachs between 1989 and 1996, for a reported $45 million. All for a guy who dressed like a king to sell tires. Who's laughing now?

The point is, if you are going to open a business, be prepared to market it shamelessly. Those who do are the winners. Those who don't, well, they most likely become part of those statistics we chatted about in Chapter 1.

Don't believe me? Well, if Chuck was more local and regional? What about national, or International? Does it work at those levels, too? Yes! Just ask former President Trump or Sir Richard Branson. In my opinion, arguably the two best shameless markers in the history of the planet! Let's look at former President Trump.

THE ART OF THE FREE DEAL

I know, I know, I know. About 52 percent of you may throw this book in the fire after reading this next blurb about our former President Donald J. Trump. But hey, you already bought it—or maybe got it for free—so that's fine by me! The other 48 percent probably didn't get the joke. Zing! I like to fancy myself as an equal opportunity offender.

Anyways. If you ever read President Trump's iconic *Art of the Deal*, it was very entertaining. And let me stop right here. If you have not read it, you should. Especially if you're a critic. How can you logically insult or criticize something if you have not read it? Follow me so far? Let me help you out with the answer, you can't! Don't listen to others. Don't form uneducated opinions. That's one of the things going haywire in our world right now. Too many people yell about things they have no actual, first-hand knowledge about. Just because someone said it on social media or otherwise. Do your research. Formulate your own opinions! Then, and only then, can you make comments worth more than just my parakeet's droppings at the bottom of their cage. Read it before you criticize! I did.

That said, the book is mainly autobiographical, giving his boastful insights into business and various aspects thereof. But a consistent theme for former President Trump, and one that he has brilliantly personified throughout his life, is why pay for advertising when, in the alternative, you can do things that promote your brand for free? In short, don't pay for a $50,000, full-page ad in the New York Times. Just do something that they report, and it's free advertising! Pretty simple in concept, right?

One of the best examples of this technique in *The Art of the Deal* involves New York's famed Central Park ice rink in the 1980s. At that time, the rink was in a state of significant disrepair. In short, it had not produced a skateable surface in years. The city had spent millions trying to fix it up and repair the cooling system to make ice...all to no avail. Enter a young, brash real estate developer looking to make a name for himself on the island of Manhattan. As the story goes, Trump began publicly chiding then-Mayor Ed Koch about the state of the ice rink, how NYC could not get it fixed, and how the time frame to do so by the city was simply unacceptable. The more he ramped up his condemnation, the more press he got. When Koch would respond, prompting an even nastier response by Trump, the NY press ate it up. All that free press. Sound familiar?

Eventually it got to the point that Koch dared Trump to do better. And, in so doing, played right into Trump's hands. Trump's construction crews and engineers were ready. From the day the challenge was accepted, it was a media circus. Nightly updates on the news on the progress of the rink. Daily updates in the papers. In all, Trump got millions in free advertising for his brand simply by egging on a politician. Simply by doing something newsworthy, as opposed to writing a check for advertising. Simply by being himself!

If I recall correctly, the dare was that Trump could not fix the rink and have ice on it within 90 days. Well, as the world now knows, Trump did not complete it in 90 days. He did it in about 45!! And in that now iconic photo from the book, Donald J. Trump stood on the ice in the Central Park rink, the first time anyone had done so in years, completing the cycle and a massive free press junket for his brand, one of his first truly iconic moments in NYC. Not too shabby.

Of course, former President Trump did not stop there. For years, he used the hit TV reality show *The Apprentice,* and later *The Celebrity Apprentice*, to advertise his brand further. In this regard, love him or hate him, what a genius at shamelessly marketing himself and the Trump brand. NBC Universal actually paid him to effectively create hour-long infomercials for the Trump organization, airing them in a highly-rated television series. Brilliant. Simply, brilliant. But there's more.

Although somewhat controversial, Trump would further use this technique to criticize President Barrack Obama using the now infamous "birther" argument. For those of you who do not recall, long before former President Trump decided to run for office, he was an outspoken critic of Obama both during his run for the presidency and during his two terms in office. In short, Trump claimed that former President Obama could not constitutionally hold the office of President of the United States based upon evidence he had obtained indicating that Obama had not been born in this country.

Now I don't know if Trump believed this or not. I have never met or spoken with him personally. But once again, he figured out a feud with a politician that would get him free press. Brilliant! And this time, as the Trump empire had expanded to a national and international level, picking a fight with a local politician in NYC would no longer cut it. His brand had transcended NYC. He needed a wider audience. He needed a presidential candidate. And in Obama he found the perfect target. And once again, the press ate it up.

He so perfected the technique that, by the time former Secretary of State Hillary Rodham Clinton was set to run for President as the heir apparent to the Obama administration, Trump's vicious, albeit self-serving attacks, on Benghazi and the missing emails from her computer, got him virtually drafted into the Republican National Party's debates. as the ratings for these once-stodgy events soared through the roof.

Enjoying the almost non-stop free press, then-candidate Trump merely had to show up and give press conferences about "Locking her up" for the alleged missing emails. Again, free press for his brand, on a scale never seen. Sorry to say, but simply brilliant! Well, by now we know how the story ends. Personally, I don't think he ever wanted to be President. I think he just wanted the free press and all the riches that went along with it for his organization. But he was so good at it, he got elected as President of the United States of America. And for that, well played, former President Trump, well played.

VIRGIN TERRITORY

On to a less controversial figure, Sir Richard Branson. So, if Curcio was the King of local, and President Trump the emperor of National—yeah, that was on purpose—Branson has got to be the Grand Poobah of international shameless marketing. I mean, by now, who hasn't heard of his Virgin brand of companies? Well, that wasn't always the case.

In the early 1970s, Branson was a co-founder of Virgin Records. An entrepreneur from an early age, the label truly began to blossom in the 1980s, as Branson's penchant for marketing stunts began taking shape.

One of the earliest of his grand forays was in 1985, when he constructed and helped pilot the *Virgin Atlantic Challenger* in an attempt to break the transatlantic crossing speed record, which had stood since 1952. Although the attempt ended in near tragedy when the vessel struck an underwater obstacle and sank in heavy seas nearly 100 miles from the finish line, it gained Branson, and his label *Virgin Records,* international acclaim. News reports from around the globe provided nightly updates of the three-day attempt, all with the *Virgin* label emblazoned all over the vessel. Why pay for it when you get it for free, right?

The next year, Branson returned with the *Virgin Atlantic Challenger II* in which he, and his team, set the Atlantic crossing record from New York to England in a time of 3 days, 8 hours, and 31 minutes. When pulling into the harbor in his *Virgin* branded boat, Branson, with his signature boyish smile and eternal youthful exuberance, popped his champagne and toasted the accomplishment, to the adoration of all in attendance and millions around the globe watching his *Virgin* brand get free global press. Well played, Sir Richard, well played.

Over the years, he would perform similar stunts, as *Virgin Records* expanded to his *Virgin* empire of airlines, hotels, and now spacecraft, to name a few. Some of the more notable included trying to pilot a *Virgin*-branded hot air balloon around the globe in 1995 and 1998. Both attempts failed, but brought Sir Richard millions of dollars in free advertising from the global press covering his attempts.

Driving a tank into Times Square in 1998, pre 9/11, and taking aim at the famous Coca-Cola sign to launch Virgin Cola. A great publicity stunt, however, it would take a lot more than one tank to take down the greatest distribution network in history. Bungee jumping off the Palms Hotel and Casino in Las Vegas for the first *Virgin America* flight, driving a "car" across the English Channel, and, most recently, sipping champagne as he repelled down the side of *Virgin Galactic's* space hanger.

Shameless. Simply shameless.

But effective.

Today, Sir Richard's Virgin Group controls nearly 400 companies in their vast Virgin empire, which includes, or at one time included, the *Virgin Records* label, *Virgin Megastores*, *Virgin Airlines* and now *Virgin Galactic*.

But what themes have we identified from Curcio, Trump, to Branson? First, they shamelessly marketed themselves to their consumer basis. They understood what worked. And no, not every venture formed by these men worked. I mean, Trump Steaks? Trump University? Virgin Cola? But for the most part, these gentlemen hit it big. And once they understood what worked, they doubled down and ramped it up.

For Curcio, it was playing the part of a silly guy dressed as a King and other 80s spoofs. For Trump, it was often picking fights with politicians, then showing them up. And for Branson, well, it was just cool fun stuff like hot air ballooning, power boats, and repelling off buildings with champagne. And once they figured out what worked, they doubled and tripled down on it.

Chapter Summary: Market Yourself Shamelessly

- **Shamelessly Market to Your Consumer Base:** Know where your market base is and shamelessly, relentlessly market to them. Years ago, it was print media and television advertising. Today, you are more likely to reach them via content media, blogs, vlogs, and social media posts. Whatever the medium, know where they are and blast them with your message.
- **Track What Works**: Keep track of where your business receives its business from. In short, know what works, and what does not. This is a critical piece of information that you must have to scale your business. If you don't understand what is driving business to your door, you can't focus on scaling that critical component of the scaling process.
- **Double-Down on What Works, Kill What Does Not, Repeat:** Once you figure out what is working, kill what is not and double down on what is. Repeat. And repeat again. Keep adding new avenues of marketing and never stop.

Additional Suggested Reading:
The Art of the Deal, Donald J. Trump, 1987
Family Jewels: Sex Money Kiss, Gene Simmons, 2006

YOU CAN'T PULL THE CART BY YOURSELF

Hire for Attitude. Train for Skill. Fire when Necessary.

ICE CASTLES

On January 11, 2018, Thomas Dundon became the majority owner of the NHL's Carolina Hurricanes. By season's end, the Canes, as they are known in the league, had failed to make the playoffs for a disappointing eighth consecutive year. Eight years! That just doesn't happen. I mean, this is the NHL, where something like half of the teams make it every year. Half! And to not make it for eight years. That's bad. Really bad.

Enter Mr. Dundon, a businessman in the financial sector. To say he had a more direct spin during exit interviews with the team in 2018 would be an understatement. He was blunt. He was direct. Oftentimes it was reported he was even caustic. Even to players who had been with the franchise for years. But he owned every comment he made in those interviews. In fact, in addressing the press on the comments made by many of the players after their post-season evaluations, Dundon said:

"It's our job to find players better than you,
and it's your job to make that hard.
There isn't anyone I'm trying to replace.
The players understand this is a business."

Whoa, the press responded. That was a tad more direct than the previous ownership. And I must admit, when I first heard this on the radio, all I could think was what a jack ass. I mean, damn. Did he just say what I think he said? In short, he is looking to fire all the players and get better players. And that's the taste he left an entire team with as they headed into the offseason? Wow.

But as I thought about his comments throughout the day, and they soaked in a little more, I began to understand and embrace what Mr. Dundon actually meant. But to truly understand the comment, we need to examine the history of the Canes franchise, so that we can appreciate the full context of his ownership and leadership at that moment.

The Canes franchise was established originally as the New England Whalers in November 1971 by the World Hockey Association. They first played their games in Boston, Massachusetts, you know, the wickedest awesome city on the planet? For the first two years of their existence, they played their home games at the Boston Arena and Boston Garden, pronounced Gaaaaaah-den. But with the increasing difficulty of scheduling games at Gaaaaaaah-den, owned by the NHL rival Boston Bruins, pronounced Breeeeeew-INs, the owners decided to move the team to Hartford, Connecticut in 1974.

A few years later, as one of the most stable WHA teams, the Whalers, along with the Edmonton Oilers, Quebec Nordiques, and Winnipeg Jets, were admitted to the NHL when the rival leagues merged in 1979. However, under pressure from the other team in the New England area, those wonderful Breeeeeew-INs, the Whalers were compelled to rename the team the Hartford Whalers but, in so doing, recaptured the proper pronunciation of the letter "a".

Unfortunately, the Whalers were plagued for most of their existence by limited marketability. Hartford was the smallest American market in the NHL, and was located on the traditional dividing line between the home territories for the New York Rangers and Boston Bruins. It was a recipe for low fan support, and even lower fan engagement. Further, it didn't help matters that the Hartford Civic Center was one of the smallest arenas in the league, seating under 16,000 spectators even though the Whalers rarely saw numbers approaching capacity.

In March 1997, under immense financial pressure from low ticket sales and merchandising, the majority owner Peter Karmanos announced that the team would move elsewhere after the 1996–97 season. The last proverbial straw being placed on the fragile franchise was the team's inability to negotiate a satisfactory construction and lease package for a new arena in Hartford.

On May 6, 1997, Karmanos announced that the Whalers would move to the Research Triangle area in the great state of North Carolina, and the new PNC Arena in the best little big town on the planet, Raleigh. Karmanos himself thought of and decided upon the new name for the club: the Carolina Hurricanes, further making the decision to adopt the red, white, and black color scheme of North Carolina State University, the flagship university for the State of North Carolina. They would be sharing the arena with the Wolfpack and a parking lot with NC State's iconic Carter-Finley Stadium.

Following the move, the Canes made waves for the first time in the 2002 playoffs. Get it? Waves? Anyways. Surviving a late charge from the Washington Capitals to win the division, the Canes made their first run at the Lord Stanley's Cup, eventually exiting that year without the cup to their name. Fast-forward a few seasons.

The outcome of the 2004–05 NHL lockout led to the shrinking of team payrolls to $26 million. As a result, the Canes turned out to be one of the NHL's biggest surprises, turning in the best season in the franchise's 34-year history. They finished the regular season with a 52–22–8 record and 112 points, shattering the previous franchise records of 94 points. It was the first time ever that the franchise had passed the 50-win and 100-point plateaus. The 112-point figure was good for fourth overall in the league, easily their highest overall finish as an NHL team.

The Canes also ran away with their third Southeast Division title, finishing 20 points ahead of the Tampa Bay Lightning. In game seven, before the second-largest home crowd in franchise history (18,978), the Canes won 3–1, sealing their first Stanley Cup championship in franchise history.

Shockingly, the Canes were unable to follow-up the success of their breakout season. The following season, they became the first Stanley Cup Champions since the 1938-39 Chicago Black Hawks to fail to qualify for the playoffs. One year stretched into two, then three. Before long, the streak of missed post seasons reached eight. Eight! In hockey years, that's an eternity. Every year hope would return, a mid-season run, but then, no playoffs. Year after year. But then came 2018, Tom Dundon, and his simple but very illuminating statement about every player on the team:

"It's our job to find players better than you,
and it's your job to make that hard.
There isn't anyone I'm trying to replace.
The players understand this is a business."

As I mentioned above, it took me some time to reflect on this statement. But upon that reflection, I realized that Dundon was not being a jerk whatsoever. He was simply a highly intelligent businessperson who summarized the ideal employer-employee experience in this simple statement; namely, what every employer should strive for in hiring and managing their team, be it a professional sports club or a simple mom and pop business.

What happened with that change in leadership and hiring philosophy? The Canes had an epic run in the 2019-2020 COVID season which saw them not only return to the playoffs for the first time in ages, but nearly back to the Stanley Cup finals. And as of the writing of this chapter, during March of 2021, they are leading their division in the NHL. Think a good hiring and retention philosophy can make a difference in your organization?

Your job, in assembling your team, is to continuously seek out the best members of your team, get them on your proverbial bus, and get them in the right seats on your bus. You should be constantly looking for the best employees available. Correspondingly, your employees should strive to be their best for you. Otherwise, if you can find better, it's nothing personal, it's just business. That's all Dundon was saying.

Brilliance in its simplest form.

EPIC HIRING

A few years ago, I had the pleasure of being invited to tour Epic Games in Cary, North Carolina, producer and provider of the smash on-line gaming phenomena *Fortnite*. And she may kill me for dragging her into this, but at the time my daughter was dating a young man from Argentina who, for the purposes of anonymity, we shall call Pablo. Why she was dating a guy from Argentina, long story. Long, often embarrassing story. Suffice as to say, the young man had flown in from Argentina, through Miami, all the way to Raleigh to take my little girl to her junior prom. I mean, damn, any man willing to transfer flights in Miami is man enough for my daughter. Nuff said.

As he stayed with us, we looked for things to occupy his time—I mean, aside from constantly pawing my daughter. Seriously, it was exhausting trying to keep Doc Ock, as he became known in my house, occupied. At times I thought he had eight arms wrapped around my little girl. Dude, boundaries. But I digress.

Now, Doc Ock's dad had founded what was now the largest accounting firm in Buenos Aires. So naturally, Doc Ock wanted to follow in dad's footsteps, become a CPA, and eventually take over the family business with an almost guaranteed path to riches. Right? Nah! That would be logical. Too easy. Nope, Doc Ock wanted to be a video game developer. But hey, we all must dance to the beat of our own drummer. I get it. But damn, dad's drummer was pounding out a thumping beat!

I thought to myself, "Self, who do I know in the video game industry?" Because I often refer to myself as "self" when addressing myself. I know, the logic is dizzying. And then it hit me: "Eureka! I have at least 4 neighbors who work for this company Epic Games. Again, if you are not aware, they make *Fortnite*, like, the most popular video game ever!

I know, I'm 50, and I can hear all my friends out there yelling "Hey Dude, don't disrespect the Pac-Man". I am not. But Epic's *Fortnite* did it bigger, better, and longer than almost any top-selling game in history, period. So, what was their secret sauce? What was the glue that held them together? Let us continue our journey.

I emailed one of my friends who worked at Epic. Told him the score, about Doc Ock, you know. "My daughter would like 2 to 3 minutes this weekend without getting groped. I mean, got to save something for Prom, right?" And to my amazement, my man came through in a big way. He said, "Meet me at Epic tomorrow morning." "Seriously?" I replied. "Absolutely" he said.

Now I want to pause right here and give a shoutout to my friend and Epic Games. I have known him for years, around a poker table, etc. But outside of poker, we had never done anything together. And I emailed him, and his first reaction was, "I got this for you." What a wonderful person. He was in a unique position to help, and he did. Strive to live your life in this way, and I promise you it will be rewarded, in spades. What a great guy and great company.

The next day arrives. I pried Pablo, aka Doc Ock's hands, off my daughter and pointed to the truck. "Pablo, I have una surprise for you today, Señor," I said. "We are getting a tour of Epic Games." Now, I am not going to say he had an orgasm right at that moment. But maybe. After he cleaned himself up, we took the short drive over to Epic's campus to begin our tour with my buddy.

Once there, we entered the security area and initially walked by some very pedestrian-looking offices. As he explained, "This is where accounting and the lawyers sit. We like to keep the lawyers away from, you know, the creative side." Yes, even at Epic, they recognize lawyers are a sometimes-necessary evil that must be segmented apart from the general population.

Now that I think of it, maybe we should do that on a larger scale. Perhaps all lawyers in the US should only be permitted to live, hmmm, let's see, in Montana. That way they will stop mucking the world up for the rest of us, but, when occasionally needed, and it is far less often than they will tell you, we can let one or two off the ranch.

As we walked from the legal and accounting sections, my buddy was consistently narrating the Epic history and experience. It was like nothing I had ever experienced before. I mean, I have had behind the scenes tours of the bridges of Royal Caribbean's biggest cruise ships, iconic Broadway venues, and even Walt Disney World, but none of those experiences compared with my buddy's tour of Epic. Every time we entered a new room, a new division, his eyes would get a twinkle as he told us the story of that department and their contribution to the then mega-hit *Fortnite*. His enthusiasm and pride beamed through every story that he relayed.

I had expected a 10-minute quick stop-by of their facility. Two hours later, we finally reached the end of our journey, back where we had started. We stopped in front of a plaque where, at the time, there was a photo of every Epic employee, by location, in the order in which they were hired. At the time, my buddy was in the top 20 of all hires, meaning he was one of the first 20 that had been hired by the company.

Everyone worked hard. Everyone believed in the mission. Everyone virtually idolized the owner of the company, a man who I simply heard them refer to as Tim. I had to know. I had to know their hiring secret. I mean, how do you create such a culture? How do you find people to run your business that have so bought into the system that they beam with pride when someone asks them who they work? So, I asked.

Passion. Passion, my buddy responded. He said that each member of the Epic team had to have displayed some form of passion for the position that they would be hired for, before ever being considered by Epic. He went on to tell the story of a bartender from New Orleans who had discovered a bug in an early version of *Fortnite*. The bartender had no previous coding experience. Candidly, he had never been in the gaming industry. But something about that bug got to him.

He watched YouTube videos, read some articles, and taught himself how to program. He then wrote a line or two of code to fix the issue and simply mailed it to Epic with a note explaining what he had found, that he had fixed it for them and there was the code. As legend has it, Epic was so impressed they flew him up a few days later, offering him a job on the team shortly thereafter. Passion. He didn't do it for the job. He did it because he loved the game and he wanted to see it made better. And he was not even paid or told to do it. Passion.

My buddy then said that, after they locate these people with passion, the interview process is rigorous. Once an individual is granted an interview, the fun truly begins. In the early days, they would interview with every member of Epic Games. Every person. Now, at the time, that was around 20 to 30 people. Why? Because any person could decide not to hire them. And that would conclude their interview process. Done. Finished. Kaput. He said this rigorous process weeded out the pretenders as they often do not have the stamina to complete an all-day interview cycle unless that passion is real. Passion.

Two things I took from this experience: it does not matter if you are opening a gaming company, a bakery, or a T-shirt company. Look for people to help you in your mission not only with passion, but with genuine passion for what they will be doing for you.

Now, a cool postscript to this story happened about a year later. I was at a small get-together at another friend's home. While there, I was introduced to another guy who worked at Epic. As I told him who my buddy was, it became apparent that the guy was my buddy's boss. Well, I told him about the tour and congratulated him on *Fortnite*'s continued success. Again, he was just as passionate about *Fortnite* and Epic as my buddy. It truly was amazing.

As I relayed to him what my buddy had said about the passion he said, here, let me prove it to you. And before I could say anything, he picked up his phone, at 10:45 pm on Saturday night, and texted one of his contemporaries to see if they could chat about an idea he had had for the game. Within 30 seconds the guy texted back, "You bet." Well, he explained, he was just trying to demonstrate passion and dedication, even on a Saturday night ,to a new friend. But damn. That's what you want. And kudos to Epic for perfecting it. No wonder *Fortnite* has been the mega hit it has been.

Now a quick post scrip on Doc Ock: at some point, he shifted his view of the world and went to get his accounting degree. He is poised to take over his father's accounting firm and permit his mom and dad to quietly slip into retirement. At some point my daughter and he drifted apart. But I find comfort in the fact that he found his true passion, and that his eight hands and insatiable groping are now the problem of fathers of young women throughout Buenos Aires.

AND ALOHA MEANS GOODBYE

But as *Rocky Balboa* says, "Life ain't all sunshine and rainbows." And sometimes, you will experience this in the form of poorly behaving or underperforming employees. And when it is time to say goodbye to an employee, it should be done quickly and decisively. Because once you figure out someone does not fit into your culture, you must remove them immediately or risk damaging the business in a manner that may take years to recover. Unfortunately, this section will be all too easy for me to complete, as it was a long and painful personal lesson.

Hear me loud and clear, and heed this advice: when it's time to let someone go, rip that Band-Aid off ASAP! Firing someone slowly or worse yet, letting them stay on past a fireable event, will do more long-term damage to your culture than any offsetting good that employee could ever bring. Period. Let them go!

Captains of nuclear submarines know this reality all too well. Although it is kept quiet, one of the few things that can make an unscheduled trip to surface is when one of the crew loses it. Think about it: you spend months in a pressurized steel tube with no sunlight, no fresh air. The only way you can discern the distinction between night and day is through artificial lighting pumped throughout the boat. And, from time to time, submariners go a little stir crazy.

When that occurs, if possible, a captain will surface to unload the crew member as soon as is practical, as cabin fever is contagious and can spread rapidly among even the most veteran of crews. And just like a submarine captain, you must run your business, your ship, constantly looking for workplace cabin-fever and, when spotted, eliminate it from your ranks at all costs.

DON'T GIVE EM CREDIT

So awhile back, one of my friends revealed to me the following story. They had a salesperson, we will call him Tyrone, that was, for all intents and purposes, a good salesperson. He was consistently one of their top salespeople, always recording stellar months and enjoying dinners out with the boss at some of the finest restaurants in Raleigh to celebrate his contributions to the company. However, after a while, some odd trends began to develop.

First, when the company had daily sales contests, he became very adroit at rolling in a substantial number right at the end of the day, to just barely eke out a win over the nearest competitor. I mean, this did not happen just once, or twice. But after a while, he was taking like 3 out of 4 sales contests a month in this fashion. You starting to think something smells fishy in Denmark?

Second, from time-to-time, a few credit card disputes would roll in with people claiming that someone from the company had charged their credit card without authorization to do so. Did that fishy scent just become the smell of a tidal wave of whale shit on an ice flow? And for the longest time, the accounting department just racked it up to the payment processor and that someone must have keyed in the wrong card.

Now, early on, it is important to note that although these phantom issues appeared to be random, the only salesperson two of the transactions had been traced to were ... one guess... you can do it ... I know you can ... YES - Tyrone!

Initially, management just chalked it up to a "whoops" and Tyrone apologized for charging the wrong card. And that's when action should have been taken. But it was not. Why? If you charge the wrong customer's card for a service, you are either (A) too stupid to work for an organization or (B) a criminal. Either or, and aloha should mean goodbye. But because he was a good salesperson, management looked the other way. Management wanted to believe him. Management wanted to give him another chance. What management should have done is kicked Tyrone's ass to the curb that afternoon. But they did not.

I would like to stop here and tell a little ditty from one from one of the greatest comedians of my generation, Larry Miller. Larry, perhaps best known for his role as a door attendant on the iconic show *Seinfeld*, and for his five stages of drinking routine, once quipped about people who remarry after a divorce: "It's like pulling out milk from the fridge, smelling it, and saying to yourself, whew that smells bad ... putting it back in and thinking, maybe it will be better tomorrow." Well, that's exactly how you must think about a bad employee. Unlike a fine wine, they do not improve with age. In fact, experience and data show they only get worse with time. Kick them to the curb and do it quickly.

Back to Tyrone. As with all criminals, they eventually get careless, arrogant really, and start slipping up. In this instance, it took a call from a California customer disputing a whopping $9,000 in transactions that were charged to the card on file, in average increments of $1000 each, over a period of months. $9,000! OMG! Well guess what? Tyrone had posted each one of those transactions in chat, on sales competition days, and could not explain why he had even run the card. OK, OK, OK. Once? OK. Twice? Seriously, be more careful. Like 9 times? Adios muchacho! No services were rendered. No authority given.

He was given until noon that day to resign. He did. But the ramifications and refunds continued for months thereafter. If only his employer had trusted the signs. If only.

But fireable offenses are not limited to rat bastard thieves. Culture killers also must go and go quickly. Why? Pull up a chair and listen.

SCREAM

We all have our moments of weakness. And, of course, I am no exception. When our company went through the great exodus of 2017, one salesperson sat with me and committed herself to making sure that the company did not go down, that the company would survive. In this regard, and as most should know by now, I am an extremely loyal person. With her commitment, I felt equally indebted to her as we worked tirelessly to keep The Trademark Company afloat.

In her first month as lead salesperson, she generated roughly 45% of our monthly revenues. 45%! Without that level of production, the company would not have made it through the dark times. But as the weeks turned into months, a faint shimmer of light could be seen at the end of the tunnel. And, unfortunately, characteristics that had propelled her to be that top salesperson began becoming more exaggerated.

For instance, when we first rolled up our sleeves, I was all too happy to have a team member who would stop at no cost to get that sale. If another team member wasn't working a lead properly, she would step and close the deal. But the monstrous bonuses she received at the beginning from sales that saved the company became an obsession, turning her, figuratively and somewhat literally, into a sales monster. She would berate new sales team members rather than helping to cultivate them. Even if she could not get to all her leads she would, against policy, verbally abuse anyone who dared touch her leads, even if it were completely within company policy.

Because of her loyalty in the beginning and her role in saving the company for months, I looked the other way. I should not have.

Towards the end of her tenure with our company, her manic moods had become so bad she was pushing new employees out the door. They would come on-board and within weeks, figure out that she was the queen, that the rules did not apply to her. The very trait that had led to her success and aiding in saving the company was now stunting the company's growth. But still, I remained loyal. I should not have. Loyalty must have its limits.

Finally, it ended. One fateful month, she took a week off to attend to family matters. Well, she never quite understood... (how do I say this delicately?)...math. Our salespersons commission structure paid you a percentage of the actual money you put in the door each month. But the percentage was based upon what you would put in if you worked all 21 days in a sales month. For instance, if you averaged $1,000 per day in sales and worked all 21 days, you would put in $21,000 in the month and receive a bonus for a $21,000 pace month of 10%. But let's say you missed 7 days, working 14, and put in $14,000 that month, you would still get the 10% rate but on the actual money received, namely, $14,000. Your bonus would be $1400 and not $2100. Got it? Well, she did not. She never did.

Working from home that day, she called me and the bookkeeper at the time to discuss why her bonus was missing so much. I calmly explained to her the structure that she had had a copy of from day one and once again how it worked. Clearly, it was completely over her head. I can still recall her response: "You're fucking stealing from me! Give me my fucking money you fucking asshole!" Ah, Memories... Light the Corner of my Mind... Misty Water-colored memories... of the way we were....

Now, let me pause right here. Anyone reading this may think, hmmm, maybe it was time for her to go? Maybe the complete lack of respect for her chain of command and using inappropriate language to address her boss would have been the final straw, right? So, I fired her right there, right? Nope. I tried to calm her down. I mean, the company had just clambered back from the brink of bankruptcy, and she had been a major part of it. I was loyal. I figured I owed her respect letting her blow off steam. Wrong. She would eventually leave and even file a wage dispute over the money she said I owed her. She lost, of course, because the Department of Labor, you know, understands math. But when an employee screams at you, it demonstrates a complete lack of understanding and respect for the chain of command. Time. To. Go!

BUT WHAT'S GOOD FOR THE GOOSE...

But this does not just apply to entry-level employees. It can even happen to managers and partners in the business.

In 2016, my former spouse went back to work for one of what used to be known as the Big 6 Accounting firms. For the sake of anonymity, we will just refer to them CostLandhouseAndHoopers. The "gentleman" she went back to work for had a penchant for using the "F" bomb. I mean, every morning at about 6:30 am, my kids were treated to little Stanley's cacophony of new derivations for the term as he ranted and raged about issues in the company, employees, politics. Just about anything that crossed his mind we got to hear it, in stereo. F' this. F' that. Of course, to my former spouse, "Oh that's just Stanley" she would say. To my kids, well, they got a whole new vocabulary from that little fella. On an aside, you know they have earpieces, right? Not everything needs to be on a speaker phone at 6:30 am for young children to hear?

And why do I say little fella? Well, and in my opinion, of course, he went about 5' 8", and 150lbs soaking wet. Was reasonably intelligent, just ask him. And had a little man's complex, meaning he would berate others because he was in a position of leadership and power. Well, it backfired.

From what we overheard over the years, he was an equal opportunity berater. Men, berated. Women, berated. You were not immune from his F bombs. Classy fella. Type of guy you really want in your organization. But here is where the story takes a twist. Little Stanley decided to berate the wrong gal, a young female attorney for CostLandhouseAndHoopers, from the land down under.

Well, as an attorney, she knew something about this little law we have in the U.S. called Title 7. After one particularly harsh berating by little Stanley, this feisty Sheela said enough is enough, let's throw some shrimps on the barbi and little Stanley too! Based upon what I overheard in those 6:30 am calls, Sheela filed a formal complaint with CostLandhouseAndHoopers, which led to little Stanley enjoying a hiatus away from the firm. You know, like a suspension? A walkabout, if you will.

But here is where it gets really fascinating. At the time, little Stanley made the infamous F Bomb too far—he was trying to negotiate a new contract with CostLandhouseAndHcopers to stay on in some capacity beyond his mandatory retirement age of 62. Really? I mean, really? How do you think that went? ADDOS MUCHACHO! Pass the hot Title 7 tamale!

And the best part: they didn't even have to fire him. They just let his retirement come and go and raised a glass to his foul mouth, patted him on the back, and walked him out the door. Buh-bye, little Stanley. Buh-bye!

As for CostLandhouseAndHoopers, well played. Well played, indeed. Or, as little Stanley might say, you know, if he could divorce himself from the situation, F'ing brilliant! Props out to CostLandhouseAndHoopers. But, of course, that's simply my opinion!

So, if you're scoring at home, or even if you're alone, simply understand that there are lines that cannot be crossed and when they are, an employee, even a partner, must be shown the door immediately. For me, those include:

1. **Dishonesty**: Lying to their employer in any capacity. Dishonesty is a character trait. Once revealed, it must be removed from the culture like cancer.
2. **Title 7 Offenses**: Receives a warning and re-training on Title 7 issues. A second offense, pull the trigger and send them packing. Unlike a fine wine, Title 7 offenders do not improve with age. Neither did little Stanley.
3. **Insubordination:** Anything that undermines their supervisor or the company, especially if it is in a public capacity. Adios muchacho! Vaya con Dios! Don't let the puerta hit you on the way out!
4. **Poor Work Ethic:** You can train for skill. But it's rare you can change a person's work ethic. In the history of our company, the employees who were let go the quickest were those who got hired but then, within days or weeks of being hired, demonstrated such a lack of effort or enthusiasm for the job that

they had to go immediately. When identified, they leave that day. Never tolerate laziness in any capacity. Find yourself a better hockey player!

OK. OK. We get it. Hire slowly and fire quickly. Pretty standard stuff. But if done properly, you will grow a culture in your company that produces impressive results, and when you occasionally make that misstep, get that bad apple out of the barrel before it can damage the whole culture. Period!

But once you bring them on board then what? They need to be trained, and trained well. They need to be indoctrinated into your system and your vision for your company.

HAMBURGER UNIVERSITY

In 1993, I was a first-year law student at George Mason University School of Law, infamously renamed the Antoni Scalia School of Law for like a day before someone pointed out that the acronym would be ASSOL. Sound it out. You will get there. You can bet the name was changed shortly thereafter. Although, really, can you think of a more appropriate name for a school that creates lawyers? It's as if the Universe called out and said *Name it what you produce!* And they did, and it was good.

Following your first year of law school there is always a race to get the top summer associateships at all the prestigious firms. That's where you spend a little time working for the big firms doing light legal research, a little pleading drafting, a little correspondence writing. But mainly, they wine and dine you. Yes, that's right, those big firms wine and dine those premiere summer associates to have them pick their firm over others. So that they can say to their clients: we hire only the best. The creme de la creme. The best of the best.

If you saw Tom Cruise's *The Firm,* you know what I'm talking about. In the movie, Tom plays a hot shot law student being recruited by some of the top law firms in the country. Of course, during the recruitment phase is all wining and dining. But guess what? Once he's onboard, it's 20-hour days and "You didn't think you got this big salary for nothing, right?" And of course, one thing leads to another and soon Tom is swept up into the world of big firm politics and an international criminal syndicate, so not too far off from many big firms. Bada bing!

Now, following my first semester at law school, let's just say I was not high on any of these premier law firm's lists to be a Summer Associate. So, from there, there were the second-tier firms, those working-class firms that needed actual law clerk help in the form of real legal research, real pleadings constructions, running papers to the courthouse, etc. They were not premiere firms, per se. But the experience you received at one of these firms could not be matched. And every year they would hire summer law clerks to help with their firm's day-to-day activities. Well, I didn't get any of those, either. Nope, my first summer in law school was spent scrambling for work, any work, just to pay the bills.

Having exhausted all my options, I first took a job as a car courier in the greater Washington, D.C. area. A what, you might ask? A courier would pick up documents, small packages, etc., and drive them from point A to point B for a set price established by the courier company. Now, a tad far-fetched, but, I figured, *Hey, I will meet some lawyers at a big law firm this way, picking up their pleadings. I bet they will be impressed with my work ethic. I bet this could lead to a job.*

I had seen *The Secret of My Success*. I could be Michael J. Fox and start in the mail room. Surely, they would see my work effort, my grit, my determination. Be like Mike! I would tell myself. And soon I would meet one of those lawyers. They would appreciate the blue-collar effort, and they would invite me for an interview. Yeah, no. Not at all. In fact, if I recall correctly, there were several instances where I would even try and start up a friendly conversation, and most lawyers I delivered to were either mean or just demeaning. What a great bunch! So, after a while, and knowing that this was only a temporary gig anyways, I looked for greener pastures.

The greener pasture, oddly enough, came by and through a temporary agency. Answering an ad and taking a few tests they told me they had the perfect 6-week assignment for me: McDonalds! At first, I was like, *The fry machine? The grill? Awesome!!!!* Then they were no, local corporate headquarters! I was like, Whhhhhhaaaaat? Dammmmmmmmmmn! Let's f'ing go!!!

And a day later, there I was, in McDonald's local Fairfax Corporate Headquarters working away in a nice little office job for the last couple of weeks before my second year of law school. And the people there were wonderful. Absolutely wonderful. Once I got past the fact that they had free fountain drinks in the break room (I mean, I was a struggling law student, and drank my weight in soda those weeks to the point that I swear they could hear my sloshing as I left the office each evening), I was amazed at their systems, their training.

When I first started it looked like any other corporate office. I was stoked. I mean, multi-colored filing cabinets everywhere.

Cubicles. Offices for the managers. Conference rooms. Oh yeah, and the all-important break room with the free sodas. Cha-Ching! I was in corporate office heaven. Suck it fellow law students! I'm working for Big Mac!!! All it was missing was Michael Scott.

On one shelf there was a set of binders. And I'm not talking about just a few. I mean tons. There must have been 15 to 20 5-inch binders. Five feet of binders. All filled with at least 1000 sheets of paper each. As my manager took me through what I would be doing for the coming weeks, it became apparent that much of my job would be assisting them with updating their training manuals, as corporate was constantly pushing down the latest updates for training to the regional offices, so on and so forth. In short, those binders I had been mesmerized with—ok I did not get out a lot at the time— well, it was my job to keep them current for the local area.

Now I would like to take a step back. In the late 1950s into 1960, the McDonald's Corporation recognized the need to provide consistent restaurant management training for its new franchisees and restaurant managers. Although they had spent years developing the systems by which all McDonald's restaurants would be run, these systems needed to be impressed upon new franchisees and managers by and through a consistent training program. Enter the now iconic- Hamburger University.

Hamburger University training started in 1961 with a class of just 14 people in the basement of one of McDonald's restaurants. Over the years it grew to occupy a larger and larger place in the corporate strategy of McDonald's. By training all new managers and franchisees at the same universal location and with the same universal materials McDonald's could even, to a greater extent, ensure that their product was delivered in a consistent manner bordering on fanaticism. Today, Hamburger University is located at the McDonald's Corporation global headquarters in Chicago, Illinois. It instructs high-potential restaurant managers, mid-managers and owner-operators in restaurant management. More than 5,000 students attend Hamburger University each year and over 275,000 people have graduated with a degree in Hamburgerology since 1961.

Back to our story. So what was my job to be for those few weeks at McDonald's local headquarters? Updating training materials designed to reinforce and support the lessons learned from managers' time at Hamburger University. How cool is that? I was a cog in the greatest training system in the history of the world: McDonald's.

So, what do you get when you add to this level of training to systems that are refined, perfected, improved upon, and then refined again? Near-perfection in product delivery across a global empire of roughly 38,000 restaurants in over 100 countries. That's what. See the importance of not only systems, but training on those systems? To this day I have never walked into a McDonald's and had an inconsistent experience. A Big Mac tastes the same in New York, Los Angeles, London, take your pick. Why? Systems, and fanatical training on those systems.

When you hire your employees, have your systems in place and train them well. But this concept is not limited to the iconic mega brands of our country. I used them myself while building The Trademark Company.

TRADEMARK UNIVERSITY

Borrowing from McDonald's concept, I knew that, when I began hiring employees for The Trademark Company, if I wanted them to know how to run the systems I had established in the manner I needed them run, I would need to train them every bit as well as Hamburger University for McDonalds. I knew that we needed, you guessed it, Trademark University.

Armed with my knowledge of trademarks, I set out to create a series of courses that would layer into every new hire not only a fundamental knowledge of trademark law, but also the systems we used for our customers to produce a consistent result when protecting their brands with the United States Patent & Trademark Office. What started with one PowerPoint slideshow quickly grew to 3, then 4, and kept growing. By the time I was done, I believe we had over 15 courses teaching our new hires about the day-to-day operations of the company, and what they would need to be completely successful here.

But now that we have the materials, how would we structure the training? I can still remember the first two employees that I took through the classes. At the time, The Trademark Company had moved out of its initial office space and into an Office Suites Plus in Cary, North Carolina. If you are not familiar with the business, it is a shared office space in which you have a dedicated office but also access to a conference room, and even administrative support on an a la carte basis. Candidly, a very cool concept for fledgling companies.

The first day they started, I welcomed them aboard, showed them their shared office, filled out the necessary new hire paperwork, and then we headed down the hallway to the conference room where I had the first PowerPoint slide already cued up on the big screen: "Welcome to The Trademark Company," it read.

Before getting started, I explained to them that our first two weeks together would be spent in this conference room learning the ins and outs of the business, trademarks, and how our model worked. PowerPoint slideshows would be augmented by tests, verbal review discussions, and other training all to get them to understand what we were doing, how we did it, and, most importantly, why.

I told them my now-famous mantra that I begin every training session with, since that first session in 2009:

"My goal is to train you so well that you can leave and make a fortune at some other company, but then to make The Trademark Company so wonderful that you never want to go!"

Before we move on, why would I say this? Well, in my opinion, it was a promise that I made to each person who comes on board with us. Make no mistake: an employee relationship is no different than any other relationship in your life. We all strive to grow and exist in the most enjoyable environment possible. If they can find a better place to work, they will. It's human nature...unless you make your workplace so freaking amazing that they never want to leave. And with the great training, they will have more options. But this statement has always served me well, as it creates the expectation that you will become better here. But to keep you, we have to get better, as well. And that creates the circle. The bond, if you will.

We started the first slideshow, which lasted one hour, and explained to them the history of the fledgling company, the expected core values, and the customer-first approach that we would bring back to the legal industry. Later that day, we drilled on those core values and principles. They had written as well as verbal tests. We talked about examples and scenarios where good customer service becomes known.

One of my favorite questions has, and always will remain, about the legal industry: name one other profession that rewards customer loyalty by raising its rates? Wait, what? You heard me correctly. Customer loyalty in the legal industry is rewarded annually by raising its rates. Insane! Rather than giving discounts or referral bonuses, they raise their clients' rates. And then people wonder why people hate lawyers. Ooooooh. Pick me! Pick me! I know!

Again, it has always baffled me as to why people have gone out of their way to attack The Trademark Company with wild theories as to why we were successful. That we didn't comply with rules, false advertising, and things of that nature. But there is this great scene in the movie *Contact* with Jodi Foster where she is asked to explain the Occam's Razor problem-solving principle and apply it to her own experience, as to whether she truly traveled to another planet. Ooops, sorry, spoiler alert. My bad. But when asked, Ms. Foster responds, "The simplest explanation is usually the right one".

Applying that to our circumstances, The Trademark Company simply infused a customer-first, customer-centric philosophy into the legal industry, an industry that was in desperate need of the same. That's how we did it. Nothing more. Nothing less. We simply brought back customer service to law. *Occam's Razor!* And it all started with every employee, and, on their first day ,drilling into them that customer service focus that would make us a legend in the industry.

And that was just the first seminar.

Over the next two weeks, we would go through the background on trademarks, copyrights, and patents. I would drill them on all the intricacies of every detail they would need to know to be fully successful at their job. Tests, quizzes, reviews. It was exhausting. I would tell them that, when they were done, they could go to any intellectual property law firm in the US and quadruple their salaries. They would be the most knowledgeable IP professionals in that organization. But given the culture at our company, they would never want to leave.

In the end, did it work? Hell yeah! My first two hires were two of the most amazing professionals I have ever had the pleasure of working with. To this day, I do not think that I have come across two people in the IP world who were as versed in the world of trademarks as they were. With that training in hand, one stayed with us for about 7 years and the other for close to 10. We disrupted the entire industry with our growth during that time, helping to create a market for trademark services on a level never seen before. And it all came back down to one fundamental root—we trained them well from the beginning.

THE COVID MIRACLE

But as you grow, so too must your systems. They must evolve with the times and become scalable, right? Well, although we experienced phenomenal growth for a micro company, over the years we always seemed to grow and contract, never quite exceeding 12 to 14 employees. For years it became a conundrum, one that I simply could not solve. Why did we keep hitting that ceiling? Why could we not get over that hump? And then it happened. The COVID miracle.

Now, please don't think that I am being dismissive of the tragedy that befell so many during this time: the shutdowns, the economic hardship, the illness and, of course, the loss of life. Never.

But one of the more fascinating externalities that occurred as a result of COVID was that the world learned to think differently, to work remotely, communicate completely electronically, and to survive in a way that was different than we ever thought possible. Before COVID, how many people had heard of Zoom? Microsoft Teams? But they enabled us to keep moving forward. To survive and even thrive in the new normal. The Trademark Company was no different. We blew up.

In early 2020, just before all the shutdowns, we had set a growth target for the year. Although we had heard grumblings about this new virus called COVID, who knew what we were in for? The goal was to quadruple the size of the company, as well as our revenues, by December 2020. Slightly aggressive, I know. By March 2020, we were a little off-target for the goal, but were still making progress on the same. And then we watched, state by state, as they began to impose variants of shut-down orders to quell the spread of the COVID virus. But that couldn't happen in North Carolina, could it? I mean, these were places with high density populations like NYC and Boston. Not rural North Carolina?

But then destiny caught us. And on March 27, 2020, Governor Roy Cooper of the great State of North Carolina stepped to the podium and announced that, as of March 30, 2020, all North Carolinians were required to stay at home. Further, non-essential businesses, like The Trademark Company, were required to shut the doors until the COVID emergency had passed.

Now, up until that point, our employment policy had limited work-from-home to those select employees who were fully successful in their jobs. Now, we would need to stitch together, and quickly, the delicate fiber of all employees working from home until COVID had passed. And hiring to hit growth targets? How?

That had to be a joke, given the then- state of our state and country. Candidly, when we left the office that afternoon, I did not know if the company would survive. But like any good CEO, I kept my chin up, gave everyone a positive message on the way out the door, and quietly departed.

We were officially in a holding pattern. How could you grow a team without an office? How would you train them? How would you monitor their job performance? Yup, holding pattern.

For the first month or so, we accepted the reality. We researched different methods to keep everyone engaged. Initially, we used Free Conference Call for our morning kick- offs and end-of-day meetings. After a few weeks, we moved to Zoom.

Now, let me stop and give as big a shoutout as I can to this company. When the pandemic began, two of the biggest hurdles for businesses were how to stay connected with their employees, and whether consumers would dry up hoarding their money out of fear of losing their jobs. Well, as the days turned into weeks and the weeks into months, it became apparent that if you had an online presence, you were going to be alright. Pivot and keep moving forward. Consumers largely kept spending, at least in our industry. In fact, for a multitude of reasons, The Trademark Company had its best year in the history of the company! And part of that was because of Zoom.

This service, along with others like it, stepped in and allowed us to stay together, even though we had to stay apart. We became more connected than ever. And Zoom was right there empowering us all. And it was so easy. No downloading of software. Almost nothing. Just click the link and you are there. Amazing! Just how amazing was it?

For that answer, I will turn it personal for a bit. Arguably the best Christmas Dinner I have ever had was December 25, 2020, thanks to Zoom. With the older generation in my family, well, getting older, I refused to let COVID take the holiday from us. Understand, when I was a child, my Aunt Donna and Uncle Steve (two of the greatest people you could ever meet in your life) would host Christmas dinner every year. We would go. My grandparents. Cousins. And, candidly, anyone we knew who did not have somewhere to go always had a place during Christmas at my Aunt Donna and Uncle Steve's table. That's who they were.

They had a big table that could seat probably twelve. In the big years, we'd set up a couple of card tables for the kids and friends that would join. In all, we typically sat between 16 to 24 for dinner every year, in a room filled with so much joy and love it is hard to imagine how blessed I was to be part of such a family.

For December 2020, I was not going to have my parents eat alone, or even just with my kids and me. We sent the word out to the entire family: Christmas Dinner Zoom at 7:00 pm EST, December 25, 2020! We would not be alone. As the time arrived, we opened our laptops from my parents' home and clicked the Zoom link to see who was out there. Admittedly, there was only one other person on the Zoom link when we logged on and, candidly, I had no idea who he was. But mom did. And they struck up the conversation.

In a year in which my parents had only seen myself, my children, and a select handful of other people for 9 months, it was a Christmas Miracle, as more family members joined and continued to join. Of course, the Greek part of the family were fashionably late. Hey, it's a Greek thing! But when my Aunt Donna finally joined from my cousin Tim and Cyndi's home near Monterey, California, for one brief, glorious moment, it was like we were all back in her house in Lake Clarke Shores, Florida. We were all together again, and everything else just melted away. We were family. And it was good.

As I watched the elder statesmen and stateswomen of the family do their best to hold court through the new normal brought together by this amazing service called Zoom, I was nearly overcome with emotions. In all, I think I counted over 60 family members that joined that night from over 30 locations around the country. All made possible through the miracle of Zoom. To the creator of Zoom and all the people who keep it running, we can never thank you enough. I'm sure you've done well financially. But you've changed lives in the process. Thank you all!

So back to The Trademark Company. Like others, we were forced to quickly adapt to not being in an office. I mean, from our perspective, we are not a factory, we are not in the food service industry. In fact, we have always prided ourselves on having a completely online presence. Our work is done entirely with phones and computers. We never see customers in the office. As such, the transition was far easier than we realized. Zoom kept us connected, and we went about our business. It took some getting used to. But within a few days, sales numbers stabilized, and we started to breathe a sigh of relief.

But as the days stretched into weeks and the weeks into months, it became apparent that we would not be returning to the office anytime soon. That we would be working out of our respective homes for the foreseeable future. In short, this was the new normal. But here was the thing: the new normal had forced us into a model that I had never even dreamed of. A model of 100% work-at-home for all employees. And not only was it working, but we also began to thrive.

For instance, for 16 years in a row, our industry always slowed down right around Easter. The first three months of the year are always our go time. We make between 37 to 42 percent of our annual revenue in those first three months. And then, as surely as the swallows return to Capistrano, sales abruptly plummet during the two weeks surrounding Easter. Why? No one really knows. However, we have theorized that it is because most public schools share Spring Breaks during those weeks, and it is simply a time when the masses take a holiday.

But during COVID, the cliff never came. In fact, sales went up. And up. And up. We began referring to it as the COVID Miracle. And it was good. My eyes had been opened. Working parents could be there for their kids. Less office chatter. No wasted time commuting. It was a polar shift in perspective I had never seen before, but my eyes had been opened.

As I became more and more comfortable with this new normal, my mind naturally drifted to how could we onboard people remotely and get back into our growth mode. I mean, for all the years we had been doing this, everyone had had to sit in the conference room and attend my Trademark University. How could we get this done online? Could it work?

A few years back, I had read up on creating virtual training systems. In short, manuals, tests, videos, so that your staff could be trained not entirely by individuals, but also through automation. I had never believed in this sort of thing, and so kept the training bottleneck in place through me, but now I would have to if we wanted to start hiring again.

I went online to look for articles on how to construct a virtual Trademark University, an academy in the cloud, if you will. To no surprise, there were many sites offering this service online. But as I read through the various platforms available, I kept gravitating back to one: Trainual.com.

Trainual is an online platform where you can create complete training programs online for your company and your services. Now, before I go further, let me say, I am not affiliated in any way shape, or form with Trainual. But man has it transformed the way we deliver our training.

When I first signed up, I simply thought that we would convert all our training slides onto their platform. But by viewing their tools, and watching their tutorials, we realized how much more robust our on-line training could be. And the best part: it was recorded in a tangible medium. In other words, we no longer had to do it ourselves. It was created for all time, space and every dimension! From coursework to testing, embedded videos, and a host of other features to keep the students engaged, Trainual was a quantum leap forward for the company.

Our COVID problem was solved! In fact, it was better than solved. Since we were all working out of our homes now, Trainual enabled us to hire work-at-home employees from North Carolina to California. From the great U.S. of A to the Philippines. In short, thanks to the COVID Miracle, we were forced to finally migrate to a training platform which would propel our growth. Has it worked?

As I relay this account, it is now September 2021, roughly 18 months into our COVID world. In this time our company has tripled in size. Tripled! All during COVID. And none of it would have been possible without the commitment to create a largely autonomous training system which has revolutionized the way we on-board employees. Thank you Trainual. Thank you!

WHAT HAPPENS IN VEGAS...

Alright, alright, alright! So, you've hired them. You get them on your bus. You get them in the right seat on your bus. And you train them to be the best in your industry? Is that it? Hell no! What comes next? You must keep them engaged with the business. You must take them to Vegas, baby! Vegas!

Now, you don't actually have to take them to Vegas to keep them engaged. But performance-based reward trips are great if you can swing it. It keeps the company focused on a common goal. And if they achieve it, it's magical. But be warned. If they don't, it can have the opposite of the desired effect. So always base your reward trips on a goal that is attainable.

Our first step down this road came in 2013, when we were set to celebrate the company's ten-year anniversary. I gave the company an attainable sales target to hit for a trip to Vegas, and they did it! Every day, they knew the number they needed, and if they missed it on a given day, they'd come back the next day and make up for it. It galvanized the team around a specific goal, and kept everyone hyper engaged in achieving that goal.

So, on a beautiful September morning in 2013, we boarded the Southwest direct from Raleigh-Durham International Airport to Las Vegas! I don't think there was a sober employee on that plane by the time we reached our cruising altitude. Never have so few consumed so much in such a short time. I thought I was going to have to carry people off the plane!

On an aside, if you've ever taken any Southwest Airlines direct to Las Vegas, you know what I'm talking about. It's like a fraternity party in the sky. I've often wondered if they carry less fuel on those flights to offset the extra weight of all the booze they need to make it through the flight. I mean, you don't want to run out of liquor over Missouri! Then you'll have a bunch of surly, sobering-up people by the time you hit the Rockies. And no one wants that on the descent down into the desert.

Off the plane, we poured and got ready for our first adventure: the scavenger hunt! That's right, after checking in, picking up their goodie bags, and a quick bite for lunch, our employees were given their instructions for the scavenger hunt. A Vegas-wide, 4-hour mad sprint to accumulate as many points as possible by completing tasks yours truly had set out for them. The prize? $500 per person on a winning two-person team. We counted down, and at the stroke of 1pm: Go!!!! And they raced out onto the strip.

They got points for things such as "Take a picture with 'The King'" by grabbing a selfie with an Elvis impersonator, or "The King of the Jungle" by snapping a pic of lions at MGM. One of the funniest ones was when they had to take a picture with a celebrity. Now, if you know anything about Vegas, you see celebrities all the time. I've walked by all-time leading NFL rusher Emmitt Smith, against whom I once played in his final high school game (Sorry, Al Bundy Moment). I've seen Donny Osmond walking into one of the hotels.

Of course, on this day, when my former wife and I were walking around monitoring the gang's progress, we happened upon the sports memorabilia shop at the Forum Shops at Caesars where, Jerry Rice, the greatest NFL receiver of all time. and boxing legend Leonard Spinks, were signing autographs. It was so fun to taunt my people with selfies with the two legends, as they begged me to know where we were.

On an aside, we were there at the time the NBA developmental league was playing in Vegas. One of our employees snapped a selfie with two "really tall guys" she thought must be in the NBA. Years later, I remembered the picture when watching the Golden State Warriors make their historic run for that two- or three-year period. Who was it in the picture with our account manager? None other than Michigan State's finest, and future star of the Golden State Warriors: Draymond Green.

In the end, I could have told you who would win the scavenger hunt before it started. OK, it would be one of two teams. Jessica and Jamie were our top two salespersons of all time, and they were paired together. Not far behind was the youthful exuberance of Whitney and Amanda, who was this little, fit dynamo. All day long, they went back and forth as points leaders until Jamie and Jess took it over the top as the only team to complete the one challenge I didn't think anyone would have the stones to do: The Big Shot at the Stratosphere.

For those of you unfamiliar with the Stratosphere, it's an older hotel on the mid-strip that looks like the Seattle Space Needle or CN Tower in Toronto. But what makes it uniquely Vegas is that on top of the tower is a roller coaster and other rides that swing you out over the thousand plus foot drop. Yikes. Well, on top of the needle is one of those drop rides that shoots you up a tower and then drops you for zero gravity effect, all on the tippy-top of the space needle. Whoa. It's called the Big Shot, and riding that ride, where so many of the events were 5 or 10 points, would secure the team 50 points!

Remember this always, and live by it: winners win. It's that simple. They do what it takes to win. And Jess and Jamie, they're winners. I can still remember the look on Jaime's face from the picture, after she did it. It was the personification of someone desperately holding back the urge to toss her cookies. It was the look of victory. It was the look of the winning team. The Big Shot put them over the top of Amanda and Whitney to take the prize. Winners win.

But in a larger context, the trip brought most of the company together. We bonded. We had a blast. It kept them engaged in the weeks and months leading up to it, then stoked in the weeks and months after. It cost us a pretty penny, but we were rewarded for the team's performance and bonding. Of course, there was a lot more that happened on that trip. Late night gambling. Drinking. Other shenanigans. But this isn't that kind of book. Besides, I must respect the old saying: *What Happens in Vegas Stays in Vegas!*

BUT IT'S MORE THAN JUST BIG TRIPS

Keeping your employees engaged can't be accomplished by a single big retreat once a year. It's a daily challenge you must accept and conquer to keep your company moving in the right direction.

In the past, we would always have an employee who we colloquially called our social director. They would be responsible for Happy Hours, Trolley Pubs, Bar Crawls, events in the office, Limo Lunches for Employees' 30th birthday parties, sports outings and more. Keeping any office fun is a part of modern culture. If you are not into it, your employees will not be into your company.

But it's more than just big trips and social events. You can also keep your employees engaged with quarterly, monthly, weekly, and even daily contests. And, even better, make sure these align with your strategic principles. For instance, have a monthly sales contest for a certain product, but possibly weekly sales contests for others. This removes the monotony of the sales process by having the whole thing turn into a big game.

But remember not to make it exclusively about money. Make sure to continue to impress upon the values that you've founded your company on, your mission. For us, that has always been easy. Employees hear about the vision all the time: We empower the American Dream! But what's your story? What's your mission? They need to know, they need to be reminded of it constantly, and they need to buy in. What is it? I can't write your story. You're the author of your own vision. But to truly keep them engaged, you need to have that vision and get them to buy in! Keep them engaged in it every day!

Chapter Summary: Hire Well. Train Them. Keep them Engaged.

- **Hire Slowly, Fire When You Must:** You need to get the right people on the bus, and in the right seats. Like with everything else, once you have created the Job Descriptions for your ideal Organizational Chart (referenced before), this should make it easier to hire the right people for those positions. But when you see it is not working out, or that you've made a bad higher, quickly remove them from your organization, as the long-term negative effects far outweigh any short-term benefits.
- **Train them Well:** Provide them with a world-class onboarding experience that includes training on your company,

your industry, their role in the company's mission, their specific job functions and how to accomplish them.

- **Keep Them Engaged:** Finally, you must keep your employees engaged if you want to achieve the goals you have set for your company. Develop an engagement plan that keeps them engaged on a daily, weekly, monthly, and annual basis.

Additional Suggested Reading:

McDonald's Behind the Arches, John F. Love, 1986

The Rare Find: Spotting Exceptional Talent Before Everyone Else, George Anders, 2011

The Real Secrets of the Top 20%, Mike Brooks, 2008

IGNORE THE NAYSAYERS AND WORK YOUR ASS OFF

Not Everyone Gets Your Dream. That's OK. It was Never Their Dream to Begin With.

NOT EVERYONE GETS YOUR DREAM

Let me tell you something you already knew: not everyone is going to support your dream. Not everyone is going to get your dream. Critics may mock you. Friends won't understand. Those closest to you may even turn their back on you. But I'm here to tell you something you maybe didn't know. It's all OK. It doesn't matter. Wait, what? Why? Because you must become comfortable with one simple truth about being an entrepreneur: it was never their dream to begin with. So don't expect them to get it. Don't fault them for failing to see it. And never let their lack of vision deter you from yours.

Steve Jobs said it best, "*...because the people who are crazy enough to think that they can change the world, are the ones who do.*" But have you ever really thought about what Steve was saying? I mean, when we hear Steve Jobs, most of us can look over and see our iPhone or another Apple product and think, yeah who needs college? Steve didn't, and look at all he accomplished! And in that moment, you instantly shift your focus away from understanding the true nature of what he said in his now-iconic message. It's subtle, and most completely miss it. But it is a critical component of the message Steve was expressing that underlies the larger, general successes of Apple and Mr. Jobs.

What most people focus on when reading this is you must be a little bit different to change the world, to have that vision. They focus on the first person when reading this, and not all the others mentioned in the simple statement. Wait what? Let's read it again, "*...because the people who are crazy enough to think that they can change the world, are the ones who do.*" I'd be willing to bet that you focused on yourself, Steve Jobs, maybe Bill Gates or Elon Musk when you read this. But did you focus on the subtle message regarding the naysayers in this line?

It's there. Steve knew it. So should you.

When we say "...the people who are crazy enough...", have you ever paused and asked yourself "Crazy by whose standards"? Did your eyes just open a little bit? What is often missed in this quote is the fact that it subtly references the naysayers of the world who will brand you as crazy if you, to use another one of Steve's more famous marketing lines, *Think Different*. If you're still reading this book, there's a good chance you probably do. So, are you going to let someone else stop you from realizing your vision? No!

IGNORE THE NAYSAYERS

Steve Jobs was maligned frequently during his career. Did he hurt from time-to-time over it? Absolutely. But did he pound through the critics to envision and be a part of creating some of the greatest products in human history? Absolutely. How? Because Steve knew, as you should now, that you must ignore the naysayers to achieve your vision.

Remember Fred Smith's plan for FedEx? He was told he'd be graded poorly by his Yale professor if he didn't come up with a more feasible concept. So, do you think the proof of concept worked? 3.4 million packages per day, a veritable private air force of jets encircling the globe, and an army of workers swarming the world like ants making sure you get your packages delivered, all overnight, and many now within hours of pickup. What if Fred had listened to his professor? What if Fred had given in to his naysayer? No FedEx. And that guy was a professor at Yale University. One of the top universities in the world. By all accounts, probably an intelligent guy. But like Steve, Fred knew to ignore his naysayers.

One of the things that you must understand when going down the path to entrepreneurship is that not everyone is wired for that lifestyle. We're taught from an early age to go to school, get good grades, build a great resume, get a good job with a company and progress with that company. Most people will take this advice and walk that path.

It is from this viewpoint that most critics emerge. They are not risk takers. They are not dreamers. They are not the ones who are wired to change the world. They come from the conventional thought process of getting that education, getting that safe job, conforming. Just look at Fred Smith's naysayer, a professor at Yale. Was he out in the business world? No. Could he have been? Yes. Rather, he was throwing shade on an idea that would lead to greatness from the comfort of a tenured, conventional path.

But here's the ironic reality hidden deep in that convention: when you do that, you're just helping to build someone else's dream. Wait, what? Yeah, you heard me right. When you're taught to conform and march to the beat of the corporate path, that's simply someone else's vision. It doesn't matter if it is a small company or Walmart, the largest employer in the world and the vision of Sam Walton. At some point, you're surrendering your vision to help someone else's dream.

Oh yeah, and that professor from Yale who I keep coming back to, he was just helping to build James Pierpont's and the other founders of the Collegiate School's dream, a dream that would eventually be known as Yale University. So, while they criticize the courage, you have to walk down your own path, and always remember that such protests come from people who did not have the courage to walk down their own.

When I think about Fred's moment with his Yale professor, I'm invariably drawn back to a scene in the movie *Back to School* starring the late, great comedian Rodney Dangerfield. In the movie, Rodney plays Thornton Melon, a successful businessman who never attended college. When his only son threatens to drop out of school, Dangerfield's character promises to go back to school with his son so they both can get their college degrees. Having only learned from the school of life, Dangerfield's character immediately comes into conflict with the stodgy old-school business professor,

Dr. Phillip Barbay, played brilliantly by Paxton Whitehead. In their first confrontation, Whitehead's character is attempting to lecture his class about start-up costs for businesses. Dangerfield, having been in the real world, keeps interrupting the professor by adding in his personal experiences. Finally, to the roaring laughter of the class, the scene ends with the following dialog:

Dr. Phillip Barbay: "*...now, notwithstanding Mr. Mellon's input, the next question for us is: where to build our factory?*"
Thornton Melon: "*How 'bout fantasyland?*"

So don't get me wrong. I love teachers. I love professors. But whenever I have thought of Fred Smith's dream and the Yale professor's response, I think of *Back to School.*

WHEN TO LISTEN TO CRITICS (AND ADVISORS)

Coming full circle: don't blame the naysayers for their critiques. They chose a different and, admittedly, safer path to help build someone else's dream, whether they realize it or not. But when you understand their point of view, it's easier to accept their comments, and keep moving forward. Now this is not to say that all naysaying is bad. In fact, there is a lot of naysaying that can be helpful, in the right circumstances. So how do you know when to ignore the naysayers and when to listen, if even just a little? By asking two simple questions every time someone gives you advice or criticizes your vision.

1. Does the critic know what they are talking about? and
2. What's their motivation?

DO THEY KNOW WHAT THEY ARE TALKING ABOUT?

Let's look at the first question: does the naysayer know what they are talking about? There is no shortage of people out there willing to critique your dream. I mean, we've all heard the adage that there are only two things for certain in life, death and taxes. If you're an entrepreneur there are three: death, taxes, and people who will criticize your dream. If you've already gone down the entrepreneurial path, you know what I mean. This is especially true if your model finds you being an industry disruptor with an invention or application of some new technology that fundamentally shifts the way business is done. But if they simply do not know what they are talking about, why should you listen to them?

Here's what I mean. A few years back, we began developing software that creates sophisticated legal documents from a customer's answers to simple questions. To understand why this will become relevant, I need to provide you with a little background about the practice of law, and who is, and is not, allowed to do so in any given state.

When you go to law school, they teach you a simple acronym that largely defines what the practice of law is. I.R.A.C. The acronym stands for:

I Issue
R Rule
A Application
C Conclusion

The practice of law largely involves being able to identify a legal issue, knowing or being able to research the rule or law which is applicable to that issue, applying the rule to the issue, and then reaching a conclusion and advising your client as to the same. Still awake after all that? If not, grab some coffee, as it's about to get real! Let's look at how this works with a practical example.

Bob runs a stop sign and is pulled over by the local police. To no one's surprise, Bob gets a ticket for blowing the stop sign. With me so far? But Bob's the type that loves to spend money and waste people's time, like the fine judges in our traffic court system. Guessing Bob drives a BMW. Anyways, Bob hires a lawyer to get him out of the ticket. When hearing the facts of what happened, here's how the lawyer's mind should work:

Issue: Bob ran a stop sign. Bob admits he ran the stop sign.

Rule: Code Section 1234 of the State Ordinance states that you must come to a complete stop at a stop sign.

Application: It is illegal to run a stop sign. Bob admitted to running the stop sign.

Conclusion: Bob is guilty of running the stop sign. Pay the ticket and stop wasting everyone's time. Now give me $1,000 for my opinion. Cha-Ching!!!

So anytime you hear about the practice of law, it mostly boils down to the acronym IRAC, and who is qualified and legally permitted to take you through all four steps to reach a conclusion about the issue you need addressed. Sure, there are a lot of other aspects, reading and writing documents, some attorneys perform trial work, but the fundamental root is IRAC.

Well, if you know anything about computer technology, it is advancing at the speed of light. Artificial Intelligence (or, AI) and machine learning are taking over the world. And having a computer run an IRAC algorithm is easy. Very easy. Sorry, lawyers. Today, most eighth graders in an introductory programming course could write a program to tell Bob that he's guilty of running a stop sign without having to have Bob drop $1,000 large. For most of us, this is a good thing. Even for BMW drivers. But let's just say that, when your entire profession depends on you making sure you maintain a monopoly on IRAC analysis for people, you're not too happy about the advancement of technology.

Richard Susskind, author of *The Future of Professions*, once estimated that more than half of all legal jobs will be lost in the next ten years due to AI, and the application of AI to service industries. With the dramatic increase in machine learning and information available online, it is only a matter of time before machines can be programmed to take over service industries like law and accounting and, specifically, perform relatively simple analysis like the IRAC methodology above.

All they need is access to the laws which are readily available online now, as well as the ability to interpret the Issue, as input by the user. Then they can easily apply the rule to the issue, reaching a consistent conclusion every time. And get this: in many cases, when interpreting the same set of facts or issues, their conclusions can be more consistent than a human's.

The Trademark Company was an early pioneer in this field. Years ago, we developed proprietary software to respond to complex legal issues encountered by our customers, when their trademark registrations are refused by the U.S. Patent and Trademark Office. The biggest challenge, however, was not creating the software. The biggest challenge was to create a front-end user interface that was easy enough for our customer to use to then permit Alan (the original name for our AI software, named after Alan Turing, the father of AI), to understand the issue and how to apply a specific rule to reach the right conclusion for the user. A big nod and thanks to TurboTax for helping us to figure that out.

The original version of the software came out in 2016. Almost immediately, we knew we had a problem. The software worked fine. It would generate the answers we wanted when specific input was entered by the user. What's was the issue, then? None of our customers could answer the questions being asked by the software. They would call, complain, and ultimately, we would have to have someone walk them through question by question, so that they could get the software to generate their legal document based upon their specific input. But then, what was the point of the software if we had to have someone work with the customer? Sort of defeats the whole purpose, right? I mean, imagine if, every time you opened your Google browser, you had to contact customer support to enter something into the search bar. Not very efficient, huh? So, as you can imagine, for years we shelved it. Until we had that Eureka moment, thanks to our friends at TurboTax.

You see, you can build something brilliant. But if it is not user-friendly, it doesn't matter. Then, in one shining moment, it hit us. We were presented with what was wrong with the software. And we knew how to fix it. Fortunately for us, TurboTax launched a new ad campaign a few years back, and it opened our eyes to a very glaring issue with our software. In the ad, TurboTax proclaimed its ease of use by asking questions such as, "If you can answer did you have a baby this year" or "buy a house this year", we can figure out the rest. In that moment, we realized what was wrong with our offering.

The whole drive of The Trademark Company has always been to bring cost-effective and easy-to-use legal solutions to everyone.

Where we failed was that the software was written in a manner only lawyers could comprehend. I mean, this was software to be used by non-lawyers. At some point during its construction, we out-thought ourselves. The questions it was asking the users were just too, well, legal.

When watching the TurboTax ads, they make it so simple. They didn't ask, "Did you qualify for an IRC Section 1234 tax credit this year?" No, because they know you have no idea. I mean, who does? Sure, a tax attorney or CPA. But how many of us have one of those just lying around the house? Nope. Rather, they asked, "Did you have a kid this year?" And most people out there, most, can figure out the answer to this question, especially if you're a woman.

Our questions on the front end were too legal. We would ask things like, "What is the commercial impression of your brand?" prompting questions like "What does commercial impression mean?" So, with our TurboTax inspiration in hand, we went back and completely re-tooled the software. By 2018, the user interface was redone, and the software has been a mega-hit for the company. Rarely, if at all, do we get questions as to how to answer the questions. The interface runs almost perfectly. But what's a good interface without a quality result?

Returning to the point of all this, our customers now have access to software that, based upon their answers to simple questions, assembles first-rate, attorney-quality documents with no input whatsoever from a lawyer or law firm.

Well, to say that this does not sit well with some is an understatement. You must understand that, in most states, it is illegal to practice law without a license. However, it is not against the law to develop software that assembles legal documents, provided it does so solely with the user's input. Now that you have a background in all of this, let's finally return to those naysayers, shall we? Need another cup of coffee yet? I can wait.

So, in 2019, we had the opportunity to address a room filled with lawyers who were "interested" in the documents produced by our software. And by "interested", I mean they could not believe that software could produce documents of this quality with detailed, factual arguments. In fairness, however, I'm not sure most of them knew what software was.

To set the stage, imagine a bull-in-the-ring environment in which about 200 feet of conference room tables were arranged in a rectangle with a huge open space in the middle, and with over 100 lawyers lining the tables. Most of the attorneys were white males who looked to be at least 60 years of age. When it came time to discuss our company's documents, they put up an image of the first page of our sample document, created by the software which we proudly display on our web site.

Almost immediately, many of the attorneys started to blurt out, "That's a complex legal document, they're not allowed to write that!" or "That's the unauthorize practice of law!" or "This is against the rules!" Are you getting the picture? All we were missing were some pitchforks and torches, and we'd have a scene right out of a movie. But wait a minute. Did you pick up on what they were saying? Their accusations all stemmed from the quality of the product, not how the product was assembled. Remember, IRAC by a human, practice of law. IRAC by a machine, no problem.

In that moment, I couldn't help but to be reminded of that iconic scene from the science fiction classic *2001: A Space Odyssey*, in which the apes start dancing around the monolith. Now, the apes did not understand what the monolith was. They just got excited about it and hooted and hollered.

Years later, Ben Stiller and Owen Wilson would parody this scene in the movie *Zoolander.* Being told the information was *"in the computer"*, high jinks ensue as they attempt to pry open the computer like apes in a jocular reference to *2001: A Space Odyssey*.

Back to our story and the tech-phobic lawyers. How did I reach this conclusion? Because the operative question is not the quality of the product, but how the product is assembled. Following me? Although the attorneys in the room may have seen their practices flash before their eyes, they jumped to the conclusion that we must be doing something wrong based solely upon quality of the work.

In candor, despite being misplaced, what a compliment to our software and its product, that they could not tell the difference between their work and the product our software assembled. But here's the question they should have all been asking: "How was this created?" That's the operative question. And they never did. For, like the apes in *2001* and of the characters in *Zoolander*, they simply lacked the requisite knowledge to even ask the proper question. And at that moment, they all simply became a bunch of howling monkeys demonstrating, beyond a shadow of a doubt, their complete lack of understanding of technology, and how it will change their profession forever.

So seemingly intelligent. I mean, they are lawyers, right? But like Fred Smith's Yale professor, they still missed the issue. And herein lies the point. Irrespective of the perceived general intelligence of the naysayer, you still need to ask, "Do they know what they are talking about?" If the answer is no, simply nod, say thank you for their input, and keep moving forward.

WHAT'S THEIR MOTIVATION?

But let's assume they *do* know what they are talking about. Let's not stop there. There are many people who are knowledgeable of facts or circumstances but, again, may not have your best interests in mind. For this, you must always ask the second question when being critiqued or given advice: *What's the person's motivation?*

When I first came out of law school in 1996, I was extremely fortunate to be hired by a great local personal injury firm for whom I had been clerking. In short, at the time it was a horrible legal market and a real scramble to get a job as a lawyer right out of law school. But D.C.-based law firm *Koonz, McKenney, Johnson, DePaolis & Lightfoot* gave me a shot. Now, I've said some very direct and not too nice things about the legal profession so far. But let me tell you, you will never find a finer group of attorneys than the lawyers I was privileged to work with at *Koonz McKenney.*

Specifically, to Peter DePaolis and Kenneth Bynum, my mentors at the firm who gave me that shot, I am eternally grateful. These two gentlemen did the legal profession proud. Fantastic lawyers. Ethical all day long. And genuinely cared about their clients. And I was fortunate enough to work under them for the first 4 years of my career.

Pete ran the Northern Virginia office where I worked. It was a small office of about 5 or 6 lawyers, secretaries, and paralegals. Like any office, there were good days and bad, good money months and those that were tighter. Internal conflicts from time to time kept it interesting. But in the end, Pete and Ken drove that office to be very successful, all the while helping people to get compensation for the wrongful acts of others. Yes, we were personal injury attorneys. And proud of it.

On an aside: personal injury attorneys are often the butt of bad jokes and allegations of what is wrong with the legal system. But to me, these criticisms are largely misplaced. Unlike other attorneys who bill by the hour and, as you have seen before, thus have the perverse incentive to be less efficient and whose interests are not aligned with their client whatsoever, personal injury lawyers only get compensated if they win or settle their clients' cases to the clients' satisfaction. Let that one soak in.

So, if you've ever paid a lawyer by the hour, wouldn't you have loved only to have paid him or her at the end of your matter, if you were satisfied with the result? And that's a personal injury lawyer. They are the most efficient and often the best lawyers I have ever come across. If they are not, quite simply, they don't get paid. So, who would you rather have on your side? Someone who doesn't get paid unless they get a result that favors you or someone who gets paid more and more the further inefficient they are, with no alignment of your best interests. I rest my case.

But the story I use to emphasize the point about only listening to people who have your best interests in mind originates from my days at *Koonz McKenney*. It was a beautifully organized and maintained small office. The attorneys' offices ringed the exterior of the floor, separated by an open walkway from the open workspaces of the secretaries that supported them. Each secretary had her own beautifully built-out space, but they were completely open so they could chat throughout the day when taking breaks from work, etc. For the most part, everyone got along. However, every so often there would be some internal conflict that would disrupt the office. The conflict almost always started between two secretaries on secretary row.

Well, on one memorable occasion, one of the secretaries was upset at something. I can't recall what it was. The amount of her raise. Working conditions. Somebody looked at her funny. Whatever. The point is, she decided to quit. Rather than just turning in her letter of resignation, she decided to spend some time badmouthing the firm and the job to two or three other secretaries on secretary row. *Can you believe this place? How can they expect us to work here?* Things I'm sure she must have said. Stirring up emotions she eventually convinced two other secretaries to walk out with their fists held high in solidarity a la Norma Rae. Go get em' girls! Girl power! Show the man!

But why? Did the other secretaries ever stop to ask what her motivation was? If they did, they most likely would have discerned that Norma Rae's ulterior motive was her driving force to push the other two to join her cause, and not to look out for their own best interests. She needed validation for her own decision, without a care in the world for her friends' economic or work situations. Wait, what? In other words, the driving motivation behind her rallying the troops was not the well-being of her friends, or even their working conditions, as they were all uniquely distinct. No, her motivation was merely to selfishly have support in her belief that she should walk out and never look back.

Anyways, all three of them stormed out on that fateful day. But what the two followers soon realized was that their fearless leader was not in the same situation as they were. More specifically, the head quitter lived in a huge home, and was married to a successful businessman in Washington, D.C. She largely worked just to get out of the house. However, her two recruits, who were largely satisfied with their working conditions prior to the revolution, lived paycheck-to-paycheck in small studio apartments, as they were younger and just getting their start in the world. Well, once they realized how tough the job market was, and that Norma Rae was in a completely different financial position than they were, they came to their senses. A few phone calls were made. They were back at work within a few days.

Now, I'd like to pause and explain something about the traditional law firm. You can get another associate attorney. You can hire a lateral partner. But the hardest thing to replace in the practice of law is a great legal secretary who becomes your work wife and your dedicated partner in running your practice for years. Almost every hyper-successful attorney I know was supported by an amazing legal secretary. The firm's namesake, Joseph Koonz, had Ruth. Peter had Judy. I had an amazing partner in Ivey.

As for Norma, I'm pretty sure no one ever heard or talked to her again. And fortunately for the two, they were good at what they did, and the boss just forgave them in their emotional moment. After all, it's hard to find a great secretary. And they were. But herein lies the second point— always ask what the person's motivation is in naysaying or giving you advice. If they had, they would never have left to begin with, risking their jobs and careers in a very difficult job environment.

Years later, I watched as this story played out again to a friend who was very close to me at the time. She was hired by a major accounting firm in their in-house tax department to largely assist with the corporate tax returns of the firm. At the time, her boss was a few years away from the mandatory retirement age of 62. When reaching this age, partners of the firm, which he was, are forced to retire. However, if the partner retains a special skill, or would otherwise still be a benefit to the company, they will retain them as an independent contractor.

Well, within weeks of her accepting this job, her conditions of employment were dramatically changed. Her boss, knowing that he was the head of a division that would likely not retain him, needed to hatch a plan. He needed to make himself indispensable to the company before his 62nd birthday, to gain that lucrative independent contractor offer. To do so, he created a plan for a new global software system that would streamline the company's current process involving the movement of employee assets (a.k.a people) across borders.

In short, when the United Kingdom needs 20 accountants from India for a special project, what do they need to do to get them into the country (e.g., work visas), and what will the cost be for the temporary assignment? This software would streamline the process. Evidently, this is a real thing among major accounting firms. But he needed a tireless, pie-eyed lieutenant to make it happen. For the adoration of her work and her boss, my friend obliged.

To secure the data for the software, each individual region of the firm would need to be contacted and negotiated with. Their base moved from Tampa to London. Rather than travelling one week out of the month, after only a year in the post, she was travelling between two and a half to three weeks every month. And sure, it was business class, and the wining and the dining that went with the role, but after a while she became so wrapped up in her work, she started to separate from her family.

At first, she stopped calling her children when traveling. She would still call her husband, but only to briefly check in out of obligation as opposed to genuine interest in trying to keep up with the day-to-day of the family. Everyone else could see how she was pulling away, but anytime it was mentioned, she would viciously defend her decisions, and act like mentioning it was an assault on her career.

She became so enamored with building her boss's vision to secure his continued employment that she completely lost touch with her own family and friends and, in the process, her own vision. To make matters worse, who did she turn to for advice on her marriage and parenting? Why, her boss, of course, who was only too pleased to tell her that her own family didn't support her, and that she needed support to be a successful career woman. He would keep her hooked, despite those who truly were supporting her every day, every week, every hour. She simply could not see it.

But because he needed her in that lieutenant's role, his motivation was different. He did not care for her family or marriage. He just needed that unquestioning person to help him keep his job. And she played the role flawlessly.

Eventually she lost her marriage, and, for some time at least, her children would not even speak to her because she had effectively left the three of them on the advice of someone who did not have her best interests in mind, only his own. In the end, his big plan failed. Ironically, not because of the plan itself. But, most likely, because of multiple Title 7 complaints lodged against him during his tenure.

Of course, he landed on his feet. He now splits time between his primary residence outside of Philadelphia, his place in the mountains of Pennsylvania, and his apartment in New York City. And where is she? Living in a small rental house, with one child just now warming back up to her after years of almost no relationship. Her 23-year marriage is now officially complete. That software that was her boss's lifeline, now rendered irrelevant by COVID-19. As of the writing of this chapter, the team that she and the boss had built have mostly been laid off. Anyone looking at this objectively can see she was merely a pawn in this man's corporate plan. Anyone but her.

Not every story in the book has a happy ending. Just think where she could have been if she could have understood his true motivation, and kept that in perspective? So, know who your advisors are, and always ask why they are telling you to do the things they are telling you to do. Is it in your best interests, or theirs?

Some of my closest advisors have always been my mother and father. Now, I cannot speak about everyone's parental situation, but I know mine have never had anything but my best interests at heart. And to make matters better, my father ran a successful small business for almost his entire career. OK, so technically, he is a physician. But if you know anything about private medical practice, he ran a small business. As such, he has been a perfect advisor to me over the years as he (1) knows what he is talking about and (2) has only my best interests in mind.

So, when listening to the advice of others, make sure not only to ensure that they know what they are talking about, but also that they have *your* best interests in mind.

WORK YOUR ASS OFF

Mind you, the advice that is forthcoming is not always the easiest. And here is where we introduce our next major concept for entrepreneurs: sometimes, if not all the time, you've just got to work your ass off. I cannot tell you how many times that has been my father's advice to me. And you know, he has always been right.

Now, I know there are some very famous business books out there that laud only working a few hours a week, and that less is more. And for some, that may work. And, in general, those books don't really say only work 2 hours a week or whatever. What they are saying is that you should work smarter, not harder. And that's great advice, don't get me wrong. But sometimes, especially when you are starting out or are having a major issue hit your company, you've just got to work harder.

One of the best examples of this comes from one of my own biggest challenges. The year is 2017, and a new business I had founded, TTC Business Solutions, was rolling along just great. Money was flowing. Sales were popping. Life was good, or so I thought.

Just prior to my annual Spring break vacation with the family, I learned that my CFO had made a mistake and, to cover it up, she had authorized roughly $20,000 in charges to one of our credit cards to remedy the issue. The worst part, if she had told me, most likely we could have recovered those costs elsewhere, without the company incurring the same.

Although I had vetted her prior to hire, and she had been nothing but an exemplary employee for the previous two years, this was the first indication of a larger issue that, in my opinion, could not be remedied. Putting aside the original $20,000 error, the larger issue was the dishonest way she had tried to cover it up. More specifically, if I had not noticed an irregularity in one of our balance sheets, it would never have been brought to my attention.

Younger and less wise then, I confronted her about the issue. However, perhaps my greatest failure in my career was in not letting her go on the spot. Rather, with certain measures in place, we would begin a job hunt for our new CFO while allowing her to transition to another job. I left for our family vacation knowing that the company would still be in good hands with my right hand—

we'll call her Ally—still on the job to oversee everything including the CFO. What could go wrong?

The day before the cruise got back, I got an email from my operations manager: all our company credit cards were declining. Odd, I thought, knowing I had left with over $300,000 in the general operating account, and all bills paid. As it was a Friday, I promised to work on it over the weekend, and would figure out the issue by Monday. Once I got home, a few calls to American Express revealed a deepening and more catastrophic mystery. American Express, who had been our primary business card and partner, if you will, for 14 years, had pulled our entire line of credit.

Now, let me explain the gravity of this. Our business model was filing for new businesses, copyrights, and trademarks for our customers. On average, we would rack up $180,000 to $200,000 per month in state and government filing fees. We needed those cards to keep the business running. Without them, we had no way to pay the states and federal government for their fees.

As I spoke with American Express, I could not believe my ears. Mind you, we had two primary accounts with them. Our Platinum charge card and our AmEx Blue. The Platinum had an unlimited spending limit. That was the card we would drop that $180,000 to $200,000 per month on. I could have gone out and bought a house with that card if I so desired. For 14 years, we never missed a payment on that card. On time, fully paid, $180,000 to $200,000 per month. The Blue, as I soon discovered, was not paid with the same regularity. Mind you, this card had a credit limit of about $20,000 and, for some reason, the CFO kept about a $2,000 balance on the same. As a result, if memory serves me correctly, we had a payment due every month in the nature of $120. $120!!!

Well, as it turns out, our CFO had failed to pay the minimum payment of about $120 to the American Express Blue Card for the last 7 months. As a result, despite timely paying them $180,000 to $200,000 per month for the other card for 14 years, American Express decided to terminate our entire line of credit, closing all our cards. In short, in one swift move, they shut down our ability to function as a company. All over a $120 bill, days after we had sent them close to $194,000! Yup, all true! No amount of begging, pleading, or going up the chain of command could get them to change their mind. We were officially dead to them, and they would not issue any further credit to our company.

Now, on an aside, I understand we missed the payments on the smaller account. But seriously? Millions, literally millions, paid to them over the years on time and without issue, and they pulled our line of credit for $120? Are you kidding me? Wow. In my opinion, not a partner that stands by you. To this day, I will never again use American Express or any of their services. Ever. Period.

At that moment, I had to come up with a solution, and fast. It was a Sunday, but most credit card application centers are still open. I methodically went through the list of credit card providers. After several calls, I found one that became the savior of our business—Capital One. Not only were they able to issue us a card that day, but they provided me with a temporary number to begin charging almost immediately. I have used Capital One since this time, and they are the greatest partner a small business could ever have. Thank you to all the wonderful people at Capital One and, especially, those in the Tampa Service Center! You all complete me! So, if you want a credit card partner for your business, I strongly recommend Capital One. But what do I know? I'm just the guy that's helped over 100,000 businesses get their start.

So having temporarily solved our credit issue sufficiently enough to keep us limping along, I headed into the office knowing that if the CFO showed up, it would only be for as long as it took me to spin her around and show her the door. When I got to the office, however, what I discovered was far more dire than the credit crisis I had to resolve the day before. To this day, I still shake my head at what unfolded over the next few hours and days.

Evidently, while I was away, and when the cards started to decline, the CFO seized her moment of revenge. A moment caused by her own ineptitude in failing to pay a bill. During a company-wide meeting they held in my absence, she told the staff that the company was near bankruptcy, we had no money, and that I had used the rest of the company's funds to take my family on a vacation. Doubling down, and knowing she was already leaving the company, she told everyone to get their resumes together, as the company would not be able to make the next payroll. She did this all with 6 months of payroll in the general operating bank account.

And it gets worse. Remember Ally, my Number 2? I had been grooming her for years to take a more prominent role in the company. She was my fail-safe. She should have done something. Anything. But all she did in that fateful moment was shrug her shoulders, say "I don't know", and let the flames the CFO had started turn into a raging inferno.

She knew how to reach me. She should have calmed the waters, walked into her office, and called me on the cruise. She did none of that. Even if she could not reach me, it was her responsibility to calm the storm. She did not. So, the redundancies I had built into the system failed, because not one but both of my top two lieutenants (one intentionally, one for reasons I still do not grasp) completely failed me and the company.

On Monday morning, I walked into the office expecting my biggest challenge to be escorting the CFO to the door, and making sure we had sufficient new credit to keep the company moving forward. What I walked into was far graver. Within the first hour, I encountered a maelstrom of resignations which saw our top producers walking out the door. By noon, 80% of our annual revenues had effectively given notice. 80%! Considering that it takes more than a year to develop a quality salesperson at our company, how would we survive? The odds seemed insurmountable.

And that's where my dad comes in. Now, you know he was a physician. More specifically, he was an OB/GYN, and a general surgeon. But he was also a fighter pilot for the US Air Force. So, as an advisor, he brought a lot to the table. First, he retained an uncanny ability to compartmentalize and systematically triage critical issues that needed to be addressed. He combined this with an unflappable work ethic.

Being a medical resident, you work hard. And being an OB/GYN, well, babies come 24 hours a day. And the patient you are seeing in the office at 9:00 am does not care if you were out delivering someone else's baby until 4:30 am. They're there for *their* appointment, so you had better be as well. I can't tell you how many nights I'd be watching a movie at 11:30 pm and dad would head out to deliver a baby. Sometimes I'd hear him roll back in just before dawn, only to have to get up after an hour or so of shut eye and head to the office. And that's the type of work ethic he has.

Did he do well? Yes. Yes, he did. But he worked hard for every penny.

So, when this maelstrom hit, as I had done so many times before, I asked him for his advice. Now, sometimes advice can be complex and detailed. But other times it can be very simple and direct. And, to this day, he gave me the best advice to get through that challenge that anyone could have given: *Son, Time to Roll Up Your Sleeves and Work Harder. Sleep is a Luxury. Now get to Work.*

The next day, I marched into the office with renewed vigor. After all, as Gene Kranz famously quipped, failure is not an option. I knew which salespeople I may have a shot at retaining. I targeted one after another. First, I sat down with one of my top producers to listen to his concerns. Understanding what they were—the lack of guaranteed commission money—I immediately offered him a new commission structure with guaranteed money. Within a day, I had retained him. Similarly, I went after those who I thought I could keep. Making deals and side deals with many in the end, about 60% of our revenue still walked out the door, including Ally, who had breached her loyalty to me and had failed to stem the tide. But dropping to 40% of revenue instead of 20% gave me a little bit more to work with. I was left to rebuild from 40%. OK, now we know the number, let's go!

I deputized the entire company to make sales, until we stabilized. Previously, if a non-salesperson took a call that could lead to a sale, they were to forward it to the sales team. No more. If you have a customer on the phone with a credit card in hand, you take that card, make the sale. Next, I myself joined the sales team. During the days, I would spend my time making sales calls, putting money into the hopper, effectively replacing at least one of the salespeople. This, of course, meant that I would have to do my normal day job at night. So be it. Work harder.

The first month, we swung from an average profit of $30,000 to a loss of $60,000. But we survived. The next month we continued to work hard towards getting it back. Hiring, training, and rebuilding a team after a few months, we re-established sufficient enough cash flow to ensure the continuity of the business. If I got 4 hours of sleep per night during that time, I would have been surprised. But we kept going. We kept fighting. We kept working harder. One salesperson, Stacy, virtually doubled her revenue to help the company. A Herculean effort.

That was now a distant four years ago. And the lessons I learned both professionally and personally will stick with me for a lifetime. Lessons that I hope to share with you. But having learned from those missteps, we are a better and stronger company for it. Our recent financial results showed that we are now not only back, but are doing better than we ever have. And now, with increased safeguards in place, we will never go down that path again. How'd we do it? I, and now my new team, worked and continued to work our asses off. It's that simple.

During such times, I would often look for inspiration beyond just the advice of my father. If you search YouTube, there are a lot of motivational speeches out there. But I always tended to gravitate towards one by an immigrant worker who wanted to make it in the United States. As he preached: have a goal, ignore the naysayers, and work your ass of. Eight hours of sleep a night? Nonsense. Sleep faster!

His was not the typical story. Born to a policeman in his native land, his parents wanted him to go into the family business, police work, marry a local girl, and have lots of children. But, as he so brilliantly explains it in the YouTube video, that was not his vision. His goal was to become a world-class athlete, then a Hollywood movie star. Yeah, right, said everyone in the small European village he came from.

But he had his goals. He ignored his naysayers. His vision was not theirs. He moved to the United States and became the greatest in his sport the world has ever seen. He then used his athletic success and work ethic to transition to film. He is now considered to be one of the most successful action heroes in the history of Hollywood. Later, he would become the governor of California and, but for Constitutional limitations, may possibly have been the president of the United States of America. His name, if you don't already know, is Arnold Schwarzenegger.

Arnold won an amazing 5 Mr. Universe titles on his way to being considered the greatest bodybuilder of all time. He worked construction to pay the bills in the early days, while enduring a training schedule that was second to none. Oh, all the while going to acting class at night. Did he listen to the naysayers? No! Did he just work his ass off? Yes.

His second career as an actor has led to worldwide box office receipts of over $4 billion U.S. This from a man whose accent was so strong that, when he originally started acting, he was told he could never make it, because no one would be able to understand him. Yet another naysayer. Again, he worked his ass off. Four billion dollars later, looks like that hard work paid off.

And let's not forget his third career as the chief executive of the State of California. Not too shabby. All this from a guy who was told to stay home in Austria, marry a girl named Heidi or something like that, have some kids, and be a local police officer.

So, in life as in business, have your goals, ignore the naysayers, and work your ass off. Steve, Fred, and Arnold did. Now it's your turn!

Chapter Summary: Ignore the Naysayers. Listen to a Select Few. Work Your Ass Off.

- **Ignore the Naysayers**: The world is filled with critics. Especially those who were not strong enough to chase their own dreams. Much of their criticism of you is their projecting their own failures. You must be comfortable living in a world where not everyone will get or support your dream. Simply understand it was never theirs to begin with. Smile. Move on.
- **Only Take Advice From a Select Few:** Listen to everyone. But only take advice from people who (1) have experience or otherwise know what they are talking about; and (2) do not have an ulterior motive. For everyone else. Listen politely. Smile. Move on.
- **Work Your Ass Off:** Hard work works. Don't let anyone else ever tell you differently. Work your ass off. Period.

CASH IS KING. EVERYTHING ELSE IS DETAILS

Money is the Most Important Thing, Period.

CASH FLOW IS *THE* MOST IMPORTANT THING

Pop quiz. What's the most important thing in your business? Inbound leads? Efficient systems to perform your work? Technology? Generally, it will depend on who you ask and what their experience is.

The VP of marketing would say it's inbound leads. The CFO would tell you it's a proper set of books. The sales manager would emphatically answer sales! And they would all be right, from their respective point of view. But as someone who has run a very successful business and helped to start thousands of others, I'm here to tell you the simple truth: Cash is King. Everything else is details.

THE PANDEMIC'S LESSON IN CASH FLOW

Perhaps at no other time in human history has this point been easier to prove. As I write this chapter, it's May of 2020. The global economy has largely been shut down since February due to the COVID-19 virus. Depending on when you read this book, you may or may not be aware of the Pandemic of 2020. If not, here's a brief synopsis of where we currently stand.

The virus originated in China and spread throughout the globe rapidly, due to air travel connecting foreign cities to the epicenter of the disease. Unlike Ebola or previous threatened pandemics, whose symptoms manifest in a relatively short period of time, the COVID-19 virus could be carried for weeks by an asymptomatic host, infecting hundreds if not thousands of people without the host ever being the wiser. With the World Health Organization, Centers for Disease Control, and other global health centers being caught largely flat-footed, most governments failed to react in a timely enough manner to prevent the spread of the virus into their respective countries.

With no cure in sight, governments were left with an agonizing decision. The only way to protect their populations and halt the spread of this killer bug was to isolate people from one another, effectively ordering them to shelter in place in their homes to avoid exposure to the virus. China, where the virus originated, was the first to react in this fashion, imposing strict stay-at-home orders. Thereafter, Europe followed suit as well as other countries around the globe. The United States, splintered into local and state governments, largely failed to have a unified voice on the issue.

However, by early March of 2020, most major cities and economic regions of the U.S. were under some form of stay-at-home order.

With people sheltering in place and avoiding contact with one another, entire industries began to suffer. The airline industry largely ground to halt, with almost no one traveling due to the pandemic. Airlines grounded their fleets at airports and even in the desert bone yards, hoping that one day we would return to normal. The cruise industry was no different.

But it is not just the travel industry that was hit hard. Bars and restaurants were closed. Retail stores largely shuttered to avoid people spreading the virus.

Returning to the agonizing decision referenced above, governments were faced with temporarily closing their economies, or doing nothing and letting the virus spread to their entire populations. For the United States, the difficult decision was generally made to shut it down.

In the initial months after the shutdown order, the economy largely limped along. Certain industries were deemed essential and permitted to keep working. Industries such as health care, food services (e.g., grocery stores and food supply) as well as shipping (FedEx, UPS, etc.) were permitted to work. As such, if your business was equipped to switch to a virtual model, you were in luck. It would go on.

But what about restaurants, retail stores, the traditional brick and mortar locations? What about airlines and cruise companies? What about the hotel industry? In the face of the crisis, the United States infused 3 trillion dollars into the economy as economic stimulus to keep it going. The primary plan was for businesses with under 500 employees to receive two and a half months of payroll, effectively for free. That way people stay on payrolls, they get their salaries, and they would continue to spend and keep money flowing into the economy.

Candidly, the plan was solid. Having studied macroeconomics at Columbia University, there is a fundamental truth underlying economies: so long as money keeps flowing in the economy, things are good. Flowing? Yes, flowing.

In short, this is how it works. Let's assume you're a barber. You cut hair for money. Your customer pays you to cut their hair. You get paid. Therefore, you now have money. You, in turn, take some of that money and go buy groceries to feed your family. The money flows.

Now, your customer's money has moved from them to you, with them receiving something they wanted (a haircut), and on to someone else receiving something you want: food. Literal cash flow. In the U.S. we have about 320 million people. Barbers, doctors, teachers, lawyers. Well, the hell with the lawyers.

Anyways, what happens to the economy when that flow stops? One day, the barber opens his shop and, for a whole day, no one comes in. No one gets a haircut. Why? Well, during the pandemic, we are not supposed to be within 6 feet of one another. And unless you want your hair cut with a telescoping hedge trimmer, the barber's business has effectively been shut down by our COVID-19 restrictions. Except for Nancy Pelosi, of course.

Sucks for him, right? Wrong. Sucks for all of us. Because the barber then doesn't go to the store to buy food. Maybe he just says to the family: we still have that 10,000 pack of hot dogs from COSTCO we bought three years ago; we'll just survive on that for a while. And so, they do. And now the grocery store has less money to pay its staff. In turn, it must lay off an employee or two. As they are laid off, their money is pulled from the economy, repeating the cycle above as we saw from the barber. And when their money is removed from the economy, someone else somewhere is getting laid off. They may not even know the person, or be in the same state. But it is a very real ripple effect.

So back to the government's plan. Rather than give the Fortune 500 companies billions in which they may still lay off workers, and just use the money to prop up their respective bottom lines, I think the Federal Government got it right. I don't know if it was Congress, the White House, or the Department of the Treasury, but infusing trillions into the economy through the hands of our barbers and store clerks is about as perfect plan as I can imagine getting us through this crisis.

But there's a hitch. We can't do it forever. And at some point, we're going to have to re-open the economy with or without a cure for COVID-19. If we don't, the ripple effect of pulling this much money from the economy for a sustained period will create a situation arguably far worse than the original virus: The Second Great Depression, with potentially millions losing their lives as a result of mass starvation and other ripple effects.

So, on a macroeconomic level, we can see cash, and, more specifically, cash flow, is king. Cash flow must continue to keep an economy going, or else people lose jobs, and the economy spirals into a recession, or, worse, a depression.

Now, in our example above, what was naturally relegated to the back seat? Did we have accurate accounting of all the money infused into the economy? Nope. About three trillion dollars went out. But an accurate accounting of every dime was not the focus. Why? Because the exact knowledge of where every penny is going at that moment was not the most important thing. The cash itself is!

Likewise, provided we get through this, as it now appears we will, we're going to have another pretty big economic hit in the future, namely, paying for all the debt that extra $3 trillion infusion cost us. How? Once we are back on our feet, someone is going to have to raise taxes. You can't just write a check for 3 trillion and pay for it with a life-long IOU. Nope, in 2022 or 2023, we are going to have to pay the piper for all that stimulus money. But, again, is that the most important thing in the crisis? Nope. We'll figure that out and put it into the budget down the road. Why? Because if we worry about debt financing now, we will stop the flow of cash today. And, as we have seen, no cash, no jobs. No jobs, big problem.

But you are likely not reading this book because you are running a government. More likely you are, or would like to become, an entrepreneur, running your own business. And that's what we call microeconomics, not macro. But the lessons hold true from above. It does not matter if you are at a macro or micro level. Cash is still king. Everything else is details.

KNOWING WHAT IS KING

From my own perspective, this was perfectly highlighted in my company's troubles a few years back. Remember, I was on a cruise with my family? My CFO stopped paying for the credit card and told everyone to quit. I came back to a company that had thrived for 14 years, but because of this malicious act, our credit was pulled and 80% of our sales walked out the door. This will be burned into my memory for the rest of my life. But there's more.

While stitching the company back together, I was consistently barraged with the opinions of others as to what they felt was the most important thing for the company. My former spouse, who was an accountant by training, would remind me daily that my top priority was to get another CFO on board with an accurate set of books. But here's the rub: she had never run a company. She was limited to her experience in large corporations, where she was given millions of dollars in a budget, then merely had to account for where it was spent. She had never had to worry about how those millions of dollars were made, or her access to those millions.

Put another way, I can't pay the salaries of the remaining employees, or pay for a new accounting firm with a great set of books. Employees, including accountants, work for money, period. So even accounting takes a back seat temporarily to cash flow in some circumstances, when every day is a grind just to keep enough cash flowing into the business, to keep the doors open.

But I knew this, because I had seen similar things happen to customers over the years and, as dire as the circumstances were, I knew one immutable truth: No matter what anyone else ever tells you, the most important thing in a business is cash! Period. End of story.

Years before my company's crisis, I had witnessed this in countless other small businesses I had helped to get up and running. Perhaps the most tragic story involves that of a California-based nutraceuticals company I helped for almost a decade until the company's demise. Here's their story.

CALIFORNICASHLESS

For those of you who do not know, nutraceuticals is a fancy term for vitamins and related health products. There is little regulation in the industry compared to prescription and over-the-counter medications. What most of you probably did not know is that, globally, nutraceuticals are a $200 Billion dollar industry per year. $200 billion, with a "B".

Years ago, I represented Mike and his company—we'll call it California Nutraceuticals. Mike was a great guy who founded the company in his home near Santa Clara. It started with one product bottled in his kitchen. A website and a toll-free number later the business started to grow. One product became two, and later three. Before long, as happens with so many home-based businesses, the assembly of the products had taken over his entire dining room. His cars had to be parked on the street to accommodate all the products being staged for shipping in the garage. In short, business was becoming, well, a business.

They rented their first space, a little warehouse-type facility with a small office and assembly area. He hired their first employees as the business grew. Three products became 8, then 12. Their distribution network expanded, and their assembly line became more refined. More employees were hired, and cash was flowing everywhere. They could do no wrong.

Within three years, they had gone from a home-based business to 15 employees, a global distribution network, and millions in sales. Over the next two years, they would double in size, then double again. Fifteen employees became 80. They built their own shipping and manufacturing plant. Their sales were off the charts. Mike's old home, well, that was traded in for a 10,000 square foot mansion with manicured lawns and a backyard pool complex that looked like it belonged on the pages of a Frontgate catalog. Life was good. But then it happened.

Mike's CFO came to him and informed him they had experienced a significant month-over-month revenue drop in their most profitable product. In fact, the revenue drop was 50%. Normally, when you have a multi-million-dollar business with over 20 products, such a drop would not be of grave concern. Normally.

But the product in question accounted for over 50% of the company's revenue. It was their bestseller. If you're decent at math, a 50% drop in revenue of the product that provides 50% of your business's revenue equates to a 25% drop in overall revenue.

OK, so 25% drop in revenue is not so bad, right? Wrong. When your margins are running at about 15-20%, a 25% drop in revenue takes you from the black to the dreaded red. And that's where they found themselves, suddenly. But why?

Well, as it turns out, the industry is very competitive, and very—for lack of better terminology—incestuous. When one person does well on a specific product and word gets out, watch out! Everyone comes up with a similar-sounding product, and starts marketing it to your customers. What they quickly unearthed by running a couple Google searches was that another competitor had not only bottled a similar product, but an identical one. Same product. Same brand name. Right down to an identical label.

Now you're probably thinking, wait a minute, can they do that? Legally, no. They cannot. But unless you have a law firm on your side ready to sue them back into the Stone Age, you have a problem. And Mike, well, he had a problem.

Remember the big new house I mentioned, and all the employees? To say the company was cash poor would be an understatement. They cleaned the bank account every month to make payroll, pay the mortgage on the big facility, and pay for that big new house. So, when a 25% hit came, it hurt. It hurt badly.

They came to me and said, "What should we do?"

"Sue em back to the Stone Age!" I said.

"Great, let's do it!" Mike replied. So, I quickly called the law firm I use in California, explained to them the situation, asked for their lowest retainer, and headed back to Mike. You see, a case like this can cost upwards of $100,000 to $300,000 to file and prosecute. So, a retainer of $20,000 for the Los Angeles area is standard. I sent it on to Mike.

A few minutes later my phone rang. It was Mike. "Matt, I don't have the cash for $20,000! Can't they do this on contingency?" The desperation came through in his voice.

"Unfortunately, not," I replied. "They're lawyers. They will only help you for cash." Sad, but true.

What occurred over the next few weeks was one of the most painful things I have ever witnessed a business owner go through. And I had a front row seat to the whole thing. Without litigation counsel in California, all they could afford to do is send letters demanding the other side stop. The bad guy, flush with all this new cash, lawyered up and said, "See you in court." Of course, Mike could not afford to go to court. He simply did not have the cash-flow due to the loss in revenues caused by the bad guy. Painfully, he had to start cutting costs.

The first to go was several of his employees. And then marketing. But as he could not address the principal issue, the issue persisted. His company continued to shrink. The bad guy got a greater and greater share of the market, until, one day, Mike went to run payroll, and there was not enough to pay all the bills. Being unable to pay his employees, he was placed in a position to merely ask them to stay on and work until their next payroll, effectively for free. You can imagine the response. Having seen two rounds of layoffs, and now missing their own paycheck, the remaining employees simply walked out. And that was it. The business went bankrupt in a period of months. He simply did not have enough cash, or access to cash, to right the wrongs that had been done to him, and to get it back.

Coming full circle. Marketing leads were in place. Mike had a perfect set of books, the books simply showed he had more bills than income. What caused the demise of the business? Ultimately, the cessation of cash. So, whenever anyone tries to tell you anything else is the most important thing, recall poor Mike. You can work through any issue in a business so long as you have cash. When you have no money, there is no more business. Period. You're out of business. Cash is king!

But not every business that gets into trouble goes down. So long as you can keep sufficient cash flowing through the business, you have time to work out the company's larger issues. And sometimes this must be through debt financing, so long as you have a plan as to how to pay it off in the end.

DEBT IF YOU DARE

As I've mentioned just a few times in this book, TTC Business Solutions was in real trouble back in 2017. With 80% of the sales walking out the door, and me having to claw it back so that we ultimately kept 40%, I had to seriously think my way through some major financial issues to ensure payroll got issued, and all our bills were paid. And they were. But it was not easy. And here is where debt financing comes in.

Debt financing is OK, so long as it is a part of a larger plan to return to profitability. For instance, in 2017, I needed to finance the company using debt because, in the short run, our sales were going to plummet; we lost 60% of a highly trained sales team. But the systems were still in place. There was a continuing market for our services. We just needed the people to perform the work. And that would take time. So, we determined that debt financing was the right move at the time for us.

What did we do? I used a combination of cash advances from credit cards in conjunction with financing through modern lending sources such as Kabbage, PayPal Loans, and even a company called Forward Line Financial to provide the company with the financial bridge to get it out of the fiscal crisis we had endured. And did I feel comfortable doing it? Absolutely. Why? Because I knew our situation was temporary. Roll up your sleeves and work harder. Eventually this will be alright. And I was right.

By May of 2020, almost all the debt we incurred in 2017 was paid off. By then we were in a strong financial position and, today, our strongest position ever. It took a few years to get here. But after what transpired, I'm happy that is the case. It was not by luck, though. It was by design. The debt had to go into the business map referenced in Chapter 1, and incorporated into our structure. Painful, but we survived.

BUILD YOUR RESERVES

So, let's look once again at Mike, and what the difference was between his company and TTC. Mike had severely overextended the company, and had little cash reserves, even in good times. In retrospect, he probably was carrying too many on payroll, and kept his cost structure too high. And that big, beautiful house, well, may not have been the best call. So, when cash flow went out the door, he didn't have anything in reserve. In fairness to Mike, this was in the days before Kabbage and PayPal Loans. So traditional bank lines of credit or loans may not have been able to have been secured in the timeframe needed to save the business. Without these more modern, speedy financing options, and given the size of his cost structure, it is doubtful that even debt financing through a credit card would have been enough to remedy his situation. In short, not only did he need to replace the lost income from his business to support the business itself, but he also needed to add in a new significant cost, in the form of a law firm charging about $20,000 per month. Crushing for most businesses. And, sadly, it crushed him.

Cash is King!

A SWEET FINANCIAL PLAN

Turning to the COVID crisis, we are seeing this play out repeatedly. One of our largest customers runs a specialty confectionery sugar company near College Station, Texas. They manufacture uniquely colored sugars for competition baking as well as everyday bakers. The business is owned and run by two brothers who are two of the greatest guys you will ever meet. Like TTC, they have endured their fair share of challenges over the years. A frivolous lawsuit, which took years to conclude, nearly drained the company completely. But they survived.

During a multi-year period, everything they earned went out the door to lawyers. Once again: lawyers, right? But this time, they learned. They learned the power of setting up reserves, be they in the form of cash on hand, or lines of credit stored away for a rainy day. When the frivolous case finally ended, it was boom time. But did they go out and buy big houses? No. Did they go out and overextend the business with fancy office buildings, company cars, or over hiring staff? No. They went out there and banked tons of cash. They went out there and secured lines of credit. They went out there and made sure, if another frivolous lawsuit ever came, or another similar crisis, their company would endure. And guess what, it has.

When COVID first hit, they were banking a great amount of money. As the shelter-in-place orders began appearing, their business started to slow. Many of us were surprised as, like the brothers, we thought people staying home more would bake more and, correspondingly, order more confectionery sugar. I know that, during our shelter-in-place orders, my daughter kept us wrapped in a seemingly endless supply of cookies, cakes, and brownies.

But their business fell by 5 - 10% in the first week California issued its mandatory order. As other major states like New York and New Jersey followed suit, business fell even further. Within 6 weeks, their business was off a shocking 95%. Let me say that again, 95%! For most businesses that would be the end. I mean, not too many can afford a loss of 95% of their revenue and keep their doors open for long.

But the brothers had been through this before. They had stored up cash reserves and had lines of credit, from their local banks to modern lenders like Kabbage. In short, even though business was almost non-existent, they were ready. Did it hurt? Absolutely. But because they had the cash to maintain the business, they used the slow times to re-imagine their production facility for even greater efficiencies, because they knew that the downturn was temporary. And it was.

As the pandemic subsided, and the economy started to reopen, their sales gradually returned. As of last count, they are still not hitting pre-COVID numbers, but the savings from the efficiencies they learned during the time have made their margins even fatter. As a result, even with sales still a little off, they are more profitable than ever. It simply could not happen to two better guys.

And why? Because cash is king, and they ensured they had cash for the lean times by storing up and lining up lines of credit during the boom times.

ONLY USE RESERVES WHEN THERE'S A PLAN TO PROFIT

But all of this is for naught if you don't have a plan to be profitable in the future. In short, cash is king. Store up reserves and credit lines for the lean times, but if you don't have a path to a profitable business in the future, don't go into debt or use your cash to keep bailing out a boat that's destined to sink.

A business's purpose is to make you money. I know, there are nonprofits out there who would contest that. But if you are an entrepreneur and you run a business, your main goal should be to put money in your pocket, period! And one of the hardest lessons to learn is that if the business model is flawed or if it is not profitable, and you do not have a map towards profitability, stop propping it up and let it go.

I had to face this question in 2017, at the height of our financial crisis. You see, in addition to lying to the staff about our financial position to induce a mass walk-out, the CFO said something to my Number 2 that did make me stop and think: "*I don't think the business model works.*" You can replace staff, given enough time. You certainly can replace a bad, malicious CFO. But if your model no longer works, how long should you keep plugging away until you throw in the towel? How long do you invest your money to get it back? All questions you may face someday.

As we were building the company back up, I would face this question repeatedly. In our industry, as you are now aware, there were traditionally three major players: the OJs, Voldemort, and us. The Trademark Company had at one time been the OJs' primary competitor in the space. However, the other guy had years ago surpassed us in key growth metrics and had occupied the number two spot, for years behind OJs.

This was largely the way it was from 2008 to 2017. During those years, several low-cost competitors entered the market. But none of them were able to sustain a market position that impacted the leaders' positions. When entering or staying in a market, you must know what your position will be. In other words, why will consumers flock to you? Perhaps the easiest way to gain a toe hold in a new market is by entering as a low-cost provider. But as most know, this often creates a "race to the bottom," where other competitors then drop prices to match or beat the competitor's price, and where everyone in the market ultimately loses—save for the new entrant, if they can hold on and grab a piece of the market share.

To further understand this: when we first launched in 2003, our average price point for a service was $225. Over the years we added packages, price points moved, and with various cost structures, that price point would fluctuate from $225, down to $149. Then, for several years, it would return to the $189 to $249 range. But that all changed in 2017.

THE HORSEMAN OF THE APOCOLYPSE

In 2017, just before the CFO issues, we started noticing a drop in our conversion rate. Well, it did not take long to realize what was going on. The new kid on the block from Houston, Texas had entered the market and had figured out a way to stick. El Caballero had a nice-looking web site, and everything flowed seamlessly. They made the trademark process appear very simple and that, after all, is the name of the game.

At that time, our lowest price point, matching other major competitors', was $99 for a basic trademark filing. The reduction from $225 to $189 to $149 and now to $99 had cut margins over the years, but at $99, and with the addition of down-the-road services, the model remained viable.

But now, we had to contend with El Caballero, Mr. 69! To make matters worse, there is a government filing fee of about $275 that goes with these packages. Traditionally, this was explained on our website, but for our $149 package, the total charge would be $425, $149 for our services and $275 for the government filing fee. Well, not only did Mr. 69 lower the fee to $69, but he did not charge them the government fee upfront, leaving that instead to a phone call or email requesting the fee, after they had signed up for the $69 service.

Well, it worked. He grabbed a chunk of our business and, from what we can tell, even larger chunks of the OJs' and Voldemort's. Some estimates show that Mr. 69 may, within one year, have moved from a market entrant to the number two and possibly number one spot in the industry. In all candor, it was impressive. But the overall effect on the industry was not.

With a market entrant offering a price point at $69, and without government filing fees, there was tremendous pressure on competition to follow suit. Now, typically, we would not have done so. However, have I mentioned our 2017 financial crisis, as a result of 80% of our sales team leaving, as a result of a CFO who had been let go and decided to light the place on fire as she walked out the door? I think I may have alluded to it once or twice thus far. Well, struggling to rebuild a sales team at the same time as this hit, we could not resist a price war and compete on customer experience alone. We just weren't there. So I made the difficult decision to drop prices to $69 on our lowest end package.

Now, if you thought margins were thin before, doing this cut margins so thin you could floss your teeth with them. At this moment, as an entrepreneur, you must ask yourself, is this worth saving? What is my plan? If we pull this off, is it all to save a failing business model, or is there a pot of gold at the end of the rainbow? In short, a business should be for profit, or at least cannot lose money forever. And if there is no path for it to begin at least paying for itself and making good money, you must make the difficult decision to pull the plug and shut it down.

For me, I was not there yet. The proof of concept had not changed. The market had evolved. But there was so much potential to be unearthed. I knew that it was not going to be easy. But if we could sustain everything the business had gone through in the preceding 2 years, it may cost me almost everything I had, but, at some point, it would come back in spades.

I re-wrote my business map, and started the journey again. Because we were larger than when we started, I had to infuse more capital into the business, just to keep her afloat. It took a significant amount of my personal financial reserves. In fact, if you looked at it from the outside, most would probably have advised me to throw in that towel. But like I said above, it was not their vision. They never believed, anyways. And I had that map, and a clear pathway back to success.

First, I had to re-assemble a top-caliber sales team. It was a start and stop process. And we had to break a bunch of eggs along the way. But as I write this today, we have the best damn sales team out there. They are passionate and methodical. They are sales killers, yet ethical and only sell what is in the customers' best interests. They are the lifeblood of the company.

Second, once we had them in place, I needed to retain them while they worked on keeping us in the black, and paying off all the red. And they have been amazing. And no matter how badly it hurt, and sometimes it would hurt badly, we went to happy hours, did corporate outings, lunches, etc., to instill in them a great sense of corporate culture, which they now have adopted. You must keep the team happy, even in the most difficult of times.

Third, once we had a great team back in place, and had returned our customer service to that of a world-class organization, we raised prices and branded El Caballero as the "you get what you pay for guy." You want the $69 package from him? Here's his number. Here's his web site. In our opinion, if you want the best service, and the best in the industry, stick with us. But if you want the lowest cost provider, all the best! Enjoy!

Wow has it worked! The company has now rebuilt and grown beyond our wildest imagination. Margins have been restored and even increased. We are rolling along with our next huge target goals now attainable. We are rolling so hard right now that I've finally had time to put this all down on paper. Because, in the end, whether you use our services or someone else's, whether you purchased this book, are reading it in that bookstore, maybe got a free copy or borrowed it from the library, I want you to succeed! I want you to get your own piece of the American Dream. And that's what this is all about. You!

Chapter Summary: Cash is King. Plan to Profit or Shut it Down.

- **Cash Flow > Costs:** Your inbound cash must exceed your outbound expenses. Too many do not get this very basic concept draining reserves until they are in a massive debt. Know your numbers and fight hard so that cash flow always exceeds costs.
- **Develop Strategic Reserves:** Develop your strategic reserves during the good times. Lenders and other forms of credit may not be available unless they exist before you truly need them.
- **Plan to Profit or Shut it Down:** If cash flow is less than your costs, *only* draw upon your strategic reserves *if* you have a realistic pathway to get back to profitability. As painful as it may sound, it is far less painful to shut it down before you go into massive debt to keep a failing business temporarily afloat.

Additional Suggested Reading:

Profit First Transform Your Business from a Cash-Eating Monster to a Money-Making Machine, Mike Michalowicz, 2014

KEEP MOVING FORWARD

You're Either Growing or You're Dying.

KEEP MOVING FORWARD

In 2007, Walt Disney Pictures released the relatively unheralded movie *Meet the Robinsons*. Set in the early 2000s, the picture tells the story of Lewis, an aspiring 12-year-old inventor, growing up in an orphanage after having been abandoned there as a baby. As the story unfolds, we quickly learn that Lewis works tirelessly, obsessing to create a machine to scan his memory, so that he can locate the one thing that he longs for most: his birth mother.

The plot takes off when Lewis meets Wilbur Robinson, a mysterious young teen who claims to be a time-traveling cop from the future in search of an evil, bowler-hat wearing individual who has stolen a valuable time-traveling device from the future, threatening to alter the very delicate time-space continuum. Hijinks ensue.

Eventually, the characters are transported to the year 2037, a magical modern world filled with flying things here and flying things there, whirling around like something out of Disney's original vision of Tomorrow Land. It's a spectacular visual achievement. As part of the race to secure the time machine from the bowler-hat man, Lewis comes face-to-face with his future self, learning that it is, in fact, his inventions that have shaped the world in which they now reside. He is the architect of this improved humanity. He has become what he had dreamt he would be. The world's greatest inventor.

Of course, there is more to the movie, plot twists, chases, and the appearance of a dinosaur in 2037! But, in the end, throughout all the fun and silliness, there is that iconic tear-jerking Disney moral. And, brilliantly, the movie weaves the iconic advice attributed to the actual late, great Walt Disney himself through the eyes of the young and older Lewis. Never dwell on your failures and . . .

Keep Moving Forward
-Walt E. Disney

There's a lot of truth in the movies if you pay attention. Why? Because they are written by writers who are merely putting their human thoughts on subjects to paper. And Walt knew, as did the writers of *Meet the Robinsons,* life, and business, is about keeping moving forward. So, keep moving forward, always. But again, don't take my word for it. Let's look at some examples of what Walt was talking about.

AN APPLE EVERY QUARTER

I can remember like it was yesterday. A thin man walking on the stage wearing glasses, a black shirt, and jeans. Not your typical corporate look. Speaking with his characteristic hand gestures, he spoke of his love of music. Of the need to store more songs in a single location. Of Apple Computer's latest innovation, the iPod! Of course, I'm referencing the late visionary Steve Jobs. And when he took the stage, you always expected something cool. Something amazing. Something that perhaps you were completely unaware of, but you knew you would need to have one, and soon.

Over the years, we came to expect Steve to take that stage for what seemed to be two or three times per year, and make some grand announcement. Sometimes they were huge! The iPod! The iPhone! The iPad! Even the Apple Watch!

On an aside, I'm sure it's a trademark thing. But ever wonder why they didn't stick to iWatch? I mean, even if somebody else had the brand, it's not like they couldn't just buy it out from under them, probably with all the $100s and $1000-dollar bills Apple could find just stuffed in the seat cushions of their corporate headquarters' couches.

Back on point: these announcements weren't just to launch entirely new products. They were also to launch updates to existing lines. For instance, as I sit here, I have just upgraded to an iPhone 12 Pro. And Just like the 11, and the 10 before it, there were press releases, marketing, and regular stage presentations announcing the new features. In fact, it's almost as if Apple innovates according to a schedule and releases their innovations to spark additional sales.

OK, it's not like that. It is that. So, in case you missed it, Apple has an innovation schedule in place so that every quarter, at a minimum, they announce some additional innovation, product, or product upgrade, to drive sales of their products.

Well, if it is good enough for Apple, it should be good enough for you. What do we mean? Well, again, as Walt would say, your business must *Keep Moving Forward.* A commitment to innovation and refreshing your products and services drives sales. Failure to make that commitment, or to fail in your efforts to innovate, will ultimately lead to the demise of your business. *Keep Moving Forward.* How do we know? Let's look.

BLACKBERRY: THE ONE HIT WONDER

In 1999, my former spouse and I moved into our first new home together—well sort of. It was a condo. But it was cool. It was a beautiful two-story corner unit with towering ceilings and a wrap-around balcony that opened to the sky above. It was perfect for entertaining with a view over the Northern Virginia treetops. Moreover, it was strategically located near the Dunn Loring Metro station of the DC Metro's coveted Orange Line in Vienna, Virginia, making our home a short 20-minute train ride to downtown D.C. It was awesome!

At the time we had yet to have kids. But we had two cats. Two big, fat cats named Doc and Grumpy. Rescue kitties from the SPCA they had come from a liter of 7, and were thus named for the Seven Dwarfs of Walt Disney Fame. Never had a name been more appropriately bestowed than on poor Grumpy. That cat only liked three people. And because we had adopted them from the SPCA, they were fully armed with claws aplenty. And man did they use them.

On one infamous occasion, I was asleep on our leather couch, sitting upright. For whatever reason, I was not wearing a shirt. At some point, Doc and Grumpy decided to see if they could do some totally awesome skater tricks off my chest. To this day, I can recall the searing pain awakening me from Doc's rear claws, digging into my flesh as he launched himself off my pecks.

As my eyes popped open, I was just able to make out Grumpy, who I can only assume pulled the short straw, in midair tracking straight at me. Before I could react, in a kick trick that would have made the legendary Tony Hawk proud, fat cat number two was bouncing off my chest and, with claws fully extended, slicing my chest like a ribbon before bounding towards my bedroom.

After that incident, we decided the cats needed to expand their horizons, effectively, so they would not kill me. So, every night after dinner, we began letting them out in our 4th floor hallway to roam and release some energy. At first, they were quite timid. But after a while they would get out and start sprinting down the hallway, running like maniacs possessed.

Eventually, they began to gravitate towards one door. And when they would get there, far down the hallway, they would stop, akin to the famous road runner in the Looney Toons shorts, and head straight to that door. They would spend minutes, as long as we allowed them, rubbing themselves all over that door. We could never understand why. But admittedly, I even became curious as to why they were so obsessed with the door.

Well, there were only 8 apartments on the top floor. As such, it was easy to keep an eye out for your neighbors. At one point, a young couple got out of the elevator while the cats were roaming. They were about our age and were very nice. I said hello and quickly gathered my cats from down the hallway. As we passed, I noticed they were the ones! They stopped at the door and reached for their keys.

Well, as a friendly neighbor should, I quickly introduced myself. "Hi, I'm Matt from down the hallway." They smiled and introduced themselves as Shane and Shelly. I continued, 'I have to know, do you all have cats?" The nice, young couple looked curiously at me, "No, in fact, Shelly is very allergic to cats," Shane replied.

And in an instant, there it was, our cats had gone from doing gainers off my chest to trying to assassinate the only person allergic to cats in the entire building. Evil little bastards! Devious, evil little bastards.

But often, even a seemingly insignificant chance meeting can change your life. And although that chance encounter with Shane and Shelly occurred as a result of two evil felines, that introduction changed my life's direction forever. Here's how.

At the time, I was a personal injury attorney working at Koonz McKenney Johnson DePaolis & Lightfoot. Now, as I've said before, I worked for two of the greatest attorneys and mentors a guy could ever hope for. That being said, I was looking forward to making a change. We were coming off a year in which my family had lost, effectively, the entire oldest generation and eldest states persons of our clan, all in a single year! Not joking, it was like 8 or 9 deaths that year. It got so bad that every time the phone rang, and it was my parents, I just started to assume I'd be heading to the airport for a funeral.

Anyways, I was having a crisis of consciousness, living so far from my parents, and somehow reasoned that I wasn't living that far away from them just to be a local PI attorney. I had to chase a career of more national prominence. I was looking to make a change.

As the days and weeks progressed, we gradually became pretty good friends with Shane and Shelly. Now, before I go on, a little about Shane and Shelly. Two of the most wonderful people you could ever hope to meet. Both highly intelligent. Both are very successful. At the time, they were both working for the same prestigious law firm in their intellectual property and other technology law fields. To say I was intrigued is an understatement.

Listening about their practices, how, rather than suing people, they were helping their clients in the creative process, protecting what they created and not merely fighting over whether someone was injured in a 3-mph car bump—I mean, accident. This, I thought, was the kind of law in which I could help to build things, and not merely the fighting and redistribution side. To me, Shane and Shelly were like legal rock stars! And I wanted to join their band!

As a tech lawyer, Shane always had the latest and coolest gadgets. In particular, he always had this black calculator-looking device clipped to his belt. It had a full little keyboard, and, from time-to-time, he would unsnap it from his belt, look at it for a second or two, and then feverishly punch a bunch of the buttons with his thumb before clicking it back onto his belt. What the hell?

The first few times he did this, it passed right by me. But after a while, I began noticing that, moments before he would reach for his bat belt, I would hear a very faint buzz sound, as if something was vibrating. Wait a minute, was his belt vibrating? Was it a secret message from Alfred at the Batcave? Was the joker up to no good again? Was he Batman? No. It was just the latest and greatest in technology. It was, in fact, a first-generation BlackBerry. And I was in awe.

Here was this magical device that promised to free us from the office! It offered an innovative technology called "push technology" that allowed you to seamlessly send and receive your emails from this little hand-held device. It was a modern-day miracle! Of course, that freedom became more of a technological chain over time, which ironically kept you always connected to the office.

When BlackBerry's first launched, they instantly snapped up a huge market share. Why? Because they effectively created the market. Their innovation changed the way we do business. Business from anywhere. And it was good. But here is the problem. BlackBerry could never top their original innovation. And they tried. But no matter how hard they worked, others caught up to them and blew them away.

Again, the original technology—their big innovation—was email push technology. But guess what? A brief period later, some product called the iPhone produced the ability to send and receive emails as well. And the iPhone wasn't clunky. It had a beautiful color screen and added web browsing capabilities.

Suddenly, the BlackBerry looked old and out of step with the state of the market. BlackBerry tried to keep pace by adding a phone and later a web browser to various models of their products. But by that time, they were no longer innovators, and were in a losing battle with the far sleeker, cooler iPhone.

By the time the Android system entered the marketplace, it all but guaranteed the long, slow demise of BlackBerry. In short, they were a one-hit wonder who relied on that one hit push technology to keep them relevant forever. But as competitors entered the marketplace with newer and sleeker products incorporating push technology and other features, BlackBerry simply could not compete. In the end, their failure to continue to innovate in a hyper competitive and technologically evolving marketplace led to their demise.

So ends the lesson. No matter where you are, you must continue to innovate. You must always remember that, even if you are on top, someone else is aiming for you. And failing to innovate and launch those innovations will spell your demise.

YOU'RE EITHER GROWING OR YOUR DYING

But wait one second, I hear you saying. You are telling me how billion-dollar companies need to innovate to stay relevant. They need to have a schedule of innovations. But what if I'm small, a mom and pop, just starting out from my basement? Well, have a seat, because the answer remains: yes you do! But more importantly, yes you can!

Understand that innovation is not relegated to simply modifying or updating an existing product. Innovation can encompass so much more. For instance, innovation can be a new way to market to an existing consumer base, or even finding and marketing to a whole new group or potential customers. It could be re-marketing to existing customers an actual product upgrade ala Apple Computers. But if you are not seeking to innovate, you are satisfied with the status quo. And when that occurs, your business will begin to die. So, innovate and thrive!

You may have heard: I founded The Trademark Company in my Northern Virginia basement, in 2003. I posted my web site and waited for the customers to materialize. No paid advertising. Not much SEO. But in those days, online services were new and we did not have many competitors. So, who needed that then? Innovation 1.

Within a year, I realized that I wanted to focus on a specific subset of trademark law, namely litigation before the US Patent and Trademark Office's Trademark Trial and Appeal Board ("TTAB"). In that regard, I looked around to figure out who would have the most potential work to refer to me. Well, it didn't take too long for me to figure out who that would be.

A young attorney was at the top of his game and filing what was then considered to be a ton of trademarks per year. I reasoned, if he is filing the most trademarks per year, he must have the most trademark disputes per year. Reasonable assumption. Soon, I convinced him to send me all his trademark dispute work. Within a few years, I had one of the largest TTAB practices in the United States. Innovation 2.

But that work was limited to what I could do. It was too complicated to systemize. But back to the original plan: trademark filings. How to get more! And by now everyone knows about content marketing. But back then, circa 2010, it was used as a gimmick, a ploy, to keep your SEO high for your website. But what if I could use it to become a recognized expert in trademark prosecutions? What if I could become the trademark guy? So, I started looking for opportunities to author articles on trademarks, business principles, and related matters. Soon, I became a contributor to Inc. Magazine's online presence.

What started as a small gig turned into more than 50 articles on business, trademarks, intellectual property, and how to start and operate a small business. My articles were picked up by the likes of *Time, MSNBC, NBC, and The Wall Street Journal.* To this day, I can honestly say one of my proudest moments was picking up the Wall Street Journal and seeing my name quoted in the iconic paper. I still have a copy in my den.

I sought out any press that would publish what I would say. And, as you have already heard, I was coined Maverick for my efforts by a British magazine. But all of it was not for me. It was to simply get the word out about our services. And it did. By spreading the word of what you could do people reached out, in droves, and we began inching up the list of top trademark filers in the world. Innovation 3.

When you're playing with the house's money, why not double down? By this time, we are coming up on 2011. For years I had dreamed of a way to reach out to people in need of trademark assistance, even if they were not a current customer. If only there was a database, a repository, if you will, of all their names and addresses and even, the Holy Grail, email addresses! If only. Well, of course there was. It was called the US Patent & Trademark Office and, at the time, if you dug deep enough, you would realize that all their data was completely open and available for public consumption.

Knowing the concept was within my wheelhouse, but the technological solution was beyond it, I searched high and low for the perfect programmer to create my vision: a mirror image of the U.S. Patent & Trademark Office's database, whereby I could sub-program the system to send targeted emails to consumers in need of our services. Now, I cannot tell you for sure that we were the first ones to think of this. But I think we were. To this day, one of the greatest innovations propelling the growth of The Trademark Company. Innovation 4.

And, of course, there were the ones that were less creative, but innovative for us just the same. I always had a philosophy that no one marketing source should account for more than 10% of your inbound leads. To this end, our innovations often focused on marketing and expanding the reach of our services into new horizontal and vertical markets. Of course, the easiest was when we decided to simply up our budget for Google AdWords, aka pay-per-click marketing. Provided your cost structure is correct, it is a worthy investment. Innovation 5.

Let us not forget as you expand, look for affiliates and strategic partners that can re-sell your goods and services to their own clientele. In this regard, you effectively deputize additional sales force, without the need to increase your payroll. Innovation 6.

And it's never all about marketing. Along the way, we created software to assemble increasingly more complex legal documents by simply having our customers answer a few, simple questions in plain English. One of my other proudest moments occurred, ironically, in a hearing in front of a large commission, accusing the company of crossing the line and giving legal advice, which is the exclusive province of lawyers, even bad ones.

As mentioned before, they put one of our documents up on the big screen for all the lawyers in attendance to review. When they put it up, an audible gasp was heard throughout the room. Seriously, a freaking gasp. Then murmur. Murmur. Murmur. Yes, it was a reference to Steve Martin's classic *The Man with Two Brains!* All you could hear was them whispering to each other. And then, as if brought together by some force beyond our comprehension, in a unified voice they all cried out and said, "*There is no way a machine made these documents!*" And there is where they were wrong. It did. And it helped our customers to avoid high-priced legal fees every day. And it was good. And I was proud! And our customers were happy. Innovation 7.

These are just the ones I can remember. I'm sure there were tons more. And tweaks to each of these 7 along the way. But you don't have to be Apple to innovate. Innovation is not relegated to product innovation. And you certainly don't want to be BlackBerry. So, if you want to beat the curve and make it in the long run, once you're established, once the business is going, you can simply never, ever, be complacent. You must innovate. You must ask what's next. You must, in the words of the immortal Walt E. Disney,

Keep Moving Forward!

Chapter Summary: Add Consistent Innovation to Your Plan.

- **Create a Marketing & Innovation Schedule:** Create an innovation schedule, in which you launch some new initiative no less than twice per year. Not only will this keep you relevant in the marketplace, but it will also keep your company's name fresh in the media.
- **Innovate & Expand into Vertical & Horizontal Markets:** Involve your front-line employees to ascertain what innovations your consumer base would like to see and offer them those innovations as part of your innovation schedule.
- **Bring to Market. Repeat.** Once you have your innovation, shamelessly market it, and the rest of your services, and repeat the whole process again and again, satisfying your company's innovation schedule.

Additional Suggested Reading:

The Ten Faces of Innovation, Tom Kelley, 2005

What Got You Here Won't Get You There, Marshall Goldsmith, 2007

CAPTAIN YOUR SHIP

Determine Your Leadership Style. Lead. Prepare for the Storm.

THE ESSENTIAL INGREDIENT: LEADERSHIP

So far, we have talked about creating your product, making sure there is a demand for it, marketing it, creating systems to run and scale your business, and how to hire and train others to do so. So many people think that this is enough. That once you create it, they will come, and that you just sit back and watch the money roll in. Well, it's not. And I'm here to tell you: if you're not prepared to lead your business to greatness, or have someone who can, no matter what your product, your business will be destined to fail. So, let's dive into the next thing you'll need to have to make a successful business: leadership.

THE SHARKS

The music comes up. "Next up, we have John. John has created a product that will revolutionize the nose hair trimming industry!" We watch John walk through a dark- paneled hallway filled with LCD aquariums displaying sharks swimming. The doors open and there, like a scene from a movie, are five stern-looking individuals waiting to hear John's big idea.

The camera cuts to a new angle as John begins to address the panel. "Hello sharks. My name is John Smith. Have you ever accidentally lopped off your nose while trying to sheer your nose hair with hedge trimmers? This can be a painful and embarrassing issue that is happening all too often in our society. But I have invented a product that will revolutionize the nose hair trimming industry and save thousands of noses in the process. I present to you .... *SafetySheers*!"

So, unless you've been living in a cave for the past 10 years, or your data service is provided by Verizon, you know I'm talking about the hit television series Shark Tank. Every week, entrepreneurs present their products to a panel of five hyper-successful fellow entrepreneurs-turned-investors in hopes of securing additional capital for their fledgling companies and, more importantly, mentorship from one or more of the Sharks.

Who are these sharks? Well, some rotate in and out, but for the most part they are Kevin O'Leary, aka Mr. Wonderful, a Canadian tech entrepreneur who sold one of his original companies for millions. Robert Herjavec, another Canadian tech entrepreneur who founded and sold a cybersecurity company to AT&T for millions. Daymond John, the founder and CEO of the FUBU clothing brand. Barbara Corcoran, founder of The Corcoran Group, a real estate brokerage company in New York which she later sold for millions. Lori Greiner, an inventor and entrepreneur known colloquially as the Queen of QVC. And Mark Cuban, a tech mogul perhaps best known for his ownership of the NBA's Dallas Mavericks.

So back to the show. There are a few things the Sharks are looking for every time and, if you do not have them, you will not get a deal. First, you must have proof of concept. In other words, you must have a product that will sell, and which generally has had some track record of sales to show that there is, in fact, a market for the same.

Second, know your numbers. What are your margins? What are your production costs? What is your gross and net profit? You must be able to discuss these with ease from a place of knowledge.

Third, and equally as important, do you have passion, and the ability to lead the company you are asking them to invest in? Often this final criterion gets overlooked, but the Sharks are experts in their respective fields, and are very aware of what they will bring as an investor to a fledgling company. Not only are they investing their capital, but also their time and expertise in the person in front of them. In short, although they are investing in your company, they are also investing in you!

You see, the Sharks don't have time to run other companies. They're largely investors at this point. What they need are proven leaders to invest in who present profitable ideas, and are able to lead with minimal assistance. Simple enough. But whether you are seeking capital from a Shark or simply managing your own slice of the American dream, it's your job to captain your ship. It's your job to build a profitable business. It's your job to lead your start-up to greatness. How? Let's look at 6 different leadership styles you must become familiar with to get to where you want to be.

THE 6 STYLES OF LEADERSHIP

The Harvard Business Review has defined six leadership styles used by industry leaders. I know what you're probably thinking, come on, just tell me the best one so I can get on with it. Well, if you've read this far, you know I won't make it that easy. But here's the rub. In all candor, there is no one style that is the best. Wait, what? Let me say it again. There is no one style that is the best. Why? you may ask.

Leadership, and in particular styles of leadership, are often dependent on the situations faced by the leader. As such, to truly master captaining your ship, you must understand this concept and respect other leaders' styles, apart from yours, when dealing with diverse circumstances you may never have imagined. What am I talking about? Well, let's take a very personal look.

In 2017, the company was struggling. As was fleshed out earlier, most of our sales team had quit. Sprinkle in a few regulatory investigations as well as some personal drama, and I was working my ass off just to keep the business afloat, and my life together. Why do I mention this? Because it's OK to understand that we all struggle at some point. And sometimes you need someone who has been through the fire to light the way.

At the time, I was close with someone who had a very different corporate experience. They had been handed a large budget, a pile of money, and told to create a product from scratch within a larger, very successful entity, with the luxury of startup capital. In short, they needed a completely different type of leadership. One that had the luxury of time. One that had the luxury of having funding. One that had little to no pressure.

However, at that time, my experience was completely different. While I needed to keep an iron fist on every aspect of my business, and couldn't afford the luxury of dissension in the ranks, she was free of the pressures of surviving day-to-day. Unfortunately, rather than recognizing the distinctions between our two situations and understanding what was needed in each, she would malign my leadership style at every turn. Constant berating. Constant criticism. It became intolerable. Candidly, dealing with her daily beatings became almost more difficult than steering my company through the troubled waters itself. And, for a time, I almost began to believe the poison that would spew forth from her mouth each time we saw each other. Almost.

But, as you should know by now, I will always find the positive in almost any situation. After a year or so of this bashing, I found myself in the San Francisco International Airport, returning from an unpleasant albeit successful business trip that was part of the company's survival. While killing time waiting for my flight home, and exhausted from my day, I stumbled into the local airport bookstore in search of some light reading for my five-hour flight back to happy town.

As I sorted through all the drivel, a bright yellow book on the shelf caught my eye. The title? *On Leadership*, by the Harvard Business Review. Harvard Business Review, I thought, sounds intriguing. I mean, after all, it is Harvard. These guys must know what they are talking about, right? Not like it was from Princeton.

I bought the book and threw it in my bag to start reading on the trip home. It was classic red-eye, leaving SFO to RDU at around 9:30 pm PDT. I figured, a couple Jack and Cokes, turn a few pages, and welcome sleepy time. I'd wake up when I felt the wheels touching down at my beloved RDU.

Well, sometimes our best laid plans don't work out as we think. I mean, I settled into my chair on the United flight. The stewardess got my first adult beverage to me moments later. As I sipped my reward for a successful trip, contemplating the shitstorm that had enveloped me and the company for the preceding few years, and all that I had done to keep moving forward, I reached into my bag and pulled out my new purchase, *On Leadership*, by the Harvard Business Review.

What I thought would be a quick and easy one-way ticket to snoozeville turned into something slightly different. Within a few pages I was hooked. I mean, I could not put the book down. That night, I learned about the different styles of leadership, why they work in certain circumstances and why they fail in others. I learned that what I had done in the early years of the company was a perfect leadership style then, but when the shit hit the fan, my transition to another style was completely warranted. I learned that I was not wrong in the things I was doing, although there was always room for improvement. And finally, I learned that the person who was beating up over my leadership style simply lacked the knowledge to know there is more than one style of leadership, and different circumstances require different styles.

Rather than being gently awakened by the wheels touching down at RDU roughly 5 hours after our departure, I was just finishing and reviewing my notes when we landed. Tired, I was re-invigorated with the knowledge that, according to those guys at Harvard, I was doing it right. And feeling sorry for the basher I would soon be seeing. Perhaps she should try to read a book as opposed constantly hurling negativity towards me as I captained my ship. I stepped off that plane knowing I had this. And you know what, I did!

Understand now that there is no one leadership style as you run your business. Rather, there are, according to those guys at Harvard, six different styles, each of which can work. So, without further ado, here's my take on those styles.

The Authoritative

First up, we have the Authoritative style of leadership. The Authoritative leader inspires and mobilizes people towards a common vision. Creating that new and innovative product that will allow people to store thousands of songs in the palm of their hand. Or perhaps transforming the way people search for information by providing an online search platform that categorizes every piece of information ever assembled, making it searchable and readily accessible. Steve Jobs successfully utilized this style in creating products for Apple that revolutionized the way we live our lives. Not to be outdone, Larry Paige and Sergi Brinn did the same thing with a little search engine called Google. Ever heard of them?

In short, I have a vision. We are going to change the world. Come along, and let's do it together!

If you can adopt this leadership style, it's great for when your company has a strong vision and can inspire others to believe in and help you to reach that goal. However, other styles may be better suited when, for instance, dealing with a crisis, or if your company is saturated with employees who are simply interested in a day-to-day paycheck and not at all in your vision.

The Affiliative

Next, we have the Affiliate style of leadership. Affiliate leaders lead by creating team harmony and emotional bonds primarily through team bonding exercises such as trips, dinners out and other blatant misdirection from the day-to-day monotony of the work environment.

When properly done, the lines between work and home life begin to blur to the point that employees become more and more dedicated to their work and less and less dedicated to spending time away from work. Again, why do you think Google provides world-class chefs, dry cleaning, and all the perks they do for their workers? Because, in the end, they blur the line so much between work and home that the workers end up never leaving and working more. Brilliant!

In short, work is fun! I'm a cool boss. We go on trips. I buy you drinks. And along the way, we get some work done!

If you can adopt this leadership style, it's great for when you have start-up capital or a budget to keep your people misdirected, and happy with the perks of the job. A significant challenge with this style, however, is that many employees will eventually get bored of the perks or, heaven forbid, something changes in the workplace (e.g., COVID lockdowns, budget issues) causing those perks to evaporate. If you solely rely on this leadership style when you face those challenges, your team may abandon ship when the perks evaporate, rather than rolling up their sleeves and helping you out of the crisis.

The Coach

Moving on, we have the Coach. The Coach-style of leadership focusing on individual attention to your subordinates and works to develop people for the future. It is a positive, mentoring-type of style which, if successful, leads to strong bonds between the coach and the mentee. In today's world, this is a valuable style, as today many younger employees are interested in their own personal development.

In short: Teach me, master. Teach me the ways of the force! OK, maybe not the force, but you get the idea.

If you can adopt this leadership style, it is great for when you have employees that value personal development and moving forward in your organization. However, if you do not have upward mobility in your company due to size limitations, or if your employees are simply not interested in personal growth, avoid this style of leadership.

The Coercive

The Coercive leader demands immediate compliance with his orders. Generally, this is viewed as a negative management style, like barking out orders to a crew and having them instantly, and mindlessly, obey. But this style is the hands-down favorite when captaining your ship through a crisis. Of note, it is imperative that, once you use this style to move through the crisis, one should generally move back into an Affiliate, Authoritative, or even Coaching style to move from a negative to a positive, prospective leadership style.

In short, the ship is sinking! Bail! Bail! Bail! Don't ask questions, I said bail!

Every leader must have this style in their repertoire. Why? Because, as we will discuss below, sooner or later it will all go sideways. And, as humans, it is our nature not to look past the immediate but to believe: this is it! Having the ability to shift into a coercive style of leadership will provide you with the tools to get through a crisis when it eventually happens. After all, anyone can captain a ship on calm waters. But a true captain knows that, when the storm comes, one no longer has the luxury of employing another style of leadership.

The Democratic

The Democratic leader drives a consensus through participation. In short, this form of management will go around the board table and ask everyone in the room their respective opinions. It is a positive style of leadership, but unless you employee a highly educated team, beware that this style often leads to endless meetings, without defined results.

In short, what do you think? And you? And how about you? Oh, almost forgot, and you as well?

Often, it is best to use a watered-down version of this. For instance, an Affiliative or Authoritative style that asks for the opinions of your subordinates but ultimately makes the decision largely based upon your own thought process. But this, too, can be dangerous, because if half your employees polled come down on the opposite side of an issue, you truly risk alienating them when you move forward with your decision.

The Pacesetter

And finally, we have the Pacesetter. The Pacesetter sets high standards for performance, and uses negative tactics to achieve those goals at all costs. I like to call it the 80s style of management.

In short, we have a revenue target. We will work until whatever time tonight until we hit it. If we don't hit it tonight, see you at 7 am Saturday morning!

This is a style of leadership that has truly faded in the last few years. Early in my career, I recall working for bosses who were Pacesetters. There was never motivation to hit your numbers, except for the hitting of the numbers themselves. You weren't helping the greater good. Hell, half the time you weren't even bettering yourself. You were just given a number for the company and told to hit that number, or else. Who knows if this style will survive as millennials become our middle managers and eventually higher-level executives.

SO, WHICH IS THE BEST?

It depends. It really does. And everyone must figure that out for themselves. However, there appears to be a growing consensus that a combination of the Authoritative and Affiliate styles, if you can afford it, works best truly to motivate your team and unify them to work towards a common goal. Sprinkle in a little of the Coaching style for those employees that want personal growth, and be ready with the Coercive for when it all hits the fan. Coming full circle, The Trademark Company is a perfect micro example of how this all comes into play.

In 2009 I hired my first 2 full-time employees. From their initial interviews, they were hit with an Authoritative leadership style. I preached to them about what The Trademark Company was going to be, how it would change the marketplace for legal services forever, and our overriding vision of finally making top caliber legal services available for all.

Almost immediately, we also utilized the Affiliate leadership style. Beginning with little things like Wednesday Bagels, it soon stretched to lunches and dinners out, birthday limousines, and trips to Las Vegas. One summer, we hosted office "dinner parties," with food and drinks from different countries every other week. Fridays we always closed for Pours at Four. For a long time, it was a fun party atmosphere, filled with high performing individuals.

Along the way, I added elements of Coaching as well, for those who wanted it. Trying to impart my years of knowledge into my more dedicated employees.

Somewhat painfully, from 2013 to 2016, when the seas got rough, we had to tighten our belts, and the Affiliative style had to take something of a hiatus. There was a loss of focus on the Authoritative style as we reached the pinnacle of our industry, and lacked a little direction. Add in a few more challenges, and soon we were in a downward spiral. This forced me to quickly shift to the Coercive style to right the ship. But, as we mentioned before, employees who have come aboard with the Authoritative or Affiliate style often do not want to hang around when, or if, you shift to the Coercive. And this can often compound the original issue.

Well, in our case, we came very close to going down. But adopting that Coercive style, we slowly began to build it back. Brick by brick, we built it back. Today, the company is not only at its largest it has ever been, but is also the healthiest it has ever been from a financial perspective. Our culture is strong, and only growing stronger. But that could not have been possible without weaving together several different styles of leadership and, more importantly, knowing when to use the various forms to ensure growth, but also the continuity of the business.

I would be remiss if I did not offer a postscript on my friend who was so critical of my journey as she moved through hers. After all, the purpose of this book is to teach you from our triumphs and our failures so that you can learn, and retain, a wealth of knowledge that has taken me a lifetime to acquire, while helping more than 100,000 businesses to get their start.

So again, recall I had mentioned the person I was close with at the time The Trademark Company endured its growing pains between 2013 to 2016, or 2017? Well, she and her boss (you may recall the name, Little Stanley) and their company, CostLandhouse-AndHoopers, had simply given them a boatload of cash to create a software package to manage human assets as they moved from country to country. Huh? Wait, what?

OK, follow me on this. When you are a global company that employs thousands throughout the world, from time to time you have a short-term project that requires, let's say, 30 accountants to fly from New Delhi to London. Well, when this occurs, there are tax ramifications. Where do they have to pay employment taxes? Does this affect whether the India partnership must pay taxes in the UK? What about Visas? Oh, and the big tamale: is CostLandhouse-AndHoopers one global entity, or a series of smaller unaffiliated partnerships that just happen to all work together under the same management structure? Hmm.

So, while I was shifting into a Coercive leadership style, she was living la vida loca, flying to London, Germany, India, Hong Kong in business and first class to wine and dine, and be wined and dined by the partners of all these various locales.

And I know what you're thinking. But Mav? How did she squeeze in time to berate you as you tirelessly attempted to galvanize support from others to help you bail out your ship? Don't worry. She found the time. Each weekend, before hitting the road again to another far off destination in one of those business-class seats, she'd squeeze in time to belittle me mercilessly. It got to the point that sometimes I'd think that's all she flew in for.

But here's where karma, but, more importantly, a failure in leadership, caught up with her. Well, if you recall from above, little Stanley was shown the door, I mean "retired," from CostLandhouseAndHoopers, in the Summer of 2019. Well, that Affiliate style of leadership just wasn't as fun without little Stanley. We'll just let that soak in for a bit, for those of you who are good at reading between the lines.

Well, my friend soldiered on into the Fall of 2019 and beyond. And then it happened. This little thing called COVID. Perhaps you've heard of it? It got a little bit of press here in the U.S. Anyways, by January 2020, the world was in full shut- down mode. First China, then Europe, and finally, the United States. I mean, not all the U.S. What's up, Florida? #Science. As the great astrophysicist Neil Degrasse Tyson would say, it was like having a designated pee zone in a swimming pool. If you don't get it, you probably live in Florida.

A style of leadership that relied almost exclusively on the Affiliate, and making their people happy with trips, dinners, and similar perks, could do nothing as all that suddenly vanished almost overnight. No longer could the team travel. No longer could they spend weeks away from their families, enjoying all the perks of the best restaurants around the globe. They, and their leadership style, were literally grounded. But wait, there's more!

Remember the point of their software? What were they doing in the first place? Creating software to manage cross-border travel for their employees? Hmmmmm. Wonder if a global pandemic that literally shuts down countries' borders affected the demand for that software? Read on young padawans, read on!

Once COVID hit, the ability to move employees from one location to another literally vanished, almost overnight, and so too did the need for that software. As various offices canceled their orders, and participation in the plan, others no longer saw the need for it. As their internal inbound revenues fell, so too did CostLandhouse-AndHoopers' overall revenues. Budgets tightened, and they lost a significant amount of their funding.

I can still recall one of our last conversations as COVID struck the world and her budget had been slashed. It had been months since she truly last spoke to me. As she sat there, her gaze was distant, a gaze I knew all too well. It was the look of a captain shell shocked and unsure of what to do as her ship had sprung a leak, and was beginning its inevitable slip below the surface of the sea. If you recall James Cameron's movie *Titanic*, it's the look of Captain Edward Smith as he realized that, no matter what he did, his boat would eventually founder. It is a look of disbelief. It is a look of impending doom. It is a look of hopelessness. It is a look of fear.

She opened her mouth, never looking at me, but maintaining her far off gaze into the unforeseen distance, and uttered, "I'll be laying off most of my team in the coming days", tacitly acknowledging the calamity of the global pandemic and its effect on her software product. With all that we had been through, it was difficult not to feel empathy for her on some level. And having been down the road I knew she was now on, and despite how she had treated me as my ship sprang a leak, I knew what lay before her. I offered her a few kind words of encouragement, and began my day.

A few days later, she moved out of the house, ending our 23-year marriage, and laid off most of her team as her ship began to sink.

I debated whether to include this personal of a story in the book. But, in the end, it serves a valuable lesson for this chapter and far beyond. First, it highlights the fact that no one leadership style is appropriate for all situations. And I could think of no better story than this one to include to make this point.

Second, and more subtly, when you are on top of your mountain, understand it may only be temporary. Others may have a completely different experience. Don't malign them. Reach back, give them a hand, help them to climb their own mountain. Sooner or later, we all need that support. And, as a new business owner, you may as well. So always be willing to give someone else a hand.

Be supportive. Be empathetic. Because someday it may be you. But with the proper utilization of these leadership styles, you will ensure your greatest chance of continued success, and success for your business. How do I know? Sit back and take a listen. Because here's the full version of what happened to The Trademark Company.

CAPTAIN YOUR SHIP

There was a time when I thought you could open a business, systemize everything, hire the right people, then just sit back and watch the money roll in. Nothing could be further from the truth. That's not to take anything away from our earlier discussion on systemization, and building a business as if it were to be franchised. But even when everything is systemized, it is built to scale, your hiring process perfected and your training impeccable, you will still always need one additional critical element to make your business a success: leadership.

Just like a ship without a captain, a business cannot reach its destination without solid leadership. Imagine what would happen if you left port on a ship without a captain. Even on the grandest and most modern of vessel, you still need a captain. If not, who would decide where the ship was going? Who would give the commands to throw the lines and set the course? Who would make the critical decisions that enable the vessel to sail from one port to another?

It's no different in business. Even if you have the best business model in the history of business models, you still must lead your team to success. Keeping the team focused on a common goal. Ensuring employee and customer satisfaction. Making sure the direction of the business stays sound and the goals of the company are met. To this end, in addition to the other principals expounded in this Chapter and, to a larger degree, in this book, here are ten critical principals you must incorporate into your leadership style to maximize your leadership effectiveness:

THE MAVERICK METHOD'S TOP 10 LEADERSHIP PRINCIPLES

1. YOU DON'T HAVE FREEDOM OF SPEECH

In the 1997 movie *Air Force One*, Harrison Ford stars as U.S. President James Marshall completing a good will trip to Moscow amid heightening tensions that a separatist, imprisoned former Soviet general is threatening to start a new cold war, should he be able to seize control of the Russian military. During the U.S. delegation's last night in Moscow, President Marshall steps to the podium and, as part of a larger speech, delivers this speech:

And tonight, I come to you with a pledge to change America's policy. Never again will I allow our political self-interests to deter us from doing what we know to be morally right. Atrocity and terror are not political weapons. And to those who would use them: Your day is over. We will never negotiate. We will no longer tolerate, and we will no longer be afraid. It's your turn to be afraid.

As he makes the impassioned speech, the camera cuts to the President's Chief of Staff and National Security Advisor in the audience. A look of disbelief crosses their faces. End scene.

As they depart in the Presidential motorcade for Air Force One the National Security Advisor and Chief of Staff address the President. As they express their concern, and although it's unscripted, once it comes from the President of the United States' mouth, it becomes policy. And we wonder why a real President perhaps should have some form of filter, or thought process, or common sense. But I digress.

The point, however, is as simple as it is important: the leader of an organization does not have freedom of speech! What, what? But it's my company? What gives?

From the onset, understand that anything that comes out of your mouth, your employees will remember. Anything that comes out of your mouth, your employees will hold you to your word. Anything that comes out of your mouth is policy.

For instance, I have often spoken about our company's 10-year anniversary trip to Vegas. And while what happens in Vegas stays in Vegas, I can tell you the origins of why we went to Vegas fit right in with this concept.

On a given night in early 2013, a certain boss may have taken some employees out for a happy hour. OK, it was me. At the time we were celebrating the end of another great sales month, so much revelry was afoot. Well, in all candor, this boss may have had a little too much revelry. As the night progressed, the topic of the company's 10-year anniversary kept surfacing.

Well, a little more revelry, and some more, then some shots of revelry. Next thing you knew, this boss had promised to take the whole damn company to Vegas, Baby! Well, once the revelry wore off and the sun rose the next day, the employees of the company recalled with surgical precision every detail of this mega trip to Vegas the boss had promised. At that point, he had a choice: shrug it off and say something like *We'll see,* which would have deflated the whole mood of the office and cast doubt on his ability to make good on his promises. In the alternative, he could live up to his revelry-fueled promises and keep his employees churning with the promise of that well-deserved vacation.

What did he do? Well, by now you know, I—I mean, he—flew the company to Vegas. Because it came out of his mouth, it was policy.

But not every example and every situation involve promises made under the influence of revelry. In fact, if they do, call AA today! No. It's the little things that you must guard against. Discussions about salary increases, benefits, work expectations. Recall, if it comes out of your mouth, it is policy.

Unlike others, when running a business, you DO NOT HAVE FREEDOM OF SPEECH. You must choose your words wisely and, once they emanate from your mouth, you must stick by them, always.

2. COMPLAIN UP

The military chain of command is used to issue orders downward, and to ask for clarification and resolve problems, upward. The chain of command is such an integral part of military life that officers and the enlisted alike are required to memorize their basic training chain of command within the first week or two of arrival. The chain of command recognizes, in its very structure, a basic element of leadership that is integral to the morale of the unit: never complain down!

As a leader, your role is, in part, to maintain an air of control and knowledge sufficient to inspire your troops to confidently follow you into battle, whether literally or figuratively. Nothing destroys that confidence more quickly than a person in a leadership role who complains down. Let's look at a few examples of what I mean.

Example 1: CEO Complaining to Employee about Their Manager: In this example, our CEO is displeased with his sales manager's performance. Rather than addressing the sales manager directly, the CEO speaks in a negative tone about the sales manager's performance to other employees in the company, including employees that are directly under the sales manager's chain of command. In this instance, no matter the reason for the complaint, it damages the company and undermines confidence in the organization for several reasons.

First, the employee is being told by the CEO that the CEO themselves believes their direct supervisor is ineffective, or simply not a good employee. As such, no matter the reason for the complaint down, it has the practical effect of undermining that manager to their direct employee, reducing their effectiveness even further because the employee, having heard negative things from the CEO himself, will now openly question whether they want to work for such an ineffective person, and it will even lead them to question directives issued by the manager.

Second, in this situation, many employees will also question then if the sales manager is so bad, as CEO why have you not addressed this with the sales manager? And, in turn, by complaining to the employee about middle-management, our CEO is, somewhat unknowingly, eroding the confidence in their own abilities, as many employees will thus question why they would continue to work for a CEO that sees issues in his ranks but fails to address them directly by training or removing the sales manager. In short, only complain up.

Example 2: Middle Manager Complaining to their Employee about the CEO: In our next example we look at a slightly different but equally damaging scenario: the middle manager complaining to their employees about the CEO. What does this accomplish? First, as before, it undermines the morale of the troops because they are being told, in essence, that this is a bad place to work by their direct supervisors, because he or she does not believe in the CEO. So, what purpose does this serve except for momentary gratification? None. But the damage is significant.

Second, it undermines the belief in the complaining middle manager, as most employees will then ask the question: Well, why should I follow you, if you are not intelligent enough to work for someone you respect? So, as we can see very clearly, no matter where in the chain the complaining occurs, you simply never complain down, period!

So where does this leave us? Well, you've heard the time-honored expression "*It's Lonely at The Top*"? Guess what? Now you know why. Because leaders do not have freedom of speech, and a good leader does not complain down. So, assuming your organization exists in a standard pyramid-type structure, as most do, the higher up you get the fewer people there are that you can truly converse with. And if you're at the pinnacle of your organization, guess what? There's no one else above you. So, zip the complaints, listen to those that come up the chain of command, and address them. But as the leader, your job is to address the complaints on the way, while never sending them down.

3. PLAN AND EXECUTE IN SILENCE

For better or for worse, we are living in the social media era. Thirty years ago, keeping up with the proverbial Joneses would only be thrust into your face from time-to-time when you drove past a certain fancy neighborhood, or saw a neighbor driving around in their new Cadillac. I can recall fondly my parents telling the story about one of our neighbors in North Palm Beach, Florida. He was a successful orthodontist, and his wife was a wonderful domestic goddess. They were always very modest, until he finally could afford the big new Caddy for his lovely wife. But as the story goes, she drove that thing around for 6 months, never removing the new car price tag sticker on the rear window, letting everyone know she had her "new" caddy.

But today it's thrust at you on Facebook, Instagram, Snapchat and I'm sure tons of other outlets I'm too old to know about. Not so subtle stuff. For instance, one of my buddies loves to post pictures of the autumn leaves in front of his house. Of course, you see like one scrawny tree in front of his Ferrari and 10,000-square-foot mansion. Sigh. OK, we get it, you're doing well. And we also all get the fact the "Fall Leaves" are just a pretense for "Let me show off my shit".

In business, however, you can never afford the luxury of falling into this trap. It's so easy to get caught up in what everyone else is doing that, the next thing you know, you start posting on things that you're doing and, sometimes, are even planning to do. If you're not careful, you can even slide into the trap of posting things you are working on but have yet to complete, all to gain kudos from your online friends and family.

When you feel like you are about to do this, stop, think about why you are doing it, and simply don't post it.

Why?

It's normal to seek encouragement and praise in life. It's natural to seek kudos from those around us. But it is better to plan and execute in silence and let them hear about your success than waste time boasting about your plans which may, or may not, ever come to fruition. So rather than spending time posting on social media about what you are going to do, spend that time executing your plan. And when it hits it big, they'll know. They'll know.

So don't brag about the person you want to become. Rather, go out and focus, in silence, on becoming the person you are bragging about.

4. NO ONE CARES

The next lesson is a hard one, but very important to being a leader. No one cares. Wait, what? No, someone must care. OK, maybe someone, but most don't. Accept this fact today.

In your life, you may have a handful of people who care about you and whether you win or lose in business and your personal affairs. For most of us, these are maybe your parents, a few family members, your kids, and maybe one or two close friends. Believe it or not, that's about it. Sure, when something goes wrong in your life, most of your friends and family will express remorse for you, but they will move on. They will not be affected by it.

A few years back, a friend of mine had some regulatory challenges with his business. From most outsiders' perspective, including the international press that covered the investigation, he was being targeted by this agency trying to shut his business down in almost a malicious fashion. Although the allegations against him were not uncommon, against others they involved a quick and easy settlement of the allegations, with a minor slap on the wrist. In his case, however, they refused to even discuss resolution of the issues, in which the discussion did not end at him shuttering his doors for good. For a while, he was unsure as to whether those challenges would end the business. The investigation took an immense toll on his personal and professional life.

In the end, he and the business survived, but not before the agency had gotten their pound and a half of flesh. Defending their antics cost him a small personal fortune, affecting the way the business conducted its affairs to the point that customer service, and the product, suffered for a year or two while dealing with those wonderful bureaucrats.

After the investigation had concluded, at one point he took a customer service call from an old customer who had been with the company for years. During the investigation, the customer lamented that he had received a service from the company that, in candor, was not up to par with what had always been its standard. As my friend explained to the customer while remedying his issue, it had been a long few years, and the reason for the issue was due to the frivolous investigation. My friend remedied the customer's issue, thanked him for being a loyal customer, and went about his way.

The next day, his sales manager came to him and alerted him to a new 1-star rating on-line that had popped up overnight. It was none other than the customer with whom he had spoken the day before. The customer had left a scathing, 1-star review, despite having had a perfect experience with the company for 10 years, and then the one issue that was remedied the day before. My friend showed me the review.

The customer never mentioned the 10 years of wonderful service. The customer never mentioned the remedy that completely fixed the issue at hand. All that the customer mentioned was the issue that had led to the conversation and my friend's explanation as to why the malicious investigation had caused the hardship. At the end of his 1-star review, the customer left the ominous admonition to my friend concerning the reason for the 1-star: "*No One Cares!*"

And he was right. No one cares why you had some difficulty in your life. No one cares why the business is struggling. Why? Because excuses never paid a bill and customers expect—and deserve—what they pay for. So, if you've had it rough, never think, not even for a minute, that anyone wants to hear your sob story. Again, use that time not to complain about the past, but to work on your future.

5. GUARD YOUR TIME

Did you know there's only 24 hours in a day? I know. I know. Seems obvious, right? But no matter how hard you try, no matter what you do, there will always be just 24 hours in a day. But here's a bit of encouragement. Those 24 hours, well, they're the same for everyone. Elon Musk has the same 24 hours as you. Jeff Bezos. The same. Bill Gates. Ditto. Richard Branson. Also 24 hours. And look at what they've been able to accomplish with their time.

Elon, from computer programming and payment gateways to Tesla, and now SpaceX and the colonization of Mars. Jeff changed retail forever, creating the most dominant online marketplace in history. Bill, well, there's that whole Microsoft thing. And let's not sleep on Sir Richard who, as I write this, is boarding a space plane on his Virgin Galactic brand, heading to space after creating one of the most successful record labels, airlines, hotels and cruise lines in history. And here's the double-edged sword on this reality: they did it all with the same 24 hours a day you have had! So, what have you been up to? And remember, no excuses! They're the easiest thing in the world. Results are what matters.

A few years back at The Trademark Company, we developed our 10 Rules for Sales Success that are now posted on the walls of our offices, as well as repeatedly referred to in all sales meetings. Number 4, added by Brian—an amazing sales professional, and great guy—was simple but critical to both sales and life as an entrepreneur: Guard Your Time! What did he mean?

Most people major in minor things. In life you will have those things that are important and those that are not. Those things that are urgent and those that are not. And the concept that we preach here is not revolutionary. It's rather just a simple reminder: never confuse urgency with importance. Wait, what? Let me say it again for you all sitting in the back: Never confuse urgency with importance!

So many of us get caught up in letting other people set our priorities. Coming to us, expecting us to drop everything when they have something that they consider to be urgent. Then they try to rope you into their "urgent" matter, demanding immediate compliance. Why? It's not their fault, *per se*. It may be the most important thing they are dealing with now. But it should not reorganize your priorities. Those are set by you, and you alone. They do not know what is on your plate. Only you do. So, as Brian would say, you've got to guard your time.

So, when prioritizing your day, I suggest the following simple order of things as to how to conduct your activities:

1. Important / Urgent
2. Important / Non-Urgent
3. Non-Important / Urgent
4. Non-Important / Non-Urgent

Let's look at this in practice.

Let's say you are opening a fast-food franchise, and you are presented with four things on your to-do list today. First, we have the bookkeeper who is demanding an answer on which bills to pay for bills that are not due for another 30-days. Second, your first franchise is making money and you'd like to set a plan for how to open additional restaurants under the same model. Third, a new paper napkin provider has requested a meeting to show you how they can save you 1 cent per 100 napkins used with their new model. And finally, a grease fire has just erupted on your griddle and your employees are having difficulties extinguishing the same. How do you handle these four "priorities"?

First up has got to be the grease fire. The grease fire is both important, as it will burn the restaurant down if not extinguished, but also urgent as, well, it's a fire! I hope I don't have to go into this one in too much depth. Most people will quip they were putting out fires all day. In our example, putting out the fire for you was literal and not figurative!

Skipping ahead: last up, we have our poor napkin supplier. Sorry, but at that level of savings, his offer is neither important nor urgent. Poor guy will probably be looking for another job soon. I wonder if he can operate a fryer.

Moving on, what takes our number 2 slot? You guessed it, the franchise plan! Because although it is not urgent, it is important. And you must set time aside to work on important things every day. That is the building of the business that so many entrepreneurs lose focus upon while being caught in the false trap of urgency imposed upon them by others.

So, clumsy segue warning: why is the franchise plan more important than the accountant, asking which bills to pay that are due in 30 days? Because it's 30 days! Although this may be the most important thing to the accountant, there's really no need to pay bills if the restaurant is burned to the ground, right? So clearly the grease fire takes precedence. But also, we must prioritize the franchise plan and building of the business above the false urgency of the accountant. If not, you will never build anything. And herein is the classic example of GUARD YOUR TIME. The accountant wants to take it away from you, for something that is truly not urgent, but they are trying to force it upon you and steal your time from business development, because it's urgent to them. Guard Your Time!

So, if you're scoring at home or, if you're alone, the order I would have suggested utilizing your 24 hours as follows:

1. Grease Fire, as it is both Important and Urgent.
2. Franchise Plan, as it is Important even if not non-Urgent.
3. Dealing with stressed-out Accountant, as it is not truly Important, but they are making it Urgent.

4. Lastly, our Napkin guy should only get time if literally everything else above is done, as it is both Non-Important and Non-Urgent.

By the way, this is just an example. As an entrepreneur, you will undoubtedly have way more than four things a day to worry about. Learn to love it and guard your time. One of the principles you must learn early on is that someone else's failure to plan should never constitute your emergency! Also, the above was just an example. Pay your bills. Pay them on time. But what's important is the accountant asked to pay bills that are due in 30 days, not the bills themselves. Hard to run a restaurant these days without electricity and water.

Guard your time!

6. SET GOALS. TAKE MASSIVE ACTION. WORK YOUR ASS OFF.

Two of my favorite motivational speakers on the planet are former California Governor and mega action star Arnold Schwarzenegger and the now iconic motivational coach, Tony Robbins. Now, as you're already aware from Chapter 7 in the book, former Governor Schwarzenegger is pretty much the greatest body builder of all time. He parlayed that into a blockbuster movie career. And later, with fortune and fame in hand, he successfully ran for the governorship of the great state of California, or, as Arnold would say, "Kuleyfornia." It's a phonetic accent thing.

Now, we'll soon learn more about Tony Robbins, but unless you've been living under a rock for the past decade, you probably know the man, the myth, the legend. Arguably the most famous motivational speaker and life coach of all time, Tony combines his unwavering positivity and seemingly endless energy to coach millions to a better path in life and business using his iconic smile, humor, and charisma.

Well, for anyone who knows me well, I'm very much into fitness. But I have not always been consistent in my approach. As a former college football player, my weight over the years would fluctuate between 185 and 195 lbs. I mean, I played in high school at 205 lbs. In college I was maybe 190. On a 5' 10" to 5' 11" frame, I never thought that was bad. However, no matter what I seemed to do, every year, when I would go in for my physical, my doctor would call me fat. And no, I'm not making this up. Dr. Jelly finger would be like, "Well, I see your still 187. Nice job fatty. You planning on losing weight, or are you just having a race to see which will kill you first: diabetes or heart disease?"

When I'd ask, "OK Jelly, how much do you want me to weigh?" He'd reply, "I'd like to see you at about 155 lb?" To which I would be like "With all four limbs? I'll look like a cancer patient!" To which he would invariably reply, "yes, yes you will." And no, I'm not joking. Dude was cruel. But perhaps he pegged my personality, as I do love a challenge, and get charged up by people who challenge me to do something especially something that is, well, a challenge. Like not using the word "challenge" and derivatives thereof three times in a sentence. Oooo. Challenge for the next book. But I digress.

As I approached the big 5-0, and no, I'm not referring to Hawaii's police department, I accepted Dr. Jelly Finger's fat man challenge and said this year, and forever more, I would roll into his office at no more than 175 lbs, shredded, tan, looking like a 50-year-old swimsuit model. Game on!

Well, the best way I know to drop weight is to run. And run. And when you're done running, run some more. It started off as a 5K, four times per week, and the weight came off a little. But as I would be listening to my Spotify motivational podcasts, I would listen to Tony and the Gubernator and their motivational speeches. Well, in one famous story, Arnold recounts how he had just won the Mr. Universe title, but was immediately approached by a film producer who wanted him in his movie. There was just one huge catch. He needed Arnold to be 220 lbs. At the time, he was tipping the scales at 260!

And, I know what so many of you will say, like all those other actors, he's not that big. He's only 5' 8" blah blah blah. Well, having met him and his former wife Maria in Palm Beach Gardens once, I can tell you he is a big guy, and stands every bit as tall, if not seems taller, than his Austrian 6' 2" frame is officially recorded. But as Arnold tells it, he had to shave an amazing 40 lbs. in just a few months, or he would not get the roll, a roll he felt would launch his film career.

Knowing that running takes it off like nothing else, he started running every day. First, a few miles a day, then 5 and then 10. As he recounts, before long, his distance was increasing every day as he watched the pounds shed away. Well, be like Arnold, I thought. And setting that goal, you know, Arnold made it, and his film career was launched. So, as I listened to this advice, I too started to run more and more. My 5K four times per week quickly became a 5K five times per week, and then six. My Saturday 5K soon became a 10K, or about 6 miles, and then moved into being Saturday runs of 10 miles up to 13.6 miles, or half marathons. The dream of being shredded at 50 was beginning to take hold.

Now, when you're out there running for 4 to 6 hours per week, you have more and more time to listen to even more motivational podcasts by Tony and Arnold. Well, you've already heard about

Arnold's "work your ass off" philosophy, from Chapter 7. But another great part of the governor's ideology is that you must have a goal, and work your ass off to achieving that plan. As he quips, you could be the greatest pilot in the world, and you'd take off in your plane, but without a plan, you'd just fly around not knowing where to go, and never get anywhere. You need a plan to know where you are going, aim for the goal, and to work your ass off.

And this is where I love to bring Tony in, as well. One of his main catch phrases is "Take Massive Action." So many of us know what we want to be. Skinnier. More in shape. More money. In a relationship. In love. Happy. Whatever the case. But hope is not a plan. When you set your goal, when you come up with what you want to accomplish. You must take massive action to achieve that goal. This is one of the fundamental premises of Tony's lessons. And if you have not listened to Tony or attended one of his seminars, it will change your life, guaranteed! Do it!

Combining Arnold and Tony's thoughts, a leader must set goals, take massive action to achieve them, and work your ass off!

Returning to Dr. Jelly Finger: I've never been one to be modest. Sorry, it's just not in my DNA. As a former athlete and someone who has been poked and prodded by doctors for years, and who is generally very comfortable with my physique, I just never see the reason to wear those little paper gowns they give you when you go in for a physical. I mean hey, they're here to examine me. Let me make it easy for them.

So, when I went in for my physical before my 50th birthday, I weighed myself that morning. 174 baby! 174! I was tanned, shredded, and, for the first time in my life, I had these things called abs. Who knew they were down there?

As Dr. Jelly Finger began his examination, I waited in anticipation for my annual fat shaming. But then, to my complete and utter surprise, as I stood before him wearing nothing but a smile, he said the following words which I will never forget . . . "Wow, you really look good . . . now turn your head and cough." Sure, his timing may have been a tad awkward. I mean really? While you're fondling my boys? But I took the compliment, nonetheless. I mean hey, I was almost 50. Gotta get them when you can!

Set Goals. Take Massive Action. Work Your Ass Off.

7. WORK HARDER AND SMARTER

One of my former neighbors grew up on a dairy farm in Michigan. Just a great guy, Dan has one of the best work ethics I have ever come across. Although he did not choose the path of the entrepreneur every day, he gives it all for the Fortune 100 chemical company he has worked for, for almost 20 years. Before they moved back to Michigan, our families were quite close. Dinners. Parties. Even vacationing at the beach was the norm.

At one point, we were conversing about partying in high school, curfews, and the like. When it came to Dan's turn to chime in, I was surprised to hear that he had never had a curfew. "No curfew?" I asked.

"Nope."

"Seriously?" I continued.

"Nope."

“Wow, so your parents were easy on you?"

"Nope. I was usually in by 10 or 11."

"Wait, what? You didn't have a curfew and you'd be in at 10 or 11 every night?"

"Yup."

"Why?" I asked inquisitively.

"Well, you see...." Dan started "... it was my job to milk the cows every morning. And my dad had a simple rule. Stay out as late as you want. Do whatever you want to do. But at 5 am, every day you're milking those cows."

"Wow. But certainly, there must have been a time or two you'd stay out late and just go on one hour of sleep, right?"

"Yeah" Dan replied, "I did that once. You see, when you're half asleep trying to hook the cow up to the milking machine and that poop-filled tail slaps you right across the face, well, that's pretty much the last time you don't get a full night's sleep."

Yup. I imagine it would be. And one more thing to know about Dan: milking the cows was a 24-7-365 affair. As anyone who has lived or worked on a farm knows, the animals don't know it's Christmas, or any other holiday. You keep working, as the cows aren't going to milk themselves!

Over the years, Dan has done quite well for his big company. As we've said before, hard work works. Work your ass off. But make sure you're doing it intelligently.

A few years back, I picked up a copy of Timothy Ferriss's now mega-hit business book *The 4-Hour Workweek*. In the book, Tim sets forth his view of the business world and how, if you set it up correctly, you can dramatically limit the amount of time you need to spend to be successful in life, your career, well, pretty much everything. Of course, the title is eye-popping. I mean, *The 4-Hour Workweek*? Who wouldn't want that life? But wait, it's got to be a joke, right? Well, for that I encourage you to pick up a copy and read it. But the thrust of the book is, in essence, don't work harder, work smarter. And by conditioning those around you not to be distractions, you can hyper-focus and get done those top-level things you need to get done!

Well, I truly respect Dan's work ethic, and those like him. And, of course, who could not help to be intrigued by Tim's concept of a 4-hour workweek? But if you're a budding entrepreneur, I will humbly suggest the following: Worker Harder (ala Dan) and Smarter (ala Tim). Imagine the volume of work that you could accomplish if you adopted both principles. Let's do the math, shall we?

Most people think of a workweek as being 40 hours, right? Not entrepreneurs. But most normal people. So what Tim is saying is that, if you apply his principals from *The 4-Hour Workweek*, you can do a 40-hour job in just 4 hours. I mean, even people who went to Florida State can understand that's a 90% savings in your time. Bada Boom! Go Gators! But what if, with Tim's efficiency in hand—a 90% savings of your time—you still worked 40, 50, or 60 hours a week, like Dan? You'd be doing the work of 10-15 people!

My advice to you as a leader: adopt both Dan and Tim's view on work and efficiency.

Work harder and smarter.

8. BE GRATEFUL, SAY THANK YOU

Say *Thank You*, and mean it. Seriously. The more you live a life filled with gratitude, the more you will see favor coming your way. I believe that with all my heart, and have endeavored to live a life true to that word.

A few years back, my former spouse had just started travelling with Little Stanley. Well, I can only surmise that he would suggest to her books to read to improve her leadership skills. She would come in from wherever she had been that week, plop down a few copies of a book, and tell me and the kids we were all going to read them together, then learn and adopt those principals. Well, at one point she brought home the iconic *How to Win Friends and Influence People* by Dale Carnegie. Again, if you have not read this book, it is an absolute must. Go to Amazon today and get your copy!

In one of the chapters, Dale speaks about the need for every person to give honest and sincere appreciation to the people around them. When the restaurant worker hands you your order, be sincerely gracious when you say thank you. Yes, you paid for the food. But you are still appreciative they brought it to you. Give sincere thanks. Extend this to everyone in your life, your friends, co-workers, employees, service providers. In short, just be grateful and let those around you know it.

Well, our book club never finished the book— not together at least. We'll just say someone may have gotten a tad hung up on that Chapter, and, as they refused to adopt it in their own life to those closest to them, well, it just didn't make much sense to continue forward with a book they were unwilling to fully adopt.

But it doesn't matter if you're the employee or the boss. When someone does something for you, even if it is a part of their job, say thank you. It goes a long way to letting them know that even though they are doing it for a paycheck, the boss appreciates and acknowledges their efforts. And, in the end, that's the recognition that most employees desperately seek out.

Just the other day, my dogs stayed at the local Pet Paradise franchise. And sure, I paid to have them board. But after the stay I received an email thanking me from the general manager of the branch and asking if there was anything that could have improved the experience. Sure, it's an attempt to solicit feedback. But by offering sincere thanks for my business, well, it just made me want to let them know how I thought the experience could improve. And I would have, save for one problem: I think it's already perfect!

So, thank you, Pet Paradise, for taking such good care of the pups. And a sincere thanks to my former spouse for recommending *How to Win Friends and Influence People*. It's a fantastic book,1983 and I recommend adopting all the principles Dale speaks of in the iconic book.

Be grateful, say thank you! And thank you for reading the book. It is greatly appreciated. See what I did there? But sincerely, thank you! I hope you are getting a lot out of it.

9. IT MAY NOT BE YOUR FAULT, BUT IT IS ALWAYS YOUR RESPONSIBILITY

There's a big difference between fault and responsibility. Most don't understand the distinction. But it's a critical distinction you must accept for you to be the best leader you can be.

Fault, at its core, is a concept that deals with blame, culpability, and retains a very negative connotation. Placing blame evokes defensiveness, denial. Responsibility, however, is a much larger concept. Responsibility doesn't care who's to blame. Responsibility doesn't care who caused the situation. Responsibility is merely about who is the person who will step forward and steer the ship to a safe harbor, no matter how the ship got into the storm.

Ultimate personal responsibility is one of the most powerful doctrines you can adopt. Once you take personal responsibility for everything in your life, you take away all other's power over you because, in the end, no matter what cards you are dealt, it's your responsibility to play them the best you can. And once you master this power, it is truly life changing.

I've previously mentioned my own personal struggles during my life as an entrepreneur, both on a personal and professional level. One of the most challenging times for me was during my business's struggles, and returning home every evening after a hard day in the trenches to a partner who, rather than offered me support, was my most vitriolic critic. The silver lining on this time, however, is that it's when I truly began to understand the distinction between fault and responsibility.

Almost every night, my critic would chastise me for the troubles the company endured. Almost every night I would hear how it was my fault, repeatedly. Fault, fault, fault. Blame, blame, blame. Of course, I could not see what I could have done to prevent my CFO from telling lies about the state of the company, and from my sales manager doing nothing to stop her or to alert me of the critical state of the office. I became defensive. I focused on whether it was my fault, and would repeatedly spend nights wondering what I could have done better. So much time was wasted.

Whether or not it was my fault, in the end, was of little consequence during the height of the crisis. As the owner of the company, it was my responsibility to right the ship. Once I realized this, the path forward became dramatically clearer. I rolled up my sleeves and got to work. I learned to ignore and relegate the blame and shame game of my harshest critics. I focused on the solutions to the problems going forward, as opposed to the blame they would relentlessly impose.

You see, excuses are easy. But excuses have never paid a bill. And once you accept ultimate responsibility for everything in your life and work your as off, it won't matter as much whose fault it is, because you are always responsible.

Forgive me in advance for the language and connotation, but one of the best lines I've ever heard on this point comes from Michael Bay's *The Rock* starring Nicholas Cage and the late, great Sean Connery. At one point, Dr. Stanley Goodspeed, played by Nicholas Cage, is complaining to Connery that he "did his best" in trying to stop an assault by mercenaries against which he had no training. And in what I now consider to be one of the greatest lines in cinematic history, Connery, in his dry-witted Scottish accent, quips, "*Losers are always whining about doing their best. Winners go home and f_ _ _ the prom queen!*"

I know, racy. But I think it is perfectly appropriate here. Don't whine about fault or who's to blame. Take responsibility and captain your ship! What, thought I was going to say something else?

It may not be your fault, but it's always your responsibility.

10. REMAIN CALM AND COLLECTED

Part of the leader's role is to remain calm and collected even in the face of the most daunting of crisis. In short, the Kobayashi Maru. Huh? you may be saying? What's Kobayashi Maru? Do I have any Star Trek fans out there? Whoop whoop! You know what I'm talking about.

Well, if it is not abundantly clear by now, or you simply opened the book to this page and started reading, I'm a big pop culture fan as well as a bit of a TV and movie buff. And if you're just opening the book to this page stop, go back, and start at the beginning!

The Kobayashi Maru refers to a training exercise in the fictional *Star Trek* universe designed to test the character of Star Fleet officers in the face of insurmountable odds. Captain James T. Kirk, played by the iconic William Shatner in the original series and reprised brilliantly on the big screen in 2009 by Christopher Pine, is the only person in Star Fleet history to have beaten the test.

Although referenced in the original series, the 2009 adaptation goes into detail as to how Kirk beat the test by programming a subroutine into the program that allows him and his crew to triumph in a purported unwinnable situation. Kirk is then hauled before the ethics counsel to face discipline for cheating on the test. In a famous admonition, Kirk is lectured by Dr. Spock at the ethics inquiry, saying:

> *The purpose [of the Kobayashi Maru] is to experience fear,*
> *fear in the face of certain death, to accept that fear,*
> *and maintain control of oneself and one's crew.*
> *This is the quality expected in every Starfleet captain.*

In short, no matter the circumstances, no matter what adversity. It is a leader's role to maintain their composure, and to always exude quiet confidence. In short, you must stay calm and collected as your employees will look to you and your state for guidance.

Well, once again, recall the series of events that led to our company's greatest hardship. The accountant said we were broke when we were not. My right-hand did nothing to stop the sales team from quitting. Loosing 80% of our revenue in a matter of days. What did I do? I rolled up my sleeves, psyched myself up, and every day walked into that office calm and collected. I knew the books were dripping with red ink. I knew we had exhausted every line of credit we had. I knew we had to make a certain amount of money every day or we would have folded. But did we? No. No, we did not.

And how would it have gone if I walked in everyday, put my face in my hands, looked dejected, and said, "Man we are soooooo screwed unless we make a gazillion dollars today! So, get on it. NOW! NOW! NOW!" Excited. Agitated. No one wants that. I would have pushed out my last few salespeople. That would have been all she wrote. But we did not.

So, no matter what happens, it is the leader's role to remain calm and always collected. In short, The Kobayashi Maru. Remain calm and collected because, at some point, it will all go sideways.

WHEN IT ALL GOES SIDEWAYS

I once had the pleasure of representing an old, retired naval aviator who flew fighter planes off aircraft carriers in the Pacific Campaign during World War 2. In addition to teaching me about the concept of black shoes versus brown shoes— sailors wore black shoes—aviators on ship wore brown - Bruce also taught me about the credo they used whenever launching a mission: *Plan for the Worst. Hope for the Best.* It's a relatively basic concept, but brilliant in its simplicity. And the longer you're in business, you'll understand exactly how this applies to you.

[A]t some point, every thing's gonna go south on you and
you're going to say, this is it. This is how I end...
Now you can either accept that, or you can get to work.
That's all it is.

I've found this to be one of the most inspirational lines ever delivered in a film. It's from the 2015 movie *The Martian* starring Matt Damon. In the movie Damon plays astronaut Mark Watney, who is presumed dead after being left behind on Mars during a fierce sandstorm which forces the rest of his crew to evacuate the red planet. But to the team's surprise, and the administrators' chagrin, Watney survives the storm and finds himself stranded alone on the hostile planet without sufficient food or water.

A logistical and PR nightmare for the muckety mucks at NASA, a complex plan develops to save the astronaut. Mind you, unlike *Star Wars* or similar science fiction movies, you can't just spin the Millennium Falcon around and go back and get him. Nope, first he must get a message to Earth that he is alive. Next, he must figure out a way to survive by collecting water and growing enough food to keep alive until they can return to extract him. Finally, the administrators at NASA must figure out how to reprovision a spacecraft to return to get him as sending another craft would take years to get there. So many moving parts.

With only meager supplies, he must draw upon his ingenuity, brains and spirit to subsist and find a way to signal to Earth that he is alive. He must figure out how to get water. He must figure out how to grow food. But once again, and major spoiler alert, he does. Piece by piece he chips away at his mountain of troubles, until he creates a survivable scenario. In the end, Watney makes it home and utters the inspirational line to a class of young astronauts. The unbreakable will of the human spirit never ceases to amaze.

> *[A]t some point, every thing's gonna go south on you and*
> *you're going to say, this is it. This is how I end...*
> *Now you can either accept that, or you can get to work.*
> *That's all it is.*

In the real world, we are all too familiar with the drama that unfolded in April of 1970 surrounding the Apollo space program. On April 11, 1970, Apollo 13 lifted off from its launch pad hurling its 3-man crew on their date with destiny. Slated to be the third manned spaceship to ever land on the surface of the moon, fate had other plans for Commander Jim Lovell and his crew.

Now made famous by the 1995 Ron Howard film, the Apollo 13 spacecraft suffered a near catastrophic failure on its way to the moon. En route to their lunar destination, an explosion rocked the spacecraft. The ship began losing oxygen at an alarming rate. She encountered significantly reduced electrical supply. Back on Earth, teams of engineers scrambled to assess the situation and come up with a workable solution to bring our boys home, alive.

As made famous in the movie, flight director Gene Kranz, in directing the teams of other astronauts, engineers, and scientists, uttered the now iconic phrase *Failure is Not an Option.* They worked round the clock to come up with solutions to bring the crippled spaceship home.

In the end, against all odds, NASA brought the crew of Apollo 13 home, safely. Years later I watched the actual documentary of this most infamous space flight in human history. When interviewing Kranz, he explained the concept behind the famous line. Most won't get the real significance, although the gist is readily understandable.

In short, when facing a crisis, never allow failure to be one of the potential outcomes, or when working through your solutions. It may be a possibility. But if you allow it to be one of your options, you will waste valuable time thinking about *what if sce*narios that lead to failure, as opposed to structuring solutions that lead to a resolution of the issue. So, the infamous line does not mean it is not a possibility. Rather, failure is simply not something that one should focus on when working through potential solutions to a problem.

As I author this Chapter, it's now June of 2021. I'm sitting on my back patio staring up at the stars just outside of Raleigh, North Carolina, thinking about Watney's line from *The Martian* and Kranz's statement from Apollo 13. Reflecting on the past 18 months, it was a period during which the world largely shut down to stop our first global pandemic in over a century. We didn't know if our business would survive. We didn't know if our economy would survive. We didn't know if we would survive.

But as I stare off into the distant night sky, I relish the fact that I'm now fully vaccinated. The U.S., and soon the world, will be getting back to some level of normalcy. Perhaps at no time in human history, save perhaps for the Great Depression, has or will the U.S. economy face such a challenge. Restaurants and stores were shuttered. People barely left their homes. Businesses shuttered their doors left and right. Unemployment skyrocketed. Yet we survived. In fact, not only did we survive, our company, and many other online ventures like us, prospered.

Rather than to decline, The Trademark Company's revenues were up 45% year-over-year. We had a record 2020. Aside from keeping people connected from our various locations, our biggest challenge during the pandemic became how to continue to onboard new members to our company. And, six-months into 2021, how are we doing? Well, 2021 is set to make 2020 look like a drop in the bucket. How did we do it? Let's take a step back a few years to see.

It's often said that great leaders are made, not born. They are forged from experience. That the truest test of a leader comes during adversity and not by sailing on placid seas. One of the most difficult tasks faced by leaders is righting a ship that is taking on water. And, as referenced above, some will focus on the reason why the ship began taking on water, and start to blame. Was it a failure in leadership? Did you encounter a perfect storm such as the global COVID-19 pandemic of 2020? Whatever the reason is of little consequence when weathering the storm. To survive and thrive again, a leader must be able to shift between leadership styles and push their team to victory.

THE DEADLIEST SEASON

If you've read any of my articles on Inc.com, you are aware that I'm a huge fan of the Discovery Channel's *Deadliest Catch*. The show profiles modern-day crab cowboys in their quest to survive and thrive in one of the deadliest professions on earth—crab fishing in the Bering Sea.

For those of you who are unfamiliar with the show, it's called the *Deadliest Catch* for a reason. Statistically speaking, crab fishing is the most dangerous occupation in the United States, with a reported fatality rate of 141.7 per 100,000 workers. Even worse, when crab fishing in the Bering Sea, that statistic skyrockets to 300 in 100,000! Wow! Why? Well, aside from the countless dangers encountered by the crews on-board the fast-paced, cramped environments of crab boats, if you fall overboard or, worse, your vessel sinks, the water is so cold you have only minutes to survive. If you are lucky enough to have one available, you have maybe 30 minutes before hypothermia sets in and you slowly drift away.

In other words, if your ship goes down in the warm waters of the tropics, you could have days to be rescued. But if your boat goes down in the Bering Sea, it is a veritable death sentence.

One of the stars of the show is Captain Sig Hansen of the 125-foot crab boat the Northwestern. The Northwestern holds the distinction of being the only ship to have been featured in all seasons to date of the now iconic show. For me, Sig is best known for being the most reliable Captain on the show using his institutional family crab fishing knowledge to produce annual good hauls of crab, with reliable big paydays for his crew.

Thanks to the show, at one point Sig and the Northwestern's fame reached such a level that they were even included in Pixar's *Cars 2*, as well as spoofed in an episode of *South Park*. Regarding leadership styles, Sig employs several of the methods discussed above in their daily quest for Bering Sea crustacean gold.

In general, Sig is a pacesetter, as crab fishing is all about the grind and getting your quota caught in as little time as possible. But at times he is also a coach teaching his brother, also a co-owner of the boat—and now his daughter—how to be successful captains on the sea. But as we will see, he can also shift to the coercive when the situation demands it. And in one infamous episode, it did.

During one season, the Northwestern began behaving sluggishly late at night while hauling crab pots. She was becoming less responsive to his turning of the wheel, or his adding and reducing power to alleviate the hits from the constant pounding of the angry sea. She felt heavy. She felt like she was taking on water.

With his decades of experience as a Captain, Sig knew something wasn't right. Calling down to the deck boss, his brother Edgar, Sig ordered a rapid inspection of the tanks that line the inner part of the vessel. Edgar pried open the floorboards on the deck, revealing that one of the tanks below was filling with water, and filling rapidly. If they did not act soon, the boat would be at risk of becoming too heavy in violent sea and capsizing. As we know from above, this would mean a cold and icy death for the crew.

Racing about the boat, they determined that a backflow valve had been installed backwards. In short, rather than allowing seawater that spilled over the boat to flow out and back into the sea, it was locking it into the tanks of the ship and, if not quickly fixed, would soon lead to the boat rolling and sinking to the bottom of the Bering Sea.

Not everyone's business is a ship. Not everyone's business literally begins to sink. Typically, this occurs in a more figurative fashion.

In 2013, The Trademark Company was at the top of our industry and, by many publications, listed as the best company in our sector. And then our perfect storm hit. As you have now heard multiple times, while away from the office on a family vacation, our CFO enacted a plan to bring the company down. All our credit cards were shut down at the same time. But for a company that relied on running hundreds of thousands of dollars a month in government filing fees on our credit cards, a sudden and absolute lack of all credit was potentially devastating.

Worse still, nothing was said to the operations department. They literally found out about the issue as they were trying to conduct their morning filings, and their cards simply stopped working. As was later relayed to me, the initial concern of having no credit quickly fanned the flames of speculation as to why our cards had been turned off. And then when those flames started to smolder, it happened: our CFO, while leading the standard Wednesday-morning meeting in my absence, stoked the fire. Rather than calming the masses, she did the unthinkable. She lied and told the entire company that we were on the brink of bankruptcy, and that all employees should immediately seek employment elsewhere.

Then the unimaginable, part two, occurred. My sales manager, the person whom I had groomed for 4 years to take the reins of the company, did nothing to calm the troops. Nothing to counter the CFO's falsehoods. Nothing to guide the team through what was becoming a gathering storm. Nothing to put out the fire. They simply did nothing.

Rather than lead the team out of this adversity, as it was her job to do, my number two sat idly by and watched as the CFO fanned the flames, the flames intensified, and the company began to burn. In business, and in life, you expect to be challenged and pushed by people and competitors who are not in your inner circle. But the most difficult thing to foresee, the most difficult thing to stomach, is when those closest to you are the ones that fail to support you, and even turn against you. And it happened.

She could have called me on the trip to address the employees. She could have simply relieved the CFO of her duties and shown her the door. She could have done something. She did not.

By the time I returned a few days later, most of our sales team had quit or would do so in the coming days. Eighty percent of our annual revenues of the company were gone with them. In short, we were in big trouble, just like Sig and the Northwestern. And if we did not act quickly to save her, our ship would go down. But how? How do you do get through this level of adversity?

Always remember, no matter where you are in life,

[A]t some point, every thing's gonna go south on you and you're going to say, this is it. This is how I end... Now you can either accept that, or you can get to work. That's all it is.

And that's what we did. And that's how you do it. It requires an immediate shift in leadership style, but when it all goes sideways, here's how to get it back.

Step 1: Quickly and Honestly Evaluate Your Situation

First, quickly and honestly evaluate your situation. Like a doctor in an emergency room, you must ascertain the most critical element causing the problem before it can lead to disaster. This is called triage. In emergency medicine, speed is often the difference between life and death, so one must quickly assess the situation and understand what the issue is, and what's causing it so the patient can be helped.

To lead your business through adversity you must act quickly like an emergency room physician in their efforts in triaging an injured or sick patient. Once your business crisis is revealed, swiftly analyze the cause of the problem, so that a plan may be put into action to fix it.

In the case of the Northwestern, Sig and his crew feverishly ran about the ship looking for why it was taking on water. As stated above, based upon their quick actions and rapid response, they quickly determined the cause, an improperly installed valve allowing water to flow into the boat but not out.

In the case of The Trademark Company, the assessment was slightly different but equally as critical. By knowing which sales team members had abruptly left, we knew we had lost 60% of our sales team and 80% of our revenue. Adding insult to injury, we had a significant credit crisis with our credit cards having been shut down. Again, for a business that relies on credit to pay millions in government filing fees every year, this was a major crisis. Business had literally ground to a halt.

So quickly and honestly evaluate your situation. If done properly, you will be able to expeditiously determine the root cause so that you can move on to Step 2.

Step 2: Create a Realistic Plan

Second, you must create a realistic plan to guide your ship through the storm. Like a fighter pilot in a damaged aircraft, you must compartmentalize the issues you are facing and create a realistic plan to deal with the same. This ability was impressed upon me at an early age by my father who had been, fortuitously, a fighter pilot. Whether it is an engine failing or taking a surface-to-air missile (SAM) up the tail pipe, fighter pilots are trained to quickly take an assessment of the situation and compartmentalize a realistic course of action to give them the best chance of returning their aircraft to base.

In the early 1970s, one of my father's squadron mates was on a mission over Vietnam when his F-4 Phantom was struck by a SAM deep in hostile territory. Smoke rapidly filled the cabin. Peering through the smoke, he could see all the alarms flashing red. The audible fire alarms were deafening. But as he evaluated his situation, he was still airborne. He was still upright. And he discovered that although his right engine was aflame somehow his left engine was still working. He still had thrust!

Due to the significance of the damage to his aircraft and the fire spreading through his right engine he had precious little time to come up with his plan before his aircraft erupted into a ball of flames. If he ejected now, over enemy territory, he would likely spend his remaining days in the Hanoi Hilton, a notorious prison made famous by the late Senator John McCain who was imprisoned there when his Navy A-4 Skyhawk was shot down in 1967.

Calling out to his wingman, he yelled how bad is it? His wingman yelled back "Eject, eject, eject!" He called out again, "No, how bad is it?" His wingman reported back quickly. “You're on fire. Looks like it went right up your right engine’s exhaust. It could hit your fuel any second. Eject!” He didn't.

Compartmentalizing the issues, he realized that, although the aircraft was on fire, she continued to be airworthy. And although she could erupt at any moment into a ball of flames, cascading the stricken aircraft into the jungle below, if he ejected now he would not survive a slower, more painful death. As such, and having quickly assessed his situation, he came up with his plan.

First, he would remain in his aircraft for as long as possible to get him back to U.S. controlled territory. Second, he would begin dropping his altitude so that when he bailed out, it would be at an ideal height for the always risky maneuver. Third, he would keep his hands ready to eject as soon as he felt the aircraft was moments away from its ultimate demise. Plan in mind, he pointed the nose of his Phantom towards the demilitarized zone (DMZ) and safety.

As this was the first world conflict largely broadcast on television, the story has it that a CBS news helicopter was flying near the DMZ and caught what follows on tape. Off in the distance, two F-4 Phantoms could be seen streaking back to base, one trailing a huge plume of black smoke. His wingman never leaving his side, he kept dropping altitude as his damaged aircraft continued to fight the forces of gravity before her inevitable plunge to the ground.

The planes approached the DMZ, lower and lower. Five-thousand, then 4,000, then 3,000 feet. Finally, as he crossed into the DMZ, his aircraft barely above the treetops and a safe bailout altitude, he punched out. Before the canopy of his parachute could even open, his Phantom disintegrated into a ball of flames as she crashed through the jungle below. As he floated down to earth, a Marine recovery helicopter was already on her way, having been alerted to the scene by the squadron. He was picked up with minor injuries and returned to base. His realistic plan was, in a nutshell, executed to perfection. Always remember, when in your planning phase, in dealing with a crisis honestly, it's critical to evaluate your situation and create a realistic plan.

Do you remember The Miracle on the Hudson when the commercial airliner lost both engines shortly after takeoff from New York's LaGuardia airport and had to ditch into the Hudson River? Within moments of losing both engines, Captain Sully Sullenberger, a graduate of the U.S. Air Force Academy, assessed the situation, and determined that a return to the airport without functioning engines was not feasible.

In a decision which would later be heavily scrutinized by the FAA, in those critical moments after the bird strike, Sully determined that if he attempted to return to LaGuardia his aircraft would fail over Manhattan. Hundreds of lives could be lost both on the crippled aircraft as well as on the ground. So, rather than forming an unrealistic plan of returning to the runway, he quickly constructed a more realistic plan: ditch the crippled aircraft in the Hudson River.

When some may have relied upon hope alone and an unrealistic plan in desperation, a military pilot knows to compartmentalize, determine what works and what does not, and map out that realistic plan. In the end, because of his quick thinking, training, and adoption of a plan knowing what worked and what did not, Sully saved the lives of all passengers and crew aboard as well as countless lives on the ground in midtown Manhattan by executing to perfection a daring water landing. His realistic plan saved the day.

Back to the case of the Northwestern, the realistic plan quickly materialized into a simple, albeit critical, two-step process. First, plug the malfunctioning valve completely so it would stop seawater from entering the vessel. Second, pump the excess water out of the boat to return it to full seaworthiness.

In the case of The Trademark Company, our plan was equally simple to devise. First, stabilize sales by deputizing every remaining employee to make sales even if they were not in the sales department. A business needs cash flow to stay afloat, and it was no time to quibble about who would get credit for the same. All hands on deck for sales!

Second, we needed to secure alternative lines of credit and credit cards to eliminate our credit crisis which had brought the operations side of our business to a grinding halt. If we did not, the business would fail within days. Third, and finally, we had to rebuild the sales team, member by member, team by team, to get us back to where we once were, and beyond.

So, create a realistic plan to address your situation. Once the plan is in place, it's time to roll up those sleeves and get to work!

Step 3: Take Action!

Third, take action! Once you have assessed the situation and come up with your realistic plan you must take action to address the situation. Methodically execute your plan by staying focused on your goal. If any part of your plan is delegated to others, you must lead and oversee your team so that they effectuate the plan that you established within the parameters you set forth. Now is not the time to casually delegate. If you delegate, it must be with specific, periodic updates so that you can continue to evaluate the progress of the plan to ensure it is executed to perfection.

Regarding the Northwestern, Sig's plan was to plug the valve and then pump out the water until the ship stabilized. He barked orders at the crew from the wheelhouse demanding updates as to the progress of the sealing of the valve. He ordered other members to make sure the pumps were functioning and dispensing with the excess water. His crew, working feverishly at his direction, complied. And his plan and oversight worked to perfection.

In our case, it became all hands-on deck for a few months regarding sales. Everyone was deputized to assist in the process, and I would watch the daily sales on an hourly basis. If sales slowed down, reminders would go out to increase our efforts. During the first two months of our crisis, I don't recall sitting down for more than 10 - 15 minutes per day while I constantly checked on everyone's performance, providing moral support and pep where needed, and leading us to our goal.

I moved my desk from a private office to the center of our sales floor to be more accessible to the troops. If I went 3 minutes without a question or interruption during the day, it was a miracle. We were able to secure new credit cards to resume the day-to-day operations of the business. And bit-by-bit, piece-by-piece, we began to stabilize our ship.

So once your plan is set, take massive action!

4. Stay Positive as Failure is Not an Option

Fourth, stay positive and remove failure as an option. The great Gene Kranz of Apollo 13 fame reminds us, failure is simply not an option. In short, never focus on failure as one of the possible outcomes of your stormy seasons because then effort will be wasted on a "what if" worst-case scenario rather than dedicating your entire energy towards solving the issue at hand.

Not to be outdone, in a speech that has received significant acclaim on the Internet, former governor and movie icon Arnold Schwarzenegger professed that one should never have a Plan B. He reasoned that if you have a Plan B, it distracts from your primary mission—Plan A. So don't waste time thinking on what if Plan A fails, that's all Plan B is, a plan for failure. Instead, work harder and make sure Plan A is successful.

Finally, adding to this focus on a winning solution, I would further like to add some more from the great Tony Robbins. Tony preaches that, no matter the circumstances, stay positive. That's not to say negative things aren't occurring. But always focus on the positive outcome you are working towards. Combining these philosophies, we come up with a powerful tool to keep in your arsenal when dealing with a crisis: Stay Positive, as Failure is Not an Option.

Turning back to the Northwestern, failure was never an option. Find the leak. Fix the leak. Save the boat. If there was a thought of negativity, it was quickly shoved to the wayside in favor of getting the task done at hand. Working feverishly, they did so with a positive attitude all the way to the finish.

At The Trademark Company, it was my job as the leader to stay positive and keep the troops motivated towards our required objectives, namely, making enough money to keep the doors open while we rebuild our depleted sales team. The pressure was intense and unrelenting. Making matters worse, my marriage was disintegrating, and rather than having support at home, my former spouse was my harshest critic.

But in the face of the challenges at work, and the unrelenting personal negativity of my former spouse, every day I forced my mind to stay positive. I willed myself to be inspirational. As I parked the car to head into the office I would take several deep breaths, whisper under my breath *Show Time*, and step out of the car, head into the office, and greet everyone with a huge The Trademark Company smile. *Today's going to be a great day!* I would tell anyone who saw me. And we willed it to be. And we did it!

So, as the leader, you do not have freedom of speech. Your words must be chosen carefully and deliberately. Stay positive in those words and your actions, because failure is simply not an option!

Step 5: Learn from the Past

Fifth and finally, learn from the past. And let me say this again, for those of you sitting in the back: *Learn from the Past!!!!*

Years ago, when my father went to medical school at the University of Florida (yeah, he was a fighter pilot then a doctor, real under achiever), he told me that the medical school used to have a process called *postmortem*. In short, after any crisis in the emergency room, after any particularly complex case they encountered in the hospital, the medical students, residents, and their instructors, would convene from time-to-time in an open forum to discuss the facts of the case, what happened, how it was treated, and whether there was anything else they could have done to treat the patient to assist them in their recovery process.

Well, we have not had a good bashing of the legal profession in some time, so away we go! Once personal injury attorneys discovered postmortem, and how they could use it against doctors in malpractice cases, the practice was largely abolished. I mean, if you cannot speak openly about what you could have done better while asking for advice from your peers without it costing you your livelihood, why would you? So again, thank you lawyers, for damaging the way we train our doctors. One more feather in the legal profession's cap they don't want you to know about.

But borrowing from this time-honored tradition, once you can see light at the end of the proverbial tunnel, you must begin a self-evaluative process to learn from the past, what went wrong, and how it could have been done better. So, remember to incorporate this into your routine. Never get past a crisis and simply forget about it, or put it out of your mind. You must review every detail about the same and memorialize it so that (1) you can understand what led to the crisis and (2) take action to make sure the same is never repeated.

In the Northwestern's case, they failed to check the work that had been performed at the docks by a third party. Why would they? It had always been reliable in the past? But this time it was not. Think they will ever leave dock again without double checking the work of a third party? No way.

In the case of The Trademark Company, a series of failures began with a trusted relationship with a CFO dead set on destroying what we had built with a series of lies. Doubling down on that, my second-in-command did nothing, and I mean nothing, to plug the hole and keep the ship from taking on water. So, an unforeseen possibility left unchecked by a failure in trustworthy management. Perhaps it is impossible to systemize away the malicious intent of a few compounded by the inaction of others. But having learned from the past, we have implemented systems that have led to massive growth in our company, all the while keeping in check other's malice against our legitimate efforts.

Thanks to these 5 critical steps we took to right our ships, the Northwestern is catching more crab than ever before, and our company is now growing at a record pace. We will always have the scars from our experiences, but they are hidden away behind our smiles knowing that ultimate victory was achieved. So, the next time you're faced with a perfect storm in your business, utilize these 5 steps not only to survive, but to once again thrive.

Chapter Summary: Captain Your Ship

- **Determine Your Leadership Style:** Determine the type of leader you will become.
- **Lead**: A leader's job is, quite simply, to lead! Once you know your style it is incumbent upon you to lead your company to greatness.
- **When it All Goes Sideways**: But be prepared to shift styles if it ever all goes sideways. Anyone can captain a boat in calm seas. Only a true leader can do so when it gets rough.

Suggested Additional Reading:

Good Boss, Bad Boss, Robert I. Sutton, Phd, 2010
On Leadership, Harvard Business Review, 2010
On Managing People, Harvard Business Review, 2010
The 4-Hour Workweek, Timothy Ferriss

PLAN TO SUCCEED

Discipline, Completing Daily Tasks and an Evolving Business Map Are Your Keys to Success.

OVERNIGHT SUCCESS STORIES

There's an old saying that most overnight success stories were 20 years in the making. Personally, I know this all too well. Remember all the way back to when I started you down this journey? How I got the nickname *Maverick?* It's because I planned in silence, watched what others were doing, and eventually built the proverbial better mousetrap. Was it easy? Hell no. If you think that the life of an entrepreneur is easy, someone somewhere has given you the wrong idea. But if you enjoy creating things, working hard, and being the master of your domain, it may be right for you!

We've talked about many concepts in this book to assist you in your journey in launching your own slice of the American Dream.

And everything that we have chatted about has been important. From your initial concept, to testing it, creating systems to market it, supply it, and find it. But as we move towards the end of our journey, we must add into your repertoire one final element critical to entrepreneurial success: systematic discipline.

One of my favorite quotes comes from a contemporary who played his college ball at The University of Miami, aka "The U". A troubled kid coming out of high school, his size and athleticism gained him a full ride to The U in the early 1990s. Sitting on multiple national titles in the decade, The U *was* then what Alabama is today—dominant. After a largely successful junior campaign, he was poised to play out his senior year and, like most before him, slide right into a lucrative career in the NFL. But during the summer camp before his senior year, he was beaten out by a chubby kid who had converted from tight end to defensive line. That year he recorded no tackles, no sacks, nothing. He didn't get drafted.

Searching for his spotlight he went into the family business, professional wrestling. Almost immediately his charm and charisma, to say nothing of his size, captivated audiences. Within a few years he was the WWE's most bankable star. Audiences simply ate up what he was cookin'. But even when he became the most bankable star in the WWE other, bigger, aspirations were calling him. He no longer wanted to be the biggest star for Vince McMahon and in sports entertainment, he wanted to be the biggest star in all of entertainment, in Hollywood.

In the late 90s he took a minor role in the sequel *The Mummy Returns*. That role led to a starring role in the *The Scorpion King*. A few years later he appeared in what is widely considered his breakout role in *The Run Down* followed by a remake of *Walking Tall*. Today, after appearing as Hobbs in the *Fast & Furious* franchise, and too many fun-filled action comedies to list, Dwayne "The Rock" Johnson is at the top of his game and is. by most accounts, the biggest star in Hollywood. Wait, so why have I included all this background? So that you will appreciate the context of some of Dwayne's advice.

Success isn't always about 'Greatness', it's about consistency. Consistent, hard work gains success. Greatness will come.

So how do you stay consistent in your quest as an entrepreneur? In my experience, there are three levels of organization that you need to stay focused on your goals and achieve the greatest success in your endeavors:

1. **Organizational Tool 1: Business Map:** A Road Map for Business Success to keep you focused and moving towards your long-term goals;
2. **Organizational Tool 2: Monthly Planner:** A Monthly Planner to remind you of important events; and
3. **Organizational Tool 3: Daily Checklist:** A Daily Checklist to keep you pounding through your tasks.

Below, we will look at how each will propel you and your vision to greatness. Oh yeah, and that chubby kid that beat out The Rock his senior year, it was none other than Hall of Fame defensive lineman Warren Sapp. So away we go!

DOESN'T EVERY CHILD LOVE CARTOGRAPHY?

When I was a child, I was always fascinated with maps. From a very early age I would look at the maps and globes we had in the house and just study them, looking for little things and destinations. You see, back in my day, you could not just click on an app on your phone, punch in directions, and have a voice start telling you how to get there. OMG! Did I just use the phrase "back in my day!" Soon I'll be yelling at kids to get off my lawn and endlessly looking for the greatest soft yogurt.

Back on topic, wouldn't that be amazing, especially when starting a business? "*Hey Siri, how do I get more customers?*" And rather than say "Still working on it", "Still working on it", or give you the answer "*Here's what I found on the web,*" Siri gave you a specific, detailed, customer-acquisition strategy? But I'm getting ahead of myself; that's simply not out there right now. Heck, half the time Siri doesn't even understand the words coming out of my mouth. I feel like the secretary from *Being John Malkovich*.

But when I was a child, we had tons of maps in the house. Always did. Why? My parents were and remain avid world travelers. Always have been. Sometimes they would take my brother and me with them. Sometimes they would just head out on their own for a few weeks and enjoy themselves. To this day, the natives still sing songs about the legendary parties that occurred at our house when mom and dad were away. But you know the rule: what happened at 1030 Pine Point Road stays at 1030 Pine Point Road.

Anyways, by the time I was 10, I had climbed the great pyramids of Giza, stood on top of the Acropolis in Athens, hung out in the Vatican, and viewed the Crown Jewels in the Tower of London. Fall trips to New York City to see the latest Broadway musicals were standard and Spring Break trips skiing in the Colorado Rockies or to Switzerland were also commonplace. Oh, and let's not forget Hawaii. If you've ever been there, it's not easy to forget. The point is, mom and dad were wonderfully generous, and we got around. A lot.

But in the days before the iPhone when you went to a location you needed a map. This was especially true if you were not hiring a guide, or were not on a specific tour in which they simply load you in a van or a bus a take you to your destinations. Now, for all of you not old enough to remember paper maps, there was a company by the name of Rand McNally that made these amazing maps that would come all folded up in the size of what today would be considered a large pamphlet. And they were always specific to the destination to which you were travelling. To use the maps, however, you would need to unfold them. Each time you pulled it apart it would double in size, and double again, and again, until this pamphlet of a map covered an entire kitchen table.

Once unfolded, they would display the location in such amazing detail. Everything was on the maps from local points of interest, major destinations, and, of course, what looked like a spiderweb of lines crisscrossing the entire paper in various shades of reds and blues. There were tiny little thin lines that sometimes ended without connecting to anything. Then, slightly thicker lines that seemed to always intersect with other lines. Finally, there were the big thick red lines that always went through major destinations, with the smaller lines branching off from them in a seemingly endless web.

By now, most of you should know that these lines represented roads. The thinner the line, the smaller the road. Correspondingly, the thicker the line, well, those typically represented major highways.

If you could decide where you wanted to go back in the 1970s, no matter where, the cartographers at Rand McNally had a map for you. And if you wanted to get from point A to point B, you needed that map, because those maps showed the spider web of intersecting roads. And without the road map, you wouldn't know which road to take to get to your destination. Paying attention? Are you starting to see how I'm going to wrap this around into your business? Well, read on!

Returning to my childhood, like I said, I was always fascinated with maps. But that's also a function of the fact we had so many. I would think about the places I wanted to go in life. I would locate the map. Unfold it. If it was in the United States, I would trace my finger along those red lines from my childhood home in Florida to the Interstate Highway and then out to destinations like the Grand Canyon or San Francisco. Or, if it were international, from the airport I would land at, or the port and the shipping lane across the ocean, and from there how to get to the Taj Mahal or the Great Wall of China. And yes, I really did this.

When I first moved to Washington, D.C. my apartment overlooked the infamous beltway better known as I-495. Even though it was a 14-hour drive home, I can always remember comforting myself by thinking home was simply 5 turns away. Right onto Gallows Road. Right onto I-495 South. Right onto I-95 South. Take that for about 14 hours. East onto Blue Heron Boulevard in Riviera Beach, Florida. Left onto Pine Point Road on Singer Island. That was it. Fourteen hours. Five turns. Nothing complicated. I was only 5 turns from home.

But the point is this, even from an early age, be it fate, curiosity, who knows, I understood the point of a map, and the need to have a map to get from point A to point B. And listen, because this is very important. Business, and life are no different. You need a map. A business map. A life map. What's that, you may ask? Allow me to explain.

When you start a business, the traditional, old-school thought is to first create a business plan, test the model and, if successful, move forward after proof of concept. In a business plan, you include fundamentals, such as the name of the business and what the business will do. It should also include a market or competitor analysis, where you fit into the marketplace, and how you will compete, fund the business, and make money. Then, as the old school dictates, refer to your business plan whenever making decisions. and the overall tenor of what you first wrote down will guide those decisions throughout the life of the business.

When I was first introduced to the business plan concept back when I was taking a business course at Columbia University in 1991, the then-prevailing logic was to update your business plan once every year or two. Well, the prevailing logic is always subject to change.

TODAY YOU NEED A BUSINESS MAP

I was first introduced to the concept of the business map by the great motivational speaker, business consultant and entrepreneur Tony Robbins. While listening to one of his thousands of podcasts and informational videos on life and business, Tony began preaching about how dynamic business today has become. In that regard, Tony teaches that the concept of the traditional business plan has become obsolete as the traditionalists' view of drafting up a business plan, updating it every two to three years, and simply using it as a point of reference to guide your decisions is simply not dynamic enough to keep pace with today's rapidly changing world.

In short, the world has changed since the traditionalists went to school. A little thing called the Internet now dominates our economies. Maybe you've heard of it? Thirty years ago, you could largely see a competitor coming. You'd see them launch and enter your space and have time to react to their marketing campaigns and even their products, once launched.

Today, however, a competitor can launch a business on-line seemingly in an instant. Through pay-per-click advertising, they can quickly get their name and product in front of your consumers, even above your rankings in search engines and in on-line advertising, provided they are willing to pay the price. Within days, your market share could be severely impacted and, within weeks, without rapid counter measures, you could be looking at bankruptcy. All in the blink of an eye. All before traditionalists would tell you, well, it's time to look at and amend your business plan!

And this, ladies and gentlemen, is why you must move away from a traditional business plan model and towards that of the more modern, dynamic business map. And, as I will explain below, you should refer to it and amend it no less than three times per day. That's right, three times per day!

Let's look at two of my favorite movies to help us illustrate the point: Jerry Bruckheimer's 2003 *Pirates of the Caribbean: The Curse of the Black Pearl* and his 2004 *National Treasure.* Both movies demonstrate a few key elements to keep in mind when creating your own business map to success.

In *National Treasure*, Nicholas Cage plays the role of Benjamin Gates, a historian and part-time treasure hunter whose family has been obsessed with finding a mythical treasure of epic proportions allegedly passed down throughout the millennium and ultimately hidden somewhere in the United States during colonial times. The challenge, however, is that there is no map, per se, to the treasure. Rather, our forefathers left a series of clues to the location of the same strewn across the country, and only the cleverest of souls could decipher the riddles leading them to the riches.

As the plot unfolds, there is no one simple map where X marks the spot. And for our purposes, I equate this to an antiquated business plan where you write down a concept and stick to your guns, following your plan to get to your business success. Now, in *National Treasure*, their direction is constantly changing depending upon the new clues they unearth along the way. And that is akin to a modern business map. In today's world, as referenced above, your business must be nimble enough to shift directions, pivot, if you will, in the blink of an eye. Equating an old treasure map to an antiquated business plan today, you need to embrace the concept of an ever-changing business map to ultimately secure your *National Treasure*.

Likewise, in *Pirates of the Caribbean: The Curse of the Black Pearl* Johnny Depp brilliantly portrays Captain Jack Sparrow, possibly the greatest pirate anyone has ever seen, as he is stalked across the Caribbean by the British Navy, while hunting for the mythical lost treasure of Cortez. Throughout the movie, and the multiple sequels, Sparrow occasionally pulls from his pocket his closely guarded special compass that directs him where to go. Simple right? It's just a compass! Well not so.

The compass often spins wildly and sends him in a completely different direction from whence he started. Does he fret? Nope. He just knows that sometimes the direction he is supposed to follow is going to change. And when it does, you need to be ready for it. And that's why you have a business map and not an old, stodgy plan. Because today, now more than ever, you need to be nimble and able to adjust quickly in our Internet economy. If not, your empire, like British Empire of Old, could vanish in an instant.

CREATE YOUR MAP. UPDATE IT EVERY DAY.

Tying our concepts together from Dr. Gates and Captain Sparrow, first you need to create your business map to get your start up from point A to point B, however you define success. Most should define it as a profitable business with a robust balance sheet and nice, fat margins! But recognize that, along the way, often daily, how you get there may change. So, your map needs to be dynamic and constantly updated to keep you moving in the right direction along your journey.

So how do you create and update your Annual Business Map (ABM)? Here's your Quick & Easy 1, 2, 3 guide.

Step 1: Chronological Map with Pertinent Categories

First, create a Chronological Map into which your categories of metrics will be added. Personally, I find a simple timeline, starting with your beginning point on the left and moving from left to right as time progresses, to be a very simple way to construct our ABM. On the left is where we are when we start the map. On the right is where I will be at the end of the map. *See* Figure A.

Figure A

Annual Business Map

Jan >>Dec

Jan Mar May Jul Sept Nov Dec

Second, define the categories of what makes a successful business, then add your specific subcategories thereunder. For most businesses, your general categories should include: (1) Finances; (2) Marketing; (3) Sales (4) Products; (5) Delivery of Products or Operations; (6) Customer Experience; and (7) Employee Experience. Take note, by no way is this intended to be an exhaustive list. Rather, it is merely an example of what most businesses I have assisted with over the years tend to focus upon when creating an initial business map. Add any other categories you deem relevant.

Finances (Fin). Under Finances, most will include Net Revenue (Rev), Operating Costs (OpC), Net Profit (NetP), and, in today's world, debt financing, if any.

Net Revenue (Rev): Include what you anticipate your revenue will be for each month as you move along your plan.

Operating Costs (OpC): Include what you anticipate your costs to operate the business will be.

Net Profit (NetP): Include what you anticipate your Net Profit will be simply defined as Net Revenue minus Operating Costs.

Marketing (Mark): Under marketing, most will include the present number of inbound leads, lead sources, present and planned future marketing for the business.

Leads (Lead): Include the number of people that will contact you for your goods or services. To effectively understand if your marketing is working, this is the best metric.

Products: Include existing products, but also new products or services that will be rolled out as part of your plan.

Delivery of Products: How will your products or services be delivered within your Terms of Service, and what improvements do you plan throughout the year?

Customer Experience: What does your customer experience look like and how will you continuously improve it?

Employee Experience: What does your employee experience look like, and how will you continuously maintain and improve it?

Once done, add your categories and sub-categories as set forth below. Layering in these categories, we can start to see our map taking shape. *See* Figure B.

Figure B

Annual Business Map

Jan >>>Dec

Jan Mar May Jul Sept Nov Dec

Fin
Rev
OpC
NetP

Mark
Leads

Prods
DofPs

CE
EE

Third, include where you currently are for each category and subcategory as well as your annual target goal for each category and subcategory. When doing this, it is critical that you take an honest assessment of the business (or future business) for an accurate portrayal of the present situation. After all, this is not for a bank or investors. This is so you can truly visualize where you are today and where you are heading, so that you can begin the process of filling in the blanks as to how you are going to get from here to there. Note, some categories will be easier having measurable figures. Others will be softer concepts. See Figure C.

Figure C
Annual Business Map

Jan >>>Dec

	Jan	**Mar**	**May**	**Jul**	**Sept**	**Nov**	**Dec**
Fin							
Rev	$100K						$200K
OpC	$75K						$150K
NetP	$25K						$50K
Mark							
Leads	600/mo						1200/mo
Prods	15						17
DofPs	3 Days						1 Day
CE	4.3 Rating						4.9 Rating
EE	60% Retention						90% Retention

Fourth, and finally, add in the components of your plan which you believe will get you from your Start to Finish for each category and subcategory. Include sub-goals and initiatives for each month along the way. Personally, I like to add check boxes to them, so I quickly know what I have, and have not, completed along my map. See Figure D.

Figure D

Annual Business Map

Jan >>Dec

	Jan	**Mar**	**May**	**Jul**	**Sept**	**Nov**	**Dec**
Fin							
Rev	$100K	$120K	$140K	$160K	$180K	$200K	
OpC	$75K	$90K	$105K	$120K	$135K	$150K	
NetP	$25K	$30K	$35K	$40K	$45K	$50K	

Mark

Leads 600/mo 1200/mo

__ Increase Pay-Per-Click Budget

__ Launch Email Marketing

__ Start Facebook Ads

Prods 15 17

__ Launch New Product 1

__ Launch New Product 2

DofPs 3 Days 1 Day

__ Move to 2-Day Delivery

__ Move to 1-Day Delivery

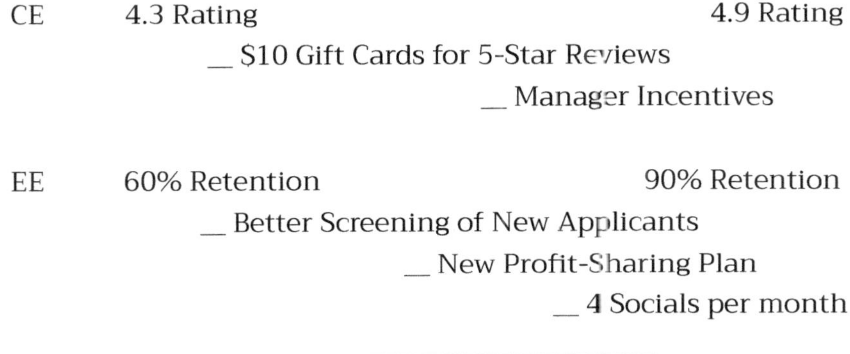

CE 4.3 Rating 4.9 Rating

__ $10 Gift Cards for 5-Star Reviews

__ Manager Incentives

EE 60% Retention 90% Retention

__ Better Screening of New Applicants

__ New Profit-Sharing Plan

__ 4 Socials per month

And there you have it. Your initial ABM is all set. And yes, this is dramatically oversimplified and yours will look very different. After all, you need to create it for your business and insert those goals and steps to get to those goals that are important to your business. My current ABM for The Trademark Company stretches to about 20 pages or more. But hopefully you've gotten the point.

Define the categories. Begin where you are and end where you want to be by the end of the year or whatever you decide should be your chronological endpoint for the ABM. Then fill in your ideas, sub-categories, and action items as to how you are going to attain these goals. Check them off as you do. Amend it as frequently as you want. Once done, you're ready for *Quick & Easy* Step 2. Away we go!

Step 2: Review Your ABM Three (3) Times a Day

Now that you have your ABM, that's just the beginning. Just like Captain Sparrow and his trusty compass, you must review your ABM at least three (3) times per day. Once in the morning, at midday, and, of course, at the end of the day or early evening.

This may seem like a significant investment of time. And it can be. But it will keep you focused on the map and doing those things to ensure you attain the goals you have set. Mind you, the timing doesn't have to be rigid. For instance, if you are out to dinner with family, don't drop everything between the guacamole and the chimichangas and whip out your map. However, do commit to the three times per day philosophy, and make sure you get it in. It will keep you focused on those critical tasks you need to hit your long-term goals.

Step 3: Amend, Update & Add to Your ABM Daily

Finally, recall that this is a dynamic process. Add and amend your ABM daily just like Captain Jack Sparrow altering his direction off the direction set by his compass. Now, that is not to say update your long-term goals three (3) times per day. No. No. No. This is just to say that, as you come up with new strategies to get from point A to point B, add them to the ABM so that you will both remember them and implement them to assist in attaining those goals.

So not only will you update intermediate goals, facts, and figures. But be sure to add in new marketing initiatives, completed tasks, canceled plans, and the like. Check off when you have completed tasks, and what needs to be done. In doing so, you will start to realize the brilliant simplicity of this all-encompassing dynamic map as it moves you to where you want your business to be.

Alas, Rome was not built in a day. Every journey begins with a first step. How do you eat an elephant? One bite at a time. Enough clichés? I hope so because I'm fresh out of them. The point is simply this, now that you have your ABM, you need a second tier of organization to make sure that you pound through the little things to accomplish your larger goals. You need a daily checklist!

A RUSSIAN DOESN'T TAKE A DUMP WITHOUT A PLAN

We've chatted about a lot of movies in this book. And spoiler alert! Now we're going to reference one of my Top 5 of all time: *The Hunt for Red October*. If you haven't seen the movie or read Tom Clancy's thrilling novel, the story follows a young CIA analyst named Jack Ryan played, by a young Alec Baldwin, one of my top four Baldwin brother actors of all time. As the plot unfolds, Ryan is attempting to unravel the mystery of a rogue Russian submarine and why it's being hunted by the entire Russian Navy.

The Russian submarine is captained by Captain Ramius, a legendary Russian seaman played by the great Sean Connery of *Shaken, Not Stirred* fame. As an unusually high number of ships in the Russian Atlantic fleet are put to sea, U.S. intelligence intercepts an ominous order to the Russian captains: find the Red October and sink her! Their own sub! Why? Has Ramius gone rogue, and does he intend to start World War III? Is he trying to defect to the U.S. with a billion dollars of Russian hardware as his dowry? Is he wondering why, as a Russian captain, he speaks with a Scottish accent? These are the mysteries Ryan is tasked with to solve before the sub can reach striking distance of the U.S.

Now, for those of you too young to remember the Cold War, this scenario would have been terrifying. Russia and the United States had been stockpiling nuclear weapons since the 1950s preparing for a conflict that would never come. Evidently, they never heard of the adage *Size Doesn't Matter*. Wonder if the generals were compensating for something? And, in retrospect, who knew that if the U.S. merely took a wait-and-see approach, Russia's Ministry of Nuclear Energy would eventually bomb itself! It's a Chernobyl joke. Too soon?

So back to the movie. As the plot unfolds Ryan becomes convinced that Captain Ramius has not gone rogue. Rather, he intends to defect and, in so doing, to offer, as a dowry of sorts, the largest intercontinental nuclear ballistic missile sub ever constructed. Talk about size matters. The powers that be—you know, those same generals who may, or may not, be compensating for something, depending on who you ask— well, they can't risk the life of every citizen on the U.S.'s Eastern seaboard on Ryan's hunch. So, a line is drawn in the sea. And if the big, long, hard Russian sub penetrates it, the U.S. Navy will blow the *Red Oktober* ... out of the water. Man, when you say it that way, sure is racy.

As such, Ryan sprints off to the Atlantic to uncover the secrets that will prove his theory correct and save the *Red Oktober* from being blown out of the water by our generals, who are definitely not compensating for anything. In one scene, our hero has flown to the stormy North Atlantic to board the USS Dallas, a Los Angeles Class attack sub that had contacted the *Red Oktober* early on in its journey out of the Russian subbase.

Dropped off on an aircraft carrier as a way point to the USS Dallas, Ryan's presence is shrouded in mystery so as not to raise the suspicions of the crew. I mean, why would some CIA-looking guy being dropped off on a ship, in the stormy North Atlantic, as tensions with Russia are at an all-time high during the Cold War, raise suspicions?

Once on board, Ryan is escorted to the captain's office, where the grizzled old Admiral of the ship awaits. Ryan explains his theory to the skipper that the captain of the *Red Oktober* is attempting to defect, and poses no harm to the U.S. The skipper of the boat, played by the late Senator Fred Thompson, is naturally skeptical of this young analyst's theory, having been on the front lines of the cold war his entire career. Eventually, they get to the seminal moment when the skipper asks, in his deep, southern drawl:

"So, what's his plan?"

"His plan, sir?" Ryan responds.

"His plan," Thompson continues. *"A Russian doesn't take a dump without a plan."*

Ryan leaves his office, befuddled and curious. The Admiral was right. Ryan was so busy trying to prove his theory about the defection that he had lost focus on what Ramius was planning to do, thereby either confirming or contradicting Ryan's analysis. Ryan eventually comes to the realization of what the captain's plan must be foreshadowing. Well, I won't spoil the rest of the movie if you have not seen it. Suffice as to say, Clancey weaves together a thrilling conclusion to this action-packed drama.

Returning to the Admiral's crass line, *A Russian doesn't take a dump without a plan,* and neither should you. Every day you need to have a plan for what you need to accomplish for your business. More specifically, you need a checklist, compiled daily, and, once created, the resolve to pound through those daily tasks to accomplish your short-term and long-term goals set forth in your ABM.

Long ago, I developed what I titled *The Trademark Company CEO Daily*. For anyone who knows me and has seen me working around the office, originally it was a single-sheet checklist I carry around on an old-fashioned clip board, which keeps me hyper-focused everyday not only on the lesser day-to-day lesser tasks, but with the higher-level long-term goals. Today, of course, it has been upgraded to an electronic checklist.

Nonetheless, every day I fill out a new *CEO Daily*, filled with the tasks I need to accomplish to make the company run. In this regard, I am never at a loss for what I should be doing and the things I need to accomplish. Even during a momentary or longer distraction, by referencing my Daily I can quickly return to productivity, and pound through my tasks.

In short, the ABM is critical to your business's long-term focus, but so too is your daily checklist, as its role is to cut up the ABM into bite-sized pieces to work through on a daily basis.

Typically, I suggest that you divide your *Daily* into four sections: (1) Building the Business; (2) Marketing; (3) Operations; and (4) Administration. I discuss each of these four quadrants below.

(1) Building the Business (50% of Your Time)

In this section, include your daily tasks that will help you to build and grow the business. Items such as strategies for new goods or services, product development, and things of that nature. In short, the building blocks that will enable you to succeed in your ABM, and build the profitable business you desire. I suggest that you work towards spending no less than 50% of your time on these tasks, as this is the quadrant that truly leads to growth.

(2) Marketing (25% of Your Time)

The world is replete with better products that lost out to superior marketing. Ever hear of the VHS tape? That's how we old people first recorded videos. But do you also recall Sony's Betamax? It was a smaller tape than the VHS and, candidly, had vastly superior quality. But the marketing was not there, and, over time, the Betamax went the way of the dodo, largely due to inadequate marketing strategy and budget allowing an inferior product, the VHS, to dominate the industry.

The point is, marketing should be the next most important quadrant on your daily checklist, spending at least 25% of your day accomplishing your marketing tasks and new initiatives.

(3) Operations (12.5% of Your Time)

By Operations, I mean the work that gets done to fulfill the orders you receive. Ideally, you should spend no more than 12.5% of your day overseeing and/or working on improvements to your operations. Not only should you focus on oversight on the delivery of your goods and services, but also the improvement of the same during the time allotted for this quadrant.

(4) Administrative (12.5% of Your Time)

And last, but certainly not least, is performing the administrative tasks such as meetings, answering team members' questions, payment of bills, etc., for the company. Here you must be particularly careful to guard your time as this, if left unchecked, can be a large drain on your time. Suffice as to say, again, only about 12.5% of your day should be devoted here.

The great Zig Ziglar, efficiency and organizational guru, preached that every night before you go to bed, write out those things that you must accomplish to be successful the next day for your life, your business. You will be eminently more productive if you do. Taking the time to do this will change your life forever, and focus on what you need to accomplish daily.

For me, I prefer to do it in the morning when I wake up, over coffee, at about 5:30 am. Whatever works for you. Just make sure you have a daily checklist, and that it's ready to go by the normal start of your business day. It will keep you focused.

As we conclude our discussion about the importance of a daily checklist, I can't help to share a story provided by the beloved and charismatic Joel Osteen, leader of Houston's mega-church Lakewood Baptist. If you have never listened to Joel's sermons, I urge you to do so. Even if you are not Christian, they are uplifting and always cheerful. No matter your faith, I challenge you to listen to one of his many podcasts and not come away feeling a little bit better about your life and your circumstances.

As Rev. Osteen tells the story, a teacher stands in front of his class with a standard drinking glass, a few large rocks, smaller rocks, and sand. He challenges his young students to get all the rocks and sand into the glass. One by one they come up to his desk, pour the sand in, then add the smaller rocks, or the smaller rocks and then the sand, but none can get everything in the glass. After numerous failures, the teacher empties the glass and, rather than inserting the smaller pieces first, puts the big rocks in the glass. He then proceeds to drop the smaller rocks in that fill in the empty spaces left by the big rocks, finally pouring in the sand which completes the challenge, as it finds its way into even the smallest of cracks left over.

The moral of the story? Focus on getting your big things done first, then the little things. And that daily checklist we are talking about...well, that will keep you focused on the large rocks of your ABM.

AND FINALLY, A MONTHLY PLANNER

Finally, one last bit of organization that I highly recommend you add to your repertoire as you open your business: a monthly calendar. You know, one of those big, paper, monthly calendars that you can buy at any office supply store like Staples or Office Depot. Why? Because it's a great way to keep your monthly tasks organized in a very visible manner, so that important dates don't get missed. Let me explain.

Back when I was a first-year associate for my first law firm, my mentor Ken Bynum pulled me aside and taught me the value of keeping such a calendar. Now, at the time, we did not have fancy iPhones and electronic calendars. In fact, the state-of-the-art calendar system then was one of those fancy date books bound in leather, where each page was a different day. As Ken explained it, you can use these if you want. Write in your assignments or otherwise. But sometimes, just sometimes, they'll get lost. Or you'll forget to look ahead. And in litigation, you cannot afford to miss a date, an appearance, anything. It's too important.

And that's when he pulled out his big monthly calendar. On the calendar was written all his court appearances, due dates for big assignments, everything. In short, as he explained, if you only keep yourself organized with a date planner, one day you may open it up and you see that today is the due date for the Smith Appeal. The only problem is that that appellate brief may take 40 hours to write. And then what? So always keep your monthly calendar up-to-date and visible, so that you can see a month in advance and know what's due and where you need to be, ensuring you never miss anything!

As a budding entrepreneur, I suggest the mundane such as the rental payments, light bills, and other utilities be added to this calendar. Don't forget to add monthly things you do to keep the business running as well. For all of you, it will be different. And, of course, add them in pencil. Then you are free to change them when you like. But it's a great tool to add to your ABM and your daily checklist to keep you perfectly organized, and ready to conquer the world. Now it's up to you. Go out there and get your business organized!

Chapter Summary: Plan to Succeed!

- **Create, Review, and Amend Your Annual Business Map:** Use the format above to plot out your business map to success, review it no less than three (3) times per day, and alter, amend, and add to it as you see fit.
- **Create a Daily Checklist and Pound Through Your Tasks:** Focus on the important tasks and guard your time against menial distractions.
- **Use a Monthly Paper Calendar:** Finally, put your important dates on an easy-to-view monthly calendar, and glance at it a week out, once per day, to ensure you never miss something important.

Additional Suggested Reading:

Over the Top, Zig Ziglar, 1994
Joel Osteen, YouTube Podcasts

YOU CAN HAVE IT ALL

Achieving the Perfect Work-Life Balance.

IF I COULD TURN BACK TIME

One of my favorite questions people often ask is: what advice would you give to your younger self? Well, for one, buy Apple stock when it was $32 bucks a share! I mean, that company, well, it may go somewhere! Also, there's this kid named Brady—Tom Brady at the University of Michigan. He was OK there, but when he gets to the NFL, baby, go all in! Oh, and video conferencing. Make sure to invest in Zoom before 2019. I have a feeling it's going to be big! What? Too soon? But nah, that's the obvious and easy stuff.

But more specifically, I'm talking about what advice I would give to my younger self as a life-long entrepreneur? A serial businessman, an inventor, creator, and problem solver.

Well, it's the same advice that I will give to you, as our journey across these pages comes to an end. Some may disagree. But it's something that I have learned running my own businesses for nearly 20 years, while helping over 100,000 others to reach for their own American Dream. And what you may ask, is this seminal advice? What is it that I would tell my younger self if given the chance? It's quite simple, really. Almost too easy. But it is very important. And here it is: Play your cards right, and you truly can have it all!

MASTER THE PLATE WALTZ OF LIFE

Have you ever seen a plate waltz? You're probably like, "Huh, what?" But allow me to call it by its more colloquial name: Chinese plate spinning. You may now know what I'm talking about. The acrobats spin plates, bowls, and other fragile objects on multiple sticks, high up in the air. The challenge, of course, is to keep all the plates spinning, and therefor balanced, on the sticks, as more and more plates are added.

High upon the sticks they go. And as each one is added, the acrobat must continuously keep spinning all the plates to keep them balanced, even as they add more and more plates on more and more sticks. If not, and if they fail, even for one plate, it will come crashing to the ground shattering upon impact. And when this occurs, the twirler must remain focused to avoid the other plates from being sentenced to the same crashing fate as their friends.

Well, to me, I can think of no better metaphor for life than the Chinese Plate Waltz. Think about it. All those plates you keep up in the air everyday spinning, spinning, spinning. Your spouse. Your job. Your friends. Your family. Just to name a few. And now you want to add another plate, a new business. Well, you better treat this metaphor for real. Your business plate will always be full. And you must keep it spinning. But if you only focus on it, your other plates may crash to the ground. Your spouse. Your family. Your friends. Get the picture?

In order to have it all, you must be willing to commit to the Chinese Plate Waltz of life. No matter what's going on upon any one stick, you can never afford the luxury of allowing any other aspect of your life to slow down and come crashing down. You must give equal care to all to have it all.

Heed the advice of someone that has had plates crash while being focused on other plates. I firmly believe you can have it all. However, you must perfect the Chinese Plate Waltz of life. And, from my experience, here's what it takes.

WORK WHILE THEY SLEEP

There's a famous saying: *Work While They Sleep, Then Live Like They Dream*. It's a testament, and a reminder, that hard work truly does work. Many years ago, I was watching some show, probably *Entertainment Tonight* or something like that, and they had flown to Richard Branson's Necker Island to interview the self-made billionaire at his posh, private island in the British Virgin Islands.

Now, of course, Sir Richard is famous for his boyish charm and charismatic smile, as well as his playful lifestyle, typically being photographed while Jet Skiing, Kite Surfing or doing some other resort-type adventures with some scantily clad model by his side. But this segment was a little unique. How so you may ask? Well, in this segment, he referenced work. And, more specifically, when he works.

Specifically, no matter what time the revelry would end on Necker Island, Sir Richard could often be found early in the morning, before children, grandchildren, or guests awoke, holding conference calls with his lieutenants back in London. Sir Richard told the reporter that he routinely works early in the morning like this, always making sure to wrap up his morning duties before any of his family or friends arise.

In the afternoons, after the morning water activities would be concluded, and people often retire for an hour or two to rest up for the evening, Richard again would lay back in a hammock and work on more complex, higher thought-level matters for one of his many businesses. Again, always maintaining high visibility with his family and friends while not letting them see how hard he was working, even on vacation. Brilliant. For an entrepreneur, simply brilliant. Why?

Working on vacation, or at home, often sends a message to your friends and family that you value work over their comradery. This can be especially damaging to family life if they feel that they are constantly number 2 behind work. But adopting the Branson model, well, problem solved.

A few years after I watched this segment, we found ourselves starting to travel more frequently as a family. The issue, be I right or wrong, was that I felt I was still needed at that time with the business. That I wanted to get work done because I enjoyed growing the business. But when you have committed to time with the family you dare not interrupt that to work. What message would that send?

So, when we went on cruises, I decided to adopt Sir Richard's strategy. And it worked like a charm. Afternoons by the pool with the wife and kids, then back to the room to relax. While the family napped, I would duck out, find a cozy spot in a lounge and sip a cocktail while I got a little work done. Back to the room to dress to the nines and take the family out "on the town" to a great dinner on the ship, then a show. Walking them back to the cabin around 11 and quietly tuck them all in, then slip out to "head to the casino."

Some nights I would actually go to the casino. But most of the time I'd head to this little British pub on the ship that was usually empty at that time. I'd review the daily numbers from the office, answer emails, take care of other items for the companies. All while the family slept. Most nights I'd slip into bed around 2 or 3 am. Catch about 3 hours of sleep before the wife would nudge me and let me know it was time to hit the gym, our morning routine since we were kid-free and in our 20s. And that's pretty much how vacations went as an entrepreneur. Some may say it's crazy. Personally, I love it.

Remember where we started in this segment: *Work While They Sleep Then Live Like They Dream.* So, what did I accomplish? Three of my plates were happy as clams knowing that they, all three, were my top priority. My spouse. My family. My Business. And how did I do it? How did I keep all those plates in the air at the same time? Focus! By focusing on them all and letting them know, through a little bit of effort, that they all were my top priority, and by not allowing them to see all the other plates I had in the air at the same time.

Work while they sleep.

GIVE SINCERE GRATITUDE

And why we are on the subject, give sincere thanks to those who help you along the way. Sure, your employees may work for you. Your spouse's role may be the stay-at-home type, while you bring home the bacon. But everyone wants to receive thanks for what they bring to the table. Be it an employee. Be it a spouse. It's no different.

Now, are you required to be gracious? Absolutely not. There is no rule making it so. And you can take everything for granted, chalking it up to *Well, it's their job!* Go ahead. Let's see how far that gets you. Or you can simply add into your repertoire the ability to be gracious and give sincere thanks to those who support you in business and in life.

Divorce is sadly too common these days. And of the friends that I know who have divorced over the years, one dominant theme arises: at some point, one or both individuals in the relationship started taking each other for granted and simply stopped saying thank you. A simple gesture, really. But one that is so critical to the maintenance of positive, healthy relationships, business or personal.

To illustrate the point, one of my dearest friends recently saw her 20+ year marriage implode before her eyes. She is a public-school teacher, and her husband was a partner in a large, professional services firm. Her career path was largely chosen so that she could be the primary care giver for their children while he brought home most of the bacon.

As she relays the story, he was obsessed with his work and the gym. Every night, after school, she would take care of their kids and have dinner on the table for the family. More times than not, he would miss dinner, as he would still be at the gym, or working late on some project. When he came in as they would be clearing the plates, his first words were not "thank you" or "I apologize for being late". Rather, he would grab something out of the pantry and start munching away. Never did he say thank you for taking care of the kids. Thanks for dinner. Nothing.

One day I asked her, do you think that you would still be married if, instead of what happened, he still came home late, missed dinner, but when he walked in the door he had flowers in hand, crossed the room, and the first thing out of his mouth as he kissed your cheek was to say "Thank you for being so wonderful. I'm sorry I was late. You're amazing. Thanks for taking care of everything. What can I do to help?" Without hesitation, she replied, “Yes.” Wow.

How painful is that? A family could have been saved if just one person could have remembered all that the other person does for them and, instead of ignoring it, they simply said, *Thanks.* Stunning.

My own story is not too dissimilar. I have resisted writing about things that are too personal in the book, but I share a very similar story to that above. For years my former spouse would travel, travel some more, and when she was done travelling, it was time for her to hit the road again. It got to the point that the kids would ask “Any clue where mom is this week?” Sometimes, I'll admit, I did not even know.

When she traveled, not only was I charged with 100% of the duties of running The Trademark Company, but 100% of taking care of the kids, the dogs, the house, etc. And I was fine with it. At least initially, she was gracious to those supporting her. But over time, her gratitude dissipated. At one point she simply stopped saying thank you for all the things that we, and I include myself, the kids, and my parents, did to support her in her career. And if we mentioned “Hey, you're welcome for all we did to support your career this week,” trying to get her to be gracious, it would simply infuriate her even more. And rather than to simply say thank you and have the emotional intelligence to understand the value of these simple words, she chose never to say it again.

You see, most of us don't mind hard work. Most of us want to support something larger than ourselves. But that comes with a simple cost. It's not that expensive. It's very affordable. It's two just little words that everyone must use to have in their repertoire and use frequently. All together now: Thank You!

Showing sincere gratitude is perhaps the most powerful thing you can do in a relationship, whether it be with an employee, an employer, a friend, or, especially, a spouse. So, no matter the situation, make sure to do so. It takes so little effort, but the rewards are almost immeasurable. Just do it!

If you want it all, be sincerely thankful to those who are assisting you in your journey. Give them sincere gratitude when you see them. It's one of the most critical components to keep your plates spinning in perfect rhythm.

Give Sincere Gratitude.

STAY POSITIVE AND BE JOYFUL

Happiness is a choice. Never forget that. In life and in business, there will be good days and bad. But as the adage goes, it is not what happens to us that defines us. It is how we react to what happens to us that defines us.

Think about it. You had a bad day at work. You didn't get that good grade you studied for. She said no when you asked her out. Whatever the issue, you decide how you will react to these challenges in life. You can either let it get you down and be depressed about the circumstance, or you can mentally dust yourself off, get up, and say to yourself, “I'll do better next time", while smiling your way through it.

I have often thought that a higher power will send me signs in my life from time to time. And one of my favorite signs will often come when I'm sore or aching after a long run, or some other form of exercise. You see, as a former college athlete, I have always kept myself in moderately good shape. At least I think so. I mean, sure, there was the time in law school I gained about 20 pounds largely on Hamburger Helper and boxed wine. By the way, if you're ever wondering what wine pairs well with Hamburger Helper, it would be of the boxed variety. You're welcome!

But after a long run or other strenuous exercise, when I'm achy or perhaps strained a muscle, or my knees hurt from my 50-year-old body, and I'm feeling tired and wishing I had my 20-year-old physique back, someone will go rolling by in a wheelchair with a big smile across their face. And here I am, blessed to have all my extremities functioning, and the person in the wheelchair has a broader smile than I do. And in that moment, I am always reminded to focus on the positive and smile through anything because, in the end, happiness is a choice.

Over the years, I have been blessed to be part of the Looping Straight Society, our neighborhood's local poker table that meets every Thursday night. No politics. No relationships. No work. Just a bunch of guys talking poker and getting away from the world for a few hours at a time. There's not a bad guy at the table. In fact, everyone there is just awesome. To that end, we all come from different backgrounds, different walks of life. One of the best guys at the table is a former police officer with the NYPD and, specifically NYPD's Port Authority unit. In a nod to *Die Hard*, let's just call him Roy.

Rarely have I ever seen Roy without a smile on his face. He is the first guy who asks you how you are and genuinely listens and cares when you tell him. He's a hugger, and just an amazing person. One night we were chatting on the way home, and the chat turned to his history. When I heard his story, it was hard to choke back the tears.

Roy and his twin brother were born into a lower middle-class family in the New York City area, in the early sixties. If my memory serves me correctly, by the time he was 4, his twin had passed of a childhood illness. His father split thereafter, and Roy never saw him again. Understandably depressed from the loss of a child and a departed spouse, Roy's mom hit the bottle hard. When Roy was about 7, his mom fell to her death down a flight of stairs in their walk-up apartment. Roy was sent to be raised with an older half-sibling in Pennsylvania. One day he returned to New York, and joined the NYPD Police Academy.

Now, if you know anything about history, Roy was part of the Port Authority police on September 11, 2001. Although I have never spoken directly to him about this, it's clear he lost a lot of friends and fellow officers that day. He's had 2 or 3 heart attacks and his wonderful wife, also a former NYPD, has had to battle at least one very serious medical condition, most likely attributable to her exposure to the dust and debris in the wake of that horrible day. You think you've had it hard? And yet despite all of this, Roy remains joyful. He is one of the happiest people I have ever met, and I am a better man for knowing him. Every time I see him, he has a huge smile on his face, gives you a bear hug and a kiss on the cheek, and legitimately asks you how you are doing, because he genuinely cares.

So, the next time life hands you those lemons, think about Roy, shove those lemons right back in life's face and put a smile on. It's not the lemons in life, it's how you decide to react to them that keeps you happy. So be happy, no matter what life, or business, throws at you.

Stay Positive and Be Joyful.

KEEP DIFFICULT TIMES IN PERSPECTIVE

I can't believe that we almost made it through the entire book without a reference to another great movie: *Cast Away*, starring the living legend Tom Hanks as a middle manager for FedEx who is lost from the world after his plane goes down somewhere in the South Pacific, landing him alone on a desert island thousands of miles from civilization. The movie details the progression of a castaway's life from the early days trying to find food and water to survive, to thriving on the island, to eventually the zest to escape his paradise prison, taking a chance upon the open sea to return home. Well, spoiler alert, he does.

But when he returns, he finds a world that has forgotten him. His fiancée when he left is now married to his dentist, and they have a child. All his worldly possessions are gone, as he was presumed lost. As the movie quips, it was if they literally had to bring someone back from the dead.

But years on a desert island mellowed our hero. And, in one particularly poignant moment in the film, he is asked how he can handle all of it. His reply, from all that he learned, is that, despite what today brings, tomorrow the sun will rise. And all will be renewed, with fresh hope and promise.

This line is so poetic for life and in business. And it's key to surviving challenging times when they invariably arise. No matter what happens in your life, or your business, tomorrow the sun will rise and there will be a fresh, new day with it, bringing new opportunities and manners to beat every obstacle.

Always remember, right now there is someone in a hospital bed fighting for their life, and they would give anything to have the same opportunities that you have. Keep your business's challenges, and your challenges in life, in perspective. Tomorrow the sun will rise, and, with it, fresh hope to rise above your challenges, or continue to excel as you have done.

Always Keep Difficult Times in Perspective.

AVOID NEGATIVITY AND DRAMA

The great comedian Larry Miller does a bit on people who get divorced, then remarried. As Larry puts it so brilliantly, that's like taking a carton of milk out of the refrigerator, smelling it, thinking, "Ooooh, that's bad." And then shrugging your shoulders, putting it back in the fridge, and saying, "Maybe it'll be better tomorrow." Love Larry. What a gem. And if you have not seen his *5 Levels of Drinking*, look it up on YouTube. You won't be disappointed.

Larry's joke always reminds me of negative and dramatic people, both of whom must be avoided, when possible, in business and in life. They will drag you down, suck up all your time, and, in the end, don't assist you in your journey whatsoever. And you know who I'm talking about. Let's start with the negative nellies. You know the ones. When you tell them your ideas or dreams, they are the first to present you with the obstacles to your dreams, but never help with a solution.

Never tell your big dream to a small-minded person. Nine out of 10 times, they're negative towards your vision because they never had the balls to pursue theirs. So, they tear down your dream because they did not have the courage to pursue their own. They want to prove to themselves that, if they could not do it, neither can you. And in some perverse way, this gives them satisfaction, as your success would somehow prove that they had failed by never having the heart to pursue their own dream.

Avoid this negativity like the plague. They do not get better. They are just negative. And, like Larry says, to put them back in the fridge for another day, well, that's just mad. Throw them out as soon as possible.

Likewise, you must avoid as much drama as you can in your life. Do you all remember the girls in high school that would have a beer or two, then the water works would start? It's always the same crazies, and you can practically set your watch to it. I mean, wind them up, add beer, and, "Why didn't Johnny ask me to the prom?" And no matter how much you want to use logic on them by replying, "Because you're psycho!" nothing is going to help the situation. And the worst part? All the attention they attract.

I mean, the rest of us would just be hanging and having a good time, maybe a little smooching, and suddenly it all goes to hell because Karen had too much happy juice and decided tonight was the perfect time to have her emotional release about the time her pet Hamster Fluffy died when she was 6. I mean really. He probably offed himself because he didn't want to listen to your crap anymore, ever consider that? I have. I mean, yeesh.

In business, the worst part of it is subtle. Their personal drama occupies precious time that otherwise could be spent with quality employees. My buddy once shared the following story about a drama queen in his office. And man, is it a perfect example. And no, it's not confidential, as you will see.

Anyways, the young woman who worked for my buddy had been dating a local musician for years, even though he had been hesitant to pop the question. Why buy the cow, right? But I digress. Well, at some point, she began experiencing a tingling sensation when she went number 1, you know, when she went pee.

Well, within a few days, that tingling sensation turned into a full-on fire storm, and I don't mean in a good way. El Fuego when you go number uno es no bueno! So, she went to her doctor to see what possibly the problem could be. I mean, after all, she was monogamous with her partner. And he was a local musician who steadfastly had refused to cohabitate with her, and I'm sure he was equally as zealous about the relationship, right?

It will come as no surprise to you what she caught rhymes with Slurpees. But how? After all, she was monogamous. Oh wait. No, it couldn't be that prince of a man, the wannabe rock and roller who refused to move in and commit after 8 years. No. I'm sure he was faithful, right?

Well, as she called my buddy, her boss, in tears to tell him the news, he steadfastly reminded her of the employee - employer relationship, and that she did not need to detail every aspect of her medical file. She merely needed to fill out a leave slip and check the box that said, "Medical leave." Undaunted, she replied, "I have herpes." My buddy was like, "OK, again, you don't need to tell me ..." and before he could finish, she continued that her boyfriend had given it to her.

"Evidentially he had a cold sore on his lip and when he was down there..."

"Please stop," my friend explained. "Again, I don't need the details, I'm your boss. Just submit the medical slip and we will mark it out, OK?"

And my buddy, knowing the employee all too well, though fortunately not *that* well, gave her one final piece of advice, "And please, when you come back to work, please just come in and don't tell anyone. Let's just get to work." She agreed, and planned to return the next day.

Well, do I need to even finish the story? The next day, something must have short-circuited in her brain. She showed up five minutes late, then proceeded to stop in every private office to tell her co-workers about her new medical condition. By mid-morning, she had made the rounds and told almost everyone in the office. My buddy calculated that, as a result of her theatrics, and disturbingly detailed storytelling as to how she contracted the illness, the company lost about 30 hours of productivity that morning. Hey, it's not the loss of a beloved hamster, but you get the point.

This is what you get when you allow dramatic people to remain in your organization. So, just like those negative nellies, they must go as well. Oh, and postscript on the young lady. Years later, after she was extracted from the organization, my buddy saw her and her then-boyfriend musician (now husband) at the Salt Lake City airport. Guess she had finally wore him down, and they had gotten hitched.

Avoid Negativity and Drama.

KEEP MOVING FORWARD

Since I was a child, I've always wanted to build things, to help people, and to be an entrepreneur. I often think a person must be wired just a tad differently to really get what it takes. To see a problem. Create value in a solution. Offer the solution for a price. Then market the hell out of it.

Honestly, to many of us it's second nature. And it's easier than you think. Every problem is a potential opportunity for a new business. The trick is to identify a problem in which your fix, or offering, is of sufficient value to induce a consumer to purchase your solution. Easy peasy! That's really all it is.

But in closing, the last piece of advice that you must live by, should you go down the entrepreneurial path, is as applicable to your business as it is to your life. For me, life has never been about the destination, it's about the journey. You may never get to where you want to go, so simply make sure to enjoy the ride for as long as you can. For, in the words of the immortal Walt Disney:

Around here . . . we don't look backwards for very long.
We keep moving forward, opening up new doors and doing new things, because we're curious
... and curiosity keeps leading us down new paths.

- Walt E. Disney

Now it's your turn. Do you want to be ordinary or extraordinary? Do you want to build someone else's dream, or your own? Do you want to live your life always wondering what could have been, or live the dream you were meant to live? Now go out there and do it! And along your journey, always remember:

Keep Moving Forward.

Chapter Summary: You Can Have It All

- **Balance: Understand that Your Business, Family, and Friends Can Be of Equal Priority:** Understand that your business, family, and friends can share the top spot in your life. You simply must make sure that you prioritize all.
- **Create an ABM but also an Annual Personal Map (APM):** To make sure you take care of every aspect of your personal life, create an Annual Personal Map (APM) to make sure you are checking the boxes for your friends and family as well as your business.
- **Execute them Simultaneously:** Execute your ABM and APMs simultaneously to have it all.

Additional Suggested Reading:

Over the Top, Zig Ziglar, 1994

APPENDIX A

THE MAVERICK METHOD'S STARTUP CHECKLIST

Step 1
Create A Product that People Want

1. **Provide a Product or Services People Need**: Before investing your blood, sweat, and tears develop a product or service people want and are willing to pay for. Ask yourself why people need or want to buy your product.
2. **Make it Competitive:** Know how your product or service will compete in the marketplace. Is it innovative? What problem does it solve? Will it compete on price alone?
3. **Price it Right:** Your price must be set at a point where you are both profitable and where the product will move in the marketplace.

Step 2
Make Your Business Legal

1. **Protect Your Intellectual Property**: Your trademark is your business's most valuable asset. Make sure it is available and register it! Likewise, if your product is entitled to patent or copyright protection, make sure to secure those as well. The more protection you can secure, the better.

2. **Incorporate**: Form a separate business entity. For most, the easiest structure is a Limited Liability Company (LLC). This will shelter your personal assets (e.g., car, house) from your business liabilities (e.g., bills, debts, etc.). And, if possible, avoid personal guarantees secured with your personal assets.
3. **Insure It**: Insure your business and services with standard policies. Your local insurance dealer can assist you in determining what you need.

Step 3
Build Your Business to Scale

1. **Create a Scalable Model:** Write down your business model and everything that is needed to make it work. How is your product or service made? How will it be delivered? Who are your ideal customers? Create your future organization chart, with every position required to make the business successful, and what the positions' duties and responsibilities will be. In the beginning, you yourself may need to fill some, if not all, of those positions. But as you grow, fill the positions to scale the business.
2. **Reduce it to a Manual:** Everything must be put down into a detailed "how to" manual from how you market, sales emails and scripts, how the goods or services are delivered, to the accounting aspects of the business. This will not only make sure that you develop a consistent product, but that you can hire people and scale the business consistent with the way the business is required to be run.
3. **Delegate, Manage & Hold Accountable:** Finally, provided it is profitable as we discuss below, add the cogs to your organizational chart. Make sure that you have a series of checks and balances in place to continuously ensure everyone in the organization is accomplishing the work they were hired to do. Hold them accountable to do so, and if they are not accountable, find someone else for the position who will be.

Step 4
Shamelessly Market Yourself

1. **Shamelessly Market to Your Consumer Base:** Know who your market base is and shamelessly market to them. Years ago, it was print media and television advertising. Today, you are more likely to reach them via content media, blogs, vlogs, and social media posts. Whatever the medium, know where they are and blast them with your message.
2. **Track What Works**: Keep track of from where you receive your business. In short, know what works, and what does not. This is a critical piece of information that you must have to scale your business. If you don't understand what is driving business to your door, you can't focus on scale this critical component of the process.
3. **Double-Down on What Works, Kill What Does Not, Repeat:** Once you figure out what is working, double down on what is and kill what is not. Repeat. Repeat again. And when you are done, repeat some more. Keep adding new avenues of marketing and never stop.

Step 5
Hire Well ~ Train Well ~ Keep them Engaged

1. **Hire Slowly, Fire When you Must:** You need to get the right people on the bus and in the right seats. Like with everything else, once you have created the Job Descriptions for your ideal Organizational Chart referenced before, this should make it easier to hire the right people for those positions. But when you see it is not working out or that you've made a bad hire, quickly remove them from your organization, as the long-term negative effects far outweigh any short-term benefits.
2. **Train them Well:** Provide them with a world-class on-boarding experience that includes training on your company, your industry, their role in the company's mission, their specific job functions, and how to accomplish them.

3. **Keep Them Engaged:** Finally, you must keep your employees engaged if you want to achieve the goals you have set for your company. Develop an engagement plan that keeps them engaged on a daily, weekly, monthly, and annual basis.

Step 6
Ignore the Naysayers ~ Listen to a Select Few ~ Work Your Ass Off

1. **Ignore the Naysayers**: The world is filled with critics. Especially those who were not strong enough to chase their own dreams. Learn to be comfortable living in a world where not everyone will support you. Simply understand it was never their dream to begin with, smile, and move on.
2. **Only Take Advice From a Select Few:** Listen to everyone, but only take advice from people who (1) have experience, or otherwise know what they are talking about; and (2) do not have an ulterior motive. For everyone else. Listen politely, smile, and move on.
3. **Work Your Ass Off:** Hard work works. Don't let anyone else ever tell you differently. Work your ass off. Period.

Step 7
Cash is King ~ Profit or Close It

1 **Cash Flow > Costs:** Your inbound cash must exceed your outbound expenses. So many don't get this basic concept, and drain reserves until they are in a massive debt. Know your numbers, and fight hard so that cash flow always exceeds costs.

2. **Develop Strategic Reserves:** Develop your strategic reserves during the good times. Lenders and other forms of credit may not be available unless they exist before you truly need them.

3. **Plan to Profit or Shut it Down:** If cash flow falls less than your costs, *only* draw upon your strategic reserves *if* you have a realistic pathway to get back to profitability. As painful as it may sound, it is far less painful to shut it down before you go into massive debt to keep a failing business temporarily afloat.

Step 8
Consistently Innovate

1. **Create a Marketing & Innovation Schedule:** Create a marketing and innovation schedule wherein you launch some new initiative no less than twice per year. Not only will this keep you relevant in the marketplace, but it will also keep your company's name fresh in the media.
2. **Innovate & Expand into Vertical & Horizontal Markets:** Involve your front-line employees to ascertain what innovations your consumer base would like to see, and offer them those innovations as part of your schedule.
3. **Bring to Market. Market. Repeat.** Once you have your innovation, shamelessly market it, and the rest of your services, and repeat the whole process again, and again, to satisfy your company's innovation schedule.

Step 9
Captain Your Ship

1. **Determine Your Leadership Style:** Determine the type of leader you will become.
2. **Lead**: A leader's job is, quite simply, to lead! Once you know your style it is incumbent upon you to lead your company to greatness.
3. **When it All Goes Sideways**: Be prepared to shift styles if it ever all goes sideways. Anyone can captain a boat in calm seas. Only a true leader can do so when it gets rough.

Step 10
Plan to Succeed

1. **Create, Review, and Amend Your Annual Business Map:** Use the format above to plot out your business map to success, review it no less than three (3) times per day, and alter, amend, and add to it as you see fit.
2. **Create a Daily Checklist and Pound through Your Tasks:** Focus on the important tasks and guard your time against menial distractions.
3. **Use a Monthly Paper Calendar:** Finally, put your important dates on an easy-to-view monthly calendar. Glance at it a week out, once per day, to ensure you never miss something important.

Step 11
Master the Plate Waltz of Life

1. **Master Life Balance.** Understand that your business, family, and friends can share the top spot in your life. You simply must make sure that you prioritize all.
2. **Create an ABM but also an Annual Personal Map (APM):** To make sure you take care of every aspect of your personal life, create an Annual Personal Map (APM) to make sure you are checking the boxes for your friends and family as well as your business.
3. **Execute them Simultaneously:** Execute your ABM and APMs simultaneously to have it all.

APPENDIX B

STARTUP READING LIST

Anders, George, *The Rare Find: Spotting Exceptional Talent Before Everyone Else*, Portfolio Penguin, 2011

Carnegie, Dale, *How to Win Friends & Influence People*, Simon & Schuster, 1936

Collins, Jim, *Great by Choice*, Harper Business, 2011

Dijulius III, John R., *Secret Service*, Amacom, 2003

Dijulius III, John R., *What's the Secret? To Providing a World-Class Customer Experience*, Wiley, 2008

Drucker, Peter F. *et al.*, *On Leadership*, Harvard Business Review, 2010

Ferriss, Timothy, *The 4-Hour Workweek*, Crown Publishers, YEAR

Gerber, Michael, *The eMyth Revisited*, Harper Business, 1995

Goldsmith, Marshall, *What Got You Here Won't Get You There*, Hyperion, 2007

Kim, W. Chan and Renee Mauborgne, *Blue Ocean Strategy*, Harvard Business Review Press, 2015

Kiyosaki, Robert T., *Rich Dad Poor Dad*, Business Plus, 1997

Love, John F., *McDonald's Behind the Arches*, Bantam, 1986

Michalowicz, Mike, *Profit First*, Portfolio Penguin, 2014

Michalowicz, Mike, *The Pumpkin Plan*, Portfolio Penguin, 2012

Simmons, Gene, *Family Jewels: Sex Money Kiss*, Simmons Books, 2006

Trump, Donald J., *The Art of the Deal*, Random House, 1987

Ziglar, Zig, *Over the Top*, Thomas Nelson, 1994

MORE ON THE WEB

WANT MORE FROM MATT?

CONNECT WITH HIM
Online & On Social

Get Your
Free Startup Tool Kit at TheMaverickMethodBook.com

Facebook.com/TheStartupMaverickMethod
Twitter @MatthewSwyers

www.ingramcontent.com/pod-product-compliance
Lightning Source LLC
Chambersburg PA
CBHW071539210326
41597CB00019B/3058

* 9 7 8 0 5 7 8 3 1 6 7 1 0 *